Bloom's Modern Critical Views

Bloom's Modern Critical Views

JOSEPH CONRAD
New Edition

Edited and with an introduction by
Harold Bloom
Sterling Professor of the Humanities
Yale University

BLOOM'S
LITERARY CRITICISM
An imprint of Infobase Publishing

Bloom's Modern Critical Views: Joseph Conrad—New Edition
Copyright © 2010 by Infobase Publishing
Introduction © 2010 by Harold Bloom

Bloom's Literary Criticism
An imprint of Infobase Publishing
132 West 31st Street
New York NY 10001

Library of Congress Cataloging-in-Publication Data
Joseph Conrad / edited and with an introduction by Harold Bloom.—New ed.
    p. cm. — (Bloom's modern critical views)
Includes bibliographical references and index.
ISBN 978-1-60413-808-5 (acid free paper)
1. Conrad, Joseph, 1857–1924—Criticism and interpretation.   I. Bloom, Harold.
PR6005.O4Z74992 2010
823.912—dc22

                                        2009036969

Contributing editor: Pamela Loos
Cover designed by Takeshi Takahashi
Composition by IBT Global, Troy NY
Cover printed by IBT Global, Troy NY
Book printed and bound by IBT Global, Troy NY
Date printed: February, 2010
Printed in the United States of America

10 9 8 7 6 5 4 3 2 1

Contents

Editor's Note

My introduction favors Conrad's late romanticism over his pervasive ironies, with particular attention to *Heart of Darkness*, *Lord Jim*, and his indubitable masterwork, the High Romantic and nihilistic *Nostromo*.

Martin Price finds Conrad's ironies to be without limits, after which Michael Winner examines the domestication of irony in *The Secret Agent*.

A defense of *Heart of Darkness* against its own obscurantism is mounted by Mark A. Wollaeger, while Cedric Watts adumbrates Conrad's version of the myth that Hell is a city much like London.

Christopher GoGwilt meditates on Condrad's images of subversion, after which Robert Hampson confronts the heroic pathos of *Victory*.

Nostromo receives complementary intrepretations by Terry Collits on the problematic heroism of its protagonist and the ancient sage J. Hillis Miller on Conrad's implicit critique of international capitalism.

In this volume's final essay, Tom Henthorne evokes the ambigiuties of a postcolonial stance in Conrad.

HAROLD BLOOM

Introduction

Joseph Conrad's early life was outrageous enough even for a young Polish person of letters, let alone for an English writer. At twenty-seven he helped run a munitions operation for the Carlist rebels in Spain. Before it was over, he came close to being killed, attempted suicide, fell in love with a fatal beauty, and gambled on a grand scale. Four years later, he had begun a more conventional career in the British merchant marine, which continued until 1894, during which time he commanded his own vessel. For his remaining thirty years, he was a superb and successful novelist, bringing forth such masterworks as *Lord Jim, Nostromo, The Secret Agent, Under Western Eyes,* and *Victory*.

Conrad's *The Mirror of the Sea* and *A Personal Record* give us his own vision of his years as a sailor. Though books of considerable use and value, they do not aid me much in understanding the moral complexities of the great Conradian novels, *Nostromo* and *Victory* in particular. A great and complex artist, Conrad seems to me more influenced by a magnificent imagining like *Nostromo* than by the events of his own life.

And yet where are the limits of Conrad's irony in *Nostromo*? The magnificent Nostromo is in love with his own magnificence, and though he is a hero of the people, he essentially is hollow. With few exceptions, all of Conrad's protagonists are hollow men. One of the many paradoxes of Conrad is that the mirror of the sea allows us to perceive a heroic ideal, one that is not available in Conrad's great fictions.

What are the limits of irony in Conrad? For Martin Price, a profoundly Conradian ironist, there are no limits. Price sees both the skepticism and the irony of *Lord Jim* and yet also perceives its unrelenting romanticism. Both are

1

allowed their full eloquence, and neither can balance or negate the other. Price ranks *Nostromo* lower, because he sees the irony as triumphant there. Conrad, an astonishing artist, allows the reader to decide. As I age, I abandon my ironies and join Nostromo in his Garibaldi-like romanticism. In Nostromo, it is flawed and corrupt, but what matter? What matters in Conrad is not *whether* you betray yourself: of course you must and will. Either you betray others or yourself. Those are the Conradian options. Of course, others betray you, but that is of minor interest, another mere irony. Nostromo sells himself for silver and yet betrays nothing except his own authentic splendor.

In Conrad, you submit to the destructive element, the sea of death: No character in all of Conrad has a Hamlet-like power of mind, unless it be Kurtz, in *Heart of Darkness*, and he is self-obliterated, pragmatically speaking. Edward Said shrewdly noted Conrad's persuasive insistence that we can survive, as persons and as writers, only through the agency of our eccentricities. What matters most in Conrad's view of the human is that each of us is unpredictable.

Is there a more profound reply to all historicizing and psychologizing overinterpretations than the unpredictability of the influence of a writer's own works on her or his life? *Victory*, a novel I never weary of rereading, was superbly interpreted by the late R. W. B. Lewis as a grand exploitation of "the peculiar resources of the novel." It has been suggested, by several critics, that *Victory* (1914) is haunted by *King Lear*, since it echoes Lear's "Nothing will come of nothing." The effect of Conrad's major novels on their creator was to confirm his nihilism, despite his courageous efforts to endow certain of his protagonists with a fundamental, decent integrity. The suicide of Decond in *Nostromo* seems to me the ultimate triumph of Conradian nihilism.

The major modern American novelists—Hemingway, Fitzgerald, above all Faulkner—were the heirs of Conrad's vision of the nihilistic center of all human experience. Conrad, a majestic personality, held his own against the darker aspects of life, but his own art mutated him into a Shakespearean nihilist.

* * *

In Conrad's "Youth" (1898), Marlow gives us a brilliant description of the sinking of the *Judea*:

> Between the darkness of earth and heaven she was burning fiercely upon a disc of purple sea shot by the blood-red play of gleams; upon a disc of water glittering and sinister. A high, clear flame, an immense and lonely flame, ascended from the ocean, and from its summit the black smoke poured continuously at the sky. She

burned furiously; mournful and imposing like a funeral pile kindled in the night, surrounded by the sea, watched over by the stars. A magnificent death had come like a grace, like a gift, like a reward to that old ship at the end of her laborious day. The surrender of her weary ghost to the keeper of the stars and sea was stirring like the sight of a glorious triumph. The masts fell just before daybreak, and for a moment there was a burst and turmoil of sparks that seemed to fill with flying fire the night patient and watchful, the vast night lying silent upon the sea. At daylight she was only a charred shell, floating still under a cloud of smoke and bearing a glowing mass of coal within.

Then the oars were got out, and the boats forming in a line moved around her remains as if in procession—the longboat leading. As we pulled across her stern a slim dart of fire shot out viciously at us, and suddenly she went down, head first, in a great hiss of steam. The unconsumed stern was the last to sink; but the paint had gone, had cracked, had peeled off, and there were no letters, there was no word, no stubborn device that was like her soul, to flash at the rising sun her creed and her name.

The apocalyptic vividness is enhanced by the visual namelessness of the "unconsumed stern," as though the creed of Christ's people maintained both its traditional refusal to violate the Second Commandment and its traditional affirmation of its not-to-be-named God. With the *Judea*, Conrad sinks the romance of youth's illusions, but like all losses in Conrad this submersion in the destructive element is curiously dialectical, since only experiential loss allows for the compensation of an imaginative gain in the representation of artistic truth. Originally the ephebe of Flaubert and of Flaubert's "son," Maupassant, Conrad was reborn as the narrative disciple of Henry James, the James of *The Spoils of Poynton* and *What Maisie Knew*, rather than the James of the final phase.

Ian Watt convincingly traces the genesis of Marlow to the way that "James developed the indirect narrative approach through the sensitive central intelligence of one of the characters." Marlow, whom James derided as "that preposterous magic mariner," actually represents Conrad's swerve away from the excessive strength of James's influence on him. By always "mixing himself up with the narrative," in James's words, Marlow guarantees an enigmatic reserve that increases the distance between the impressionistic techniques of Conrad and James. Though there is little valid comparison that can be made between Conrad's greatest achievements and the hesitant, barely fictional status of Pater's Marius the Epicurean, Conrad's impressionism is as extreme and solipsistic as Pater's. There is a definite parallel between the fates of Sebastian Van Storck (in Pater's *Imaginary Portraits*) and Decoud in *Nostromo*.

In his 1897 "Preface" to *The Nigger of the "Narcissus,"* Conrad famously insisted that his creative task was "before all to make you *see*." He presumably was aware that he thus joined himself to a line of prose seers whose latest representatives were Carlyle, Ruskin, and Pater. There is a movement in that group from Carlyle's exuberant "Natural Supernaturalism" through Ruskin's paganization of Evangelical fervor to Pater's evasive and skeptical epicurean materialism, with its eloquent suggestion that all we can see is the flux of sensations. Conrad exceeds Pater in the reduction of impressionism to a state of consciousness where the seeing narrator is hopelessly mixed up with the seen narrative. James may seem an impressionist when compared to Flaubert, but alongside of Conrad he is clearly shown to be a kind of Platonist, imposing forms and resolutions on the flux of human relations by an exquisite formal geometry altogether his own.

To observe that Conrad is metaphysically less of an idealist is hardly to argue that he is necessarily a stronger novelist than his master, James. It may suggest though that Conrad's originality is more disturbing than that of James and may help explain why Conrad, rather than James, became the dominant influence on the generation of American novelists that included Hemingway, Fitzgerald, and Faulkner. The cosmos of *The Sun Also Rises*, *The Great Gatsby*, and *As I Lay Dying* derives from *Heart of Darkness* and *Nostromo* rather than from *The Ambassadors* and *The Golden Bowl*. Darl Bundren is the extreme inheritor of Conrad's quest to carry impressionism into its heart of darkness in the human awareness that we are only a flux of sensations gazing outward on a flux of impressions.

Heart of Darkness

Heart of Darkness may always be a critical battleground between readers who regard it as an aesthetic triumph and those, like myself, who doubt its ability to rescue us from its own hopeless obscurantism. That Marlow seems, at moments, not to know what he is talking about, is almost certainly one of the narrative's deliberate strengths, but if Conrad also seems finally not to know, then he necessarily loses some of his authority as a storyteller. Perhaps he loses it to death—our death, or our anxiety that he will not sustain the illusion of his fiction's duration long enough for us to sublimate the frustrations it brings us.

These frustrations need not be deprecated. Conrad's diction, normally flawless, is notoriously vague throughout *Heart of Darkness*. E. M. Forster's wicked comment on Conrad's entire work is justified perhaps only when applied to *Heart of Darkness*:

Misty in the middle as well as at the edges, the secret cask of his genius contains a vapour rather than a jewel. . . . No creed, in fact.

Forster's misty vapor seems to inhabit such Conradian recurrent modifiers as "monstrous," "unspeakable," "atrocious," and many more, but these are minor defects compared to the involuntary self-parody that Conrad inflicts on himself. There are moments that sound more like James Thurber lovingly satirizing Conrad than like Conrad:

> We had carried Kurtz into the pilot house: there was more air there. Lying on the couch, he stared through the open shutter. There was an eddy in the mass of human bodies, and the woman with helmeted head and tawny cheeks rushed out to the very brink of the stream. She put out her hands, shouted something, and all that wild mob took up the shout in a roaring chorus of articulated, rapid, breathless utterance.
> "Do you understand this?" I asked.
> He kept on looking out past me with fiery, longing eyes, with a mingled expression of wistfulness and hate. He made no answer, but I saw a smile, a smile of indefinable meaning, appear on his colorless lips that a moment after twitched convulsively. "Do I not?" he said slowly, gasping, as if the words had been torn out of him by a supernatural power.

This cannot be defended as an instance of what Frank Kermode calls a language "needed when Marlow is not equal to the experience described." Has the experience been described here? Smiles of "indefinable meaning" are smiled once too often in a literary text if they are smiled even once. *Heart of Darkness* has taken on some of the power of myth, even if the book is limited by its involuntary obscurantism. It has haunted American literature from T. S. Eliot's poetry through our major novelists of the era 1920 to 1940, on to a line of movies that go from the *Citizen Kane* of Orson Welles (a substitute for an abandoned Welles project to film *Heart of Darkness*) on to Coppola's *Apocalypse Now*. In this instance, Conrad's formlessness seems to have worked as an aid, so diffusing his conception as to have made it available to an almost universal audience.

Nostromo

An admirer of Conrad is happiest with his five great novels: *Lord Jim* (1900), *Nostromo* (1904), *The Secret Agent* (1906), *Under Western Eyes* (1910), and *Victory* (1914). Subtle and tormented narratives, they form an extraordinarily varied achievement, and despite their common features they can make a reader wonder that they all should have been composed by the same artist. Endlessly enigmatic as a personality and as a formidable moral character, Conrad pervades his own books, a presence not to be put by, an elusive storyteller who yet seems to write a continuous spiritual autobiography. By the general consent of advanced critics and of common readers, Conrad's masterwork is *Nostromo*, where his perspectives are largest and where his essential originality in the representation of human blindnesses and consequent human affections is at its strongest. Like all overwhelming originalities, Conrad's ensues in an authentic difficulty, which can be assimilated only very slowly, if at all. Repeated rereadings gradually convince me that *Nostromo* is anything but a Conradian litany to the virtue he liked to call "fidelity." The book is tragedy, of a post-Nietzschean sort, despite Conrad's strong contempt for Nietzsche. Decoud, void of all illusions, is self-destroyed because he cannot sustain solitude. Nostromo, perhaps the only persuasive instance of the natural sublime in a twentieth-century hero of fiction, dies "betrayed he hardly knows by what or by whom," as Conrad says. But this is Conrad at his most knowing, and the novel shows us precisely how Nostromo is betrayed, by himself, and by what is in himself.

It is a mystery of an overwhelming fiction why it can sustain virtually endless rereadings. *Nostromo*, to me, rewards frequent rereadings in something of the way that *Othello* does; there is always surprise waiting for me. Brilliant as every aspect of the novel is, Nostromo himself is the imaginative center of the book, and yet Nostromo is unique among Conrad's personae and not a Conradian man whom we could have expected. His creator's description of this central figure as "the Magnificent Capataz, the Man of the People," breathes a writer's love for his most surprising act of the imagination. So does a crucial paragraph from the same source, the "Author's Note" that Conrad added as a preface thirteen years after the initial publication:

> In his firm grip on the earth he inherits, in his improvidence and generosity, in his lavishness with his gifts, in his manly vanity, in the obscure sense of his greatness and in his faithful devotion with something despairing as well as desperate in its impulses, he is a Man of the People, their very own unenvious force, disdaining to lead but ruling from within. Years afterwards, grown older as the famous Captain Fidanza, with a stake in the country, going about his many affairs followed by respectful glances in the modernized streets of Sulaco, calling on the widow of the cargador, attending the Lodge, listening in unmoved silence to anarchist speeches at the meeting, the enigmatical patron of the new revolutionary agitation,

the trusted, the wealthy comrade Fidanza with the knowledge of his moral ruin locked up in his breast, he remains essentially a man of the People. In his mingled love and scorn of life and in the bewildered conviction of having been betrayed, of dying betrayed he hardly knows by what or by whom, he is still of the People, their undoubted Great Man—with a private history of his own.

Despite this "moral ruin," and not because of it, Conrad and his readers share the conviction of Nostromo's greatness, share in his sublime self-recognition. How many persuasive images of greatness, of a natural sublimity, exist in modern fiction? Conrad's may be the last enhanced vision of natural man, of the man of the people, in which anyone has found it possible to believe. Yet Conrad himself characteristically qualifies his own belief in Nostromo, and critics too easily seduced by ironies have weakly misread the only apparent irony of Conrad's repeated references to Nostromo as "the magnificent Capataz de Cargadores." Magnificent, beyond the reach of all irony, Nostromo manifestly is. It is the magnificence of the natural leader who disdains leadership, yet who loves reputation. Though he is of the people, Nostromo serves no ideal, unlike old Viola the Garibaldino. With the natural genius for command, the charismatic endowment that could make him another Garibaldi, Nostromo nevertheless scorns any such role, in the name of any cause whatsoever. He is a pure Homeric throwback, not wholly unlike Tolstoi's Hadji Murad, except that he acknowledges neither enemies nor friends, except for his displaced father, Viola. And he enchants us even as he enchants the populace of Sulaco, though most of all he enchants the skeptical and enigmatic Conrad, who barely defends himself against the enchantment with some merely rhetorical ironies.

Ethos is the daimon, character is fate, in Conrad as in Heracleitus, and Nostromo's tragic fate is the inevitable fulfillment of his desperate grandeur, which Conrad cannot dismiss as mere vanity, despite all his own skepticism. Only Nostromo saves the novel, and Conrad, from nihilism, the nihilism of Decoud's waste in suicide. Nostromo is betrayed partly by Decoud's act of self-destruction, with its use of four ingots of silver to send his body down, but largely by his own refusal to maintain the careless preference for glory over gain which is more than a gesture or a style, which indeed is the authentic mode of being that marks the hero. Nostromo is only himself when he can say, with perfect truth: "My name is known from one end of Sulaco to the other. What more can you do for me?"

Toward the end of chapter 10 of part 3, "The Lighthouse," Conrad renders his own supposed verdict on both Decoud and Nostromo, in a single page, in two parallel sentences a paragraph apart:

A victim of the disillusioned weariness which is the retribution
meted out to intellectual audacity, the brilliant Don Martin Decoud,
weighted by the bars of San Tomé silver, disappeared without a
trace, swallowed up in the immense indifference of things.

The magnificent Capataz de Cargadores, victim of the disenchanted vanity which is the reward of audacious action, sat in the
weary pose of a hunted outcast through a night of sleeplessness
as tormenting as any known to Decoud, his companion in the
most desperate affair of his life. And he wondered how Decoud
had died.

Decoud's last thought, after shooting himself, was: "I wonder how that
Capataz died." Conrad seems to leave little to choose between being "a victim
of the disillusioned weariness which is the retribution meted out to intellectual audacity" or a "victim of the disenchanted vanity which is the reward of
audacious action." The brilliant intellectual and the magnificent man of action
are victimized alike for their audacity, and it is a fine irony that "retribution"
and "reward" become assimilated to each other. Yet the book is Nostromo's
and not Decoud's, and a "disenchanted vanity" is a higher fate than a "disillusioned weariness," if only because an initial enchantment is a nobler state
than an initial illusion. True that Nostromo's enchantment was only of and
with himself, but that is proper for an Achilles or a Hadji Murad. Decoud
dies because he cannot bear solitude, and so cannot bear himself. Nostromo
finds death-in-life and then death because he has lost the truth of his vanity,
its enchanted insouciance, the *sprezzatura* which he, a plebeian, nevertheless
had made his authentic self.

Nostromo's triumph, though he cannot know it, is that an image of this
authenticity survives him, an image so powerful as to persuade both Conrad
and the perceptive reader that even the self-betrayed hero retains an aesthetic
dignity that renders his death tragic rather than sordid. Poor Decoud, for all
his brilliance, dies a nihilistic death, disappearing "without a trace, swallowed
up in the immense indifference of things." Nostromo, after his death, receives
an aesthetic tribute beyond all irony, in the superb closing paragraph of the
novel:

Dr. Monygham, pulling round in the police-galley, heard the name
pass over his head. It was another of Nostromo's triumphs, the
greatest, the most enviable, the most sinister of all. In that true cry
of undying passion that seemed to ring aloud from Punta Mala to
Azuera and away to the bright line of the horizon, overhung by
a big white cloud shining like a mass of solid silver, the genius of

the magnificent Capataz de Cargadores dominated the dark gulf containing his conquests of treasure and love.

Lord Jim

Lord Jim (1900) is the first of Conrad's five great novels, followed by what seems to me the finest, *Nostromo* (1904), and then by the marvelous sequence of *The Secret Agent* (1906), *Under Western Eyes* (1910), and, finally, *Victory* (1914). Of these, it seems clear that *Lord Jim* has the closest to universal appeal; I have rarely met a reader who was not fascinated by it. Martin Price, the subtlest of Conrad's moral critics, prefers *Lord Jim* to *Nostromo* because he finds that both the author's skepticism and the author's romanticism are given their full scope in *Lord Jim* rather than in *Nostromo*. Doubtless this is true, but Jim himself lacks the high romantic appeal of the magnificent *Nostromo*, and I prefer also the corrosive skepticism of Decoud to the skeptical wisdom of Marlow and Stein. Not that I would deprecate *Lord Jim*; had Conrad written nothing else, this single novel would have guaranteed his literary survival.

Aaron Fogel, writing on *Nostromo*, sees it as marking Conrad's transition from an Oedipal emphasis (as in *Lord Jim*) to a representation of the self's struggle against more outward influences. Certainly Jim's struggle does suit Fogel's formulation of the earlier mode in Conrad: "the denial, by internalization, of the Oedipal order of forced dialogue in the outside world—the translation of inquisition into an inner feeling of compulsion to quarrel with a forebear or with oneself." Though there is much of Conrad in Marlow and a little of him in Stein, his true surrogate is surely Jim, whose dialectics of defeat are in some sense a late version of Polish romanticism, of the perpetual defeat of Polish heroism. This is only to intimate that Jim's Byronism is rather more Polish than British. Jim rarely demands anything, and he never demands victory. One way of understanding the novel is to see how incomprehensible it would be if Conrad had chosen to make his hero an American.

Marlow, our narrator, becomes something like a father to Jim, in an implicit movement that has been shrewdly traced by Ian Watt. There is an impressive irony in the clear contrast between the eloquent father, Marlow, and the painfully inarticulate son, Jim. The relation between the two poignantly enhances our sense of just how vulnerable Jim is and cannot cease to be. Marlow is a survivor, capable of withstanding nearly the full range of human experience, while Jim is doom eager, as much a victim of the romantic imagination as he is a belated instance of its intense appeal to us.

Albert J. Guerard associated *Lord Jim* with *Absalom, Absalom!* (a not un-Conradian work) as novels that become different with each attentive reading. Jim's "simplicity" takes the place of the charismatic quality we expect of the romantic protagonist, and Guerard sees Jim as marked by a conflict between personality and will. But Jim's personality remains a mystery to us, almost despite Marlow, and Jim's will is rarely operative, so far as I can see. What we can know about Jim is the enormous strength and prevalence of his fantasy-making powers, which we need not confuse with a romantic imagination, since *that* hardly excludes self-knowledge. Indeed, the deepest puzzle of Jim is why should he fascinate anyone at all, let alone Marlow, Stein, Conrad, and ourselves? Why is he endless to meditation?

Everyone who has read *Lord Jim* (and many who have not) remember its most famous statement, which is Stein's:

> A man that is born falls into a dream like a man who falls into the sea. If he tries to climb out into the air as inexperienced people endeavour to do, he drowns—*nicht wahr?* ... No! I tell you! The way is to the destructive element submit yourself, and with the exertions of your hands and feet in the water make the deep, deep sea keep you up.

That describes Stein's romanticism but hardly Jim's, since Jim cannot swim in the dream world. When he seems to make the destructive element keep him up, as in Patusan, there would always have to be a Gentleman Brown waiting for him. An imagination like Jim's, which has little sense of other-ness, falls into identification as the truly destructive element, and the error of identifying with the outrageous Brown is what kills Jim. Tony Tanner deftly compares Brown to Iago, if only because Brown's hatred for Jim approximates Iago's hatred for Othello, but Brown has a kind of rough justice in denying Jim's moral superiority. That returns us to the enigma of Jim: Why does he make such a difference for Marlow—and for us?

We know the difference between Jim and Brown, even if Jim cannot, even as we know that Jim never will mature into Stein. Is Jim merely the spirit of illusion, or does there linger in him something of the legitimate spirit of romance? Marlow cannot answer the question, and we cannot either, no matter how often we read *Lord Jim*. Is that a strength or a weakness in this novel? That Conrad falls into obscurantism, particularly in *Heart of Darkness*, is beyond denial. Is *Lord Jim* simply an instance of such obscurantism on a larger scale?

Impressionist fiction necessarily forsakes the idealist metaphysics of the earlier romantic novel, a metaphysics that culminated in George Eliot. Marlow beholding Jim is a concourse of sensations recording a flood of impressions; how can a sensation distinguish whether an impression is authentic or not? Yet Marlow is haunted by the image of heroism and finds an authentic realization of the image in Stein. The famous close of Marlow's narrative invokes Jim as an overwhelming force of real existence and also as a disembodied spirit among the shades:

"And that's the end. He passes away under a cloud, inscrutable at heart, forgotten, unforgiven, and excessively romantic. Not in the wildest days of his boyish visions could he have seen the alluring shape of such an extraordinary success! For it may very well be that in the short moment of his last proud and unflinching glance, he had beheld the face of that opportunity which, like an Eastern bride, had come veiled to his side.

"But we can see him, an obscure conqueror of fame, tearing himself out of the arms of a jealous love at the sign, at the call of his exalted egoism. He goes away from a living woman to celebrate his pitiless wedding with a shadowy ideal of conduct. Is he satisfied—quite, now, I wonder? We ought to know. He is one of us—and have I not stood up once, like an evoked ghost, to answer for his eternal constancy? Was I so very wrong after all? Now he is no more, there are days when the reality of his existence comes to me with an immense, with an overwhelming force; and yet upon my honour there are moments, too, when he passes from my eyes like a disembodied spirit astray amongst the passions of his earth, ready to surrender himself faithfully to the claim of his own world of shades.

"Who knows? He is gone, inscrutable at heart, and the poor girl is leading a sort of soundless, inert life in Stein's house. Stein has aged greatly of late. He feels it himself, and says often that he is 'preparing to leave all this; preparing to leave . . . ' while he waves his hand sadly at his butterflies."

Stein's sadness is that he had hoped to find a successor in Jim and now wanes into the sense that he is at the end of a tradition. Enigmatic as always, Marlow cannot resolve his own attitude toward Jim. I do not suppose that we can either, and I wonder if that is necessarily an aesthetic strength in Conrad's novel. Perhaps it is enough that we are left pondering our own inability to reconcile the authentic and the heroic.

MARTIN PRICE

Conrad: Satire and Fiction

In the sixth chapter of *The Shape of Utopia* Robert Elliott discussed the conflict between utopian fiction and the novel. 'The novelist's art is to metamorphose ideas into the idiosyncratic experience of complex human beings', but the utopian writer, interested as he is in the ideas for their own sakes, is content to create characters that are stylized, mechanical, flat. 'The expectations we bring to the *Satyricon*, *Gargantua and Pantagruel*, *Candide*, Barth's *Giles Goat-Boy* are very different from those we bring to *Emma* or *Sons and Lovers*: it is pointless to require of *Brave New World* that it try to be what they are.'[1]

My concern is with the way that satire and the novel may combine or conflict, and, while I shall start with a few instances from Dickens, my subject is really the uneasy mixture of satire and fiction in Joseph Conrad.[2] In his discussion of the 'great misanthropes', under the rubric 'the satirist satirized', Elliott had occasion to cite Conrad's remarks in *Nostromo* about Charles Gould: 'A man haunted by a fixed idea is insane. He is dangerous even if that idea is an idea of justice: for may he not bring the heavens down pitilessly upon a loved head?'[3] Conrad is, as I have tried to show elsewhere, essentially concerned with the 'idea' and the way in which it possesses men, turning them, as in the case of Gould, into both victims and tyrants.[4] Conrad tries to show how much our lives are governed by ideas or, as he often chooses to call

From *The Yearbook of English Studies* 14 (1984): 226–42. © 1984 by the Modern Humanities Research Association.

them, illusions. Because the idea always outruns the actual, it is threatened by calm reflection. Such reflection will make us recognize the very unrealizability of ideas. The universe is inhospitable to man's ideas; no human meanings are accommodated in the grand spectacle of nature. Man must choose among roles: he may assert and live by idea in the face of inevitable defeat; he may adapt himself to the world as it is and ignore the claims of the idea; he may remain an ironic spectator of others' efforts or obliviousness and enjoy the comic spectacle of quixotic heroism or heroic obtuseness. The first of these roles may create existential tragedy and the second the comic triumph that arises from luck rather than intention. The third comes at times very close to satiric disdain for those who cannot endure the effort of being fully aware.[5]

In Dickens's novels we often move between satire and the novelistic. Some characters exist entirely within a satiric world, and, through that world, create the obstacles, enclosures, and resistances that threaten the hero. Individually these characters may be absurd; collectively, as a world, they become formidable. These characters display, moreover, a great range of triviality, self-absorption, rigid obsession, and darker impulses of cruelty and aggression. The degree to which these characters resemble each other (in devotion to forms, in acquisitiveness, in defensive self-imprisonment) makes them the various aspects of a common identity and of a shared world. But Dickens's characters may, as one critic has put it, serve a double purpose:

> They may be simultaneously dramatic (or novelistic) and rhetorical (satiric counters), or they may move from one mode to another. More often the characters are divided into two groups, one dramatic and one rhetorical (with possibly a third group of those who are or can be both), and the difficulty is the incongruity of their appearance together in the same fictional world.[6]

Dickens tends to segregate such characters when they are most fully realizing one mode or the other. When Fanny Dorrit decides to win her revenge upon Mrs Merdle, we see her in dramatic scenes with her sister Amy, who tries to dissuade her from so empty a purpose. But when we see Fanny carry out her resolution, she enters the Merdles' world with all the reductive simplicity of purpose that this world demands. In *Our Mutual Friend* the world of the Veneerings is virtually autonomous; characters who gain their identity there may, however, open out into greater complexity, as Sophronia Lammle does in her warning to Podsnap. Within the Veneering world a major character must be reduced to a virtual triviality that he may want as a refuge from earnestness. 'Eugene Wrayburn, we note, is buried alive in this company: he is dead in the ironic sense that if they are alive the truly living must be dead; and he is dead in the straightforward sense that he is bored to death, but even more in that he has given in to their death by apathetically consenting to join them' (Manning, p. 203). The paradoxes of life and death are raised more explicitly, and in a different mode, by Jenny Wren, whom Mrs Manning likens to the 'type of primitive satirist described by R. C. Elliott': 'The relish of physical punishment, the bitterness, hatred, and abuse, and the sense of outraged justice behind these resemble the state of satire as it passed from magic to art' (p. 223). Jenny Wren can, at different moments, be tender, bitterly angry, parentally severe, radiantly prophetic; and we are somewhat startled by the reduction of her to a partner of Sloppy at the close.

Dickens's freedom in moving between modes has the confidence of an author who is not hobbled by doctrines of realism and who is constantly in touch with the supple conventions of popular art. Conrad learned much from Dickens's verbal wit, but his effects are less exuberant and far more studied. Conrad's idiom and images are saturated, even adrip, with intention. The difficulty is that the intention is sometimes uncontrolled, and what seems to be meant as Dickensian facetiousness may as readily veer into sarcasm:

> Mr Verloc went on divesting himself of his clothing with the unnoticing inward concentration of a man undressing in the solitude of a vast and hopeless desert. For thus inhospitably did this fair earth, our common inheritance, present itself to the mental vision of Mr Verloc. All was so still without and within that the lonely ticking of the clock on the landing stole into the room as if for the sake of company.[7]

One could wish away the second of those sentences, which seems more to gloat than to present Mr Verloc's state of mind.

This uncertainty of tone and effect comes from two principal sources: a conflict of attitudes that is insufficiently resolved, and an excess of assertion. There is a counterpart of these difficulties in Conrad's invention of character and situation. I should like to deal with some of these difficulties as they appear in two comparatively early stories, both in *Tales of Unrest* (1898) and as they appear again in *The Secret Agent* (1907) and *Under Western Eyes* (1911).

The first of the two stories from *Tales of Unrest* is one that Conrad himself regarded highly, 'An Outpost of Progress'; the second is a tale that won praise only from Ford Madox Ford, 'The Return'. The first of these stories was, as Conrad put it in his 'Author's Note', the 'lightest part of the loot' he carried off from Central Africa, 'the main portion being of course *The Heart of Darkness'*. The story continues to win high praise; V. S. Naipaul regards it as 'the finest thing that Conrad wrote'.[8] But, while R. A. Gekoski considers it 'the best of the stories in the volume', he is troubled, as I am, by 'the ferocity of Conrad's treatment' of his characters.[9] It is a tale of studied brilliance, and the author detaches himself from his characters from the outset. The two Belgians are put in charge of a remote and 'useless' trading station so that the director can dispose of the two 'imbeciles' sent him by the company for six months. Kayerts and his assistant Carlier are 'two perfectly insignificant and incapable individuals, whose existence is rendered possible through the high organization of civilized crowds'. Nor are they exceptional in this: 'Few men realize that their life, the very essence of their character, their capabilities and their audacities, are only the expression of their feeling in the safety of their surroundings.' All our virtues and principles, 'every great and every insignificant thought belongs not to the individual but to the crowd: to the crowd that believes blindly in the irresistible force of its institutions and of its morals, in the power of its police and of its opinion' (p. 89). This is a traditional Conradian theme: it exhibits the superior penetration and disdain of a narrator who sees through all pretensions and presuppositions. A page or two later, this general theme is localized: 'Society, not from any tenderness, but because of its strange needs, had taken care of these two men, forbidding them all independent thought, all initiative, all departure from routine; and forbidding it under pain of death. They could only live on condition of being machines.' Once these men are subjected to 'the negation of the habitual', they are at a loss, 'being both, through want of practice, incapable of independent thought' (p. 91). Although both men look back longingly to their condition as part of a mass mind, they seem at first to get along well enough 'in the fellowship of their stupidity and laziness. Together they did nothing, absolutely nothing, and enjoyed the sense of idleness for which they were paid' (p. 92). They come belatedly to read novels, in which the range of human motives surprises them.

The station is in fact run by a native clerk, who disturbs the two Belgians' serenity by secretly selling the hired station men into slavery in return for a fine lot of ivory. Not only the rather despondent and inefficient station men have been sold, but some members of the friendly local people. The Belgians are horrified. Or are they? 'They believed their words' (p. 105). And then, once more, the narrator opens up their state to suggest a general one: 'Everybody shows a respectful deference to certain sounds that he and his fellows can make.' Meanings give way to sounds; social beliefs to empty rituals. 'But about feelings people really know nothing. We talk with indignation or enthusiasm; we talk about oppression, cruelty, crime, devotion, self-sacrifice, virtue, and we know nothing real beyond the words. Nobody knows what suffering or sacrifice mean—except, perhaps the victims of the mysterious purpose of these illusions' (pp. 105–06).

For all their obtuseness and their wish not to face reality, a measure of fear steals into the two men's minds and brings with it the loss of their sense of safety. They pick quarrels with each other, until finally Kayerts accidentally shoots and kills Carlier. Kayerts now becomes totally demoralized. All he once believed in and lived by appears 'contemptible and childish, false and ridiculous' (p. 114). But, as he hears the whistle of the steamer making its delayed visit to the station, Kayerts hangs himself from the cross that marks the previous agent's grave. As the director finds him, Kayerts's corpse exhibits his late-found wisdom: 'His toes were only a couple of inches above the ground; his arms hung stiffly down; he seemed to be standing rigidly at attention, but with one purple cheek playfully posed on the shoulder. And, irreverently, he was putting out a swollen tongue at his Managing Director' (p. 117). One may feel that the corpse might have been spared this last exhibition of the narrator's intention, even if it might be read as Kayerts's repudiation of all he has unthinkingly lived by. What is troubling about the story is its steady denial of even a shadow of consciousness to its characters; such consciousness as Kayerts attains at the close is the 'wrong-headed lucidity' (p. 115) of a transvaluation of values. Even when Kayerts looks at his daughter's portrait, we are carefully made to see what Kayerts cannot. 'It represented a little girl with long bleached tresses and a rather sour face' (p. 108). The two men are allowed no thoughts but banalities, no conscience but feeble rationalizations, no feelings but clumsy projections. They become a demonstration of the anonymous urban citizen (such as we see in the Geneva of *Under Western Eyes*) becoming demoralized by solitude, unable to sustain the forms of civilization beyond the pale, worked upon by forces they cannot even imagine.

All that is missing from this story can be seen if we compare these men to Marlow and Kurtz in *The Heart of Darkness*. Kurtz is a far more outrageous and guilty figure. The evil he performs is more than tacit complicity, and the good to which he may have originally aspired is altogether beyond the conception of these two men. What we are given, then, is a demonstration performed upon and through them, and we may be led to ask ourselves how adequate the demonstration is. It has, surely, the boldness of satire in its reductive force. These men embody in almost pure form the operations of a collective mind upon the unreflective individual; they seem completely controlled by their society, in a manner which Emile Durkheim called 'mechanical solidarity'. Durkheim speaks of two kinds of consciousness or *conscience*: 'one which we share with our entire group, which, in consequence, is not ourselves, but society living and acting within us; the other which . . . represents only that which is personal and distinctive to each of us, which makes him an individual'. Mechanical solidarity is at its highest pitch 'when the *conscience collective* is exactly co-extensive' with the individual's consciousness 'and coincides at all points with it: but at this moment his individuality is non-existent'. A society created by mechanical solidarity is a system of homogeneous elements, not so much coherent as bounded territorially.[10] Here the massmen who are homogeneous elements of Western European society are isolated in Africa, which requires powers such men no longer have. Is the story a satire? Is ridicule the primary note? Do these immediate objects of satire suggest something more general in human behaviour, as we see in some of the narrator's comments? How telling or general is the import of the human deficiencies Conrad presents here? What is left out that we find in the more novelistic treatment of *The Heart of Darkness*? If this is satire, is it as forceful as it might be if it took more of man into account? Is all satiric reduction of equal value?

A second story, much the longest of those in *Tales of Unrest*, caused Conrad enormous pains of effort and seemed to him later 'a left-handed production'. It is not a story that has won much praise, or even much analysis.[11] It seems too long, somewhat as the final dialogue of Verloc and Winnie seems to have been unduly protracted for ironic effect when Conrad revised the serial version of *The Secret Agent*.[12] It is, moreover, a story which draws on the same themes as 'An Outpost', although it is set in London. Alvan Hervey and his wife are examples of the homogeneous elements of mechanical solidarity. They are suddenly isolated by a moral crisis rather than by distance. We first see Hervey coming off the commuters' train with other men: 'Their backs appeared alike—almost as if they had been wearing a uniform; their indifferent faces were varied but somehow suggested kinship, like the faces of a band of brothers who through prudence, drifting, disgust, or foresight would resolutely ignore each other.' Their eyes 'had all the same stare, concentrated and empty, satisfied and unthinking' (pp. 118–19). Hervey has been married for five years to a woman who had been 'intensely bored with her home where, as if packed in a tight box, her individuality—of which she was very conscious—had no play' (p. 120). (It should be said that Mrs Hervey's belief in her individuality is made a typical manifestation of the middle-class mind.) But they choose to belong to a world 'where nothing is realized and where all joys and sorrows are cautiously toned down into pleasures and annoyances', 'where noble sentiments are cultivated in sufficient profusion to conceal the pitiless materialism of thoughts and aspirations' (p. 121). They are like skilful skaters 'cutting figures on thick ice for the admiration of the beholders, and disdainfully ignoring the hidden stream, the stream restless and dark; the stream of life, profound and unfrozen' (p. 123). All the consciousness is false. Hervey finances a journal because it serves his ambition, because he enjoys 'the special kind of importance he derived from the connection with what he imagined to be literature' (p. 121).

Conrad finds a brilliant image for Hervey's participation in mechanical solidarity. As he stands beside his wife's pier-glass, it multiplies his image

> into a crowd of gentlemanly and slavish imitators, who were dressed exactly like himself; ... who moved when he moved, stood still with him in an obsequious immobility, and had just such appearances of life and feeling as he thought it dignified and safe for any man to manifest. And like real people who are slaves of common thoughts, that are not even their own, they affected a shadowy independence by the superficial variety of their movements. ... And like the men he respected they could be trusted to do nothing individual, original, or startling—nothing unforeseen and nothing improper. (pp. 124–25)

When Hervey finds a note in which his wife tells him that she has left him for the editor of the journal, Hervey feels 'physically sick'. But he soon works his way into a saving self-righteousness. He is defending 'life', that 'sane and gratifying existence untroubled by too much love or by too much regret' (p. 129). She has defiled it with a show of passion that 'strips the body of life'. It has 'laid its unclean hand upon the spotless draperies of his existence' (p. 130). We have virtually moved into Swift's world of *A Tale of a Tub*, where the soul is our outward clothing.

When his wife returns, unable to carry through her action but also unrepentant, Hervey seems at first to draw back from the intolerable into the safety of moral outrage. But, for all his posturing, he comes to recognize how much he needs the 'certitude of love and faith' (p. 180), and he finds the loss of it intolerable. He tries to blame the loss upon his wife: 'She had no love and no faith for anyone' (p. 183). In the midst of his self-centred grief, his conscience is born: 'It came to him in a flash that morality is not a method of happiness. The revelation was terrible' (p. 183). He wants 'help against himself, against the cruel decree of salvation. The need of tacit complicity, where it had never failed him, the habit of years affirmed itself' (p. 184). But he does not know how to ask for what he now wants, nor does she recognize any change in him. As she wards off what seems a renewed manifestation of his somewhat brutal egoism and suspects him only of 'a fresh fit of jealousy, a dishonest desire of evasion', she defies him. 'Can you stand it?', he asks, thinking of years 'without faith or love'. To what she thinks he means she shouts angrily, 'Yes!'. Thereupon he leaves, never to return (pp. 185–86).

It is a somewhat muddled narrative because it records the events within the mind of a man who is averse to self-analysis, but the story allows Hervey a growth of awareness that seems genuine enough.[13] The result is to make the satirical elements of the story a record of the self from whose constriction he finally breaks—not at once, not altogether clearly, but with sufficient force to become a complex character. 'The Return' is a more diffuse and less efficiently controlled story than 'An Outpost of Progress', but it attempts to treat more complex characters. They create, as such characters will, a narrative richer in dramatic power. Conrad shifts from sardonic exemplification of a theme his characters cannot conceive to the emergence, within the consciousness of a character, of the meaning of his experience.

Some of the puzzles and difficulties that these stories evoke are to be found in the critical response to *The Secret Agent*. Frederick R. Karl feels that the Professor, in 'a somewhat limited sense', reflects 'Conrad's own contempt for the mediocre, for the loss of nerve and vitality, for a world that has become passionless'. Somewhat earlier Karl observed that Conrad's irony appears to 'give the novelist a devastating authority, even an arrogance'.[14] H. M. Daleski seems led by Conrad's ironic levelling to draw some very questionable equivalences. The Assistant Commissioner's 'settling of scores with both the minister and his own subordinate' is a 'civilized—but almost as deadly—variant of the Professor's shovelling of his stuff at street corners'. Or again: 'In his readiness to stick at nothing in protecting himself. . . . Heat resembles nobody so much as the Professor.'[15]

F. R. Leavis described the career of Winnie Verloc after the murder of her husband as a 'gruesomely farcical coda in which the gallows-haunted Winnie, whose turn it now is to suppose herself loved for her own sake, clings round the neck of the gallant Comrade Ossipon'.[16] Leavis's use of 'whose turn it is' reduced Winnie's desperation to the same obtuseness we have seen in her husband's complacency. But Daleski sees her 'obsessive self-sacrifice' on her brother's behalf as 'moral nihilism that is similar [to that of Verloc and Heat] in its exclusive concern with an end and its bland indifference to the means employed to achieve it' (pp. 147, 149). Hers, like Stevie's, is a story of the 'disintegration that follows a prolonged state of nullity or vacancy'. Albert J. Guerard suggests that the vividness of Ossipon's 'growing horror and disgust' after finding Verloc's corpse 'effectively destroys much of our sympathy for Winnie. We may come to share his view. But this is not too high a price to pay for such a show of fictional virtuosity'.[17]

Ian Watt corrects Richard Curle's sentimental view of Stevie by insisting that Stevie is regarded with the 'same impartial perspective as everything else' in this 'black comedy of human cross-purposes'. Watt warns against too simple a reading: 'Just as we are denied the pleasure of melodrama—there is no one we particularly want to applaud or hiss—so we are denied the pleasures of parody or satire—the characters are too human for that.' And yet they are all, as Conrad put it in a letter to his French translator, 'imbéciles'. The characters, as Watt observes, do not 'understand themselves, or really know what they are doing'. Yet if we look to the author's intentions, Watt sees a 'control that approaches serenity', a tale which is 'tonic rather than depressive in its final effect'.[18] It is perhaps in this sense that Daleski (p. 151) regards *The Secret Agent* as the 'most enjoyable' of Conrad's novels or that Guerard (p. 231) finds it 'an entertaining and easy book'.

What these critics make clear is the way in which the irony seems to effect a moral levelling of all the characters and the way in which the aloofness or comic distance of the novelist makes us associate our feelings more with his virtuosity than with the minds of his characters. There are variations on each of these emphases. The first is extended by J. Hillis Miller to a view of the 'sinister connectedness of all levels of society from bottom to top'. All the 'living deaths of the novel are the same death, and ... the theme of *The Secret Agent* is the universal death which underlies life'.[19] The second emphasis has been pursued, to a different evaluation from those I have so far cited, by Irving Howe. Conrad's 'ability to make the life of humanity seem a thing of shame reaches an appalling completeness' at times. Howe regards the final scene between Verloc and Winnie as a 'dazzling *tour de force*', but he feels that Conrad's 'insistence upon squeezing the last ounce of sordid absurdity' is in conflict with 'the narrative rhythm of the book'. Conrad's studied irony is constantly 'nagging at our attention'; he 'lacks the talent for self-resistance that is indispensable to a novelist for whom irony has been transformed from a tactic into a total perspective'.[20]

Perhaps the most comprehensive criticism of the novel is that of R. A. Gekoski. He also compares it to 'An Outpost of Progress' and feels that most of the characters in *The Secret Agent*, like those in the story, are 'finally unworthy even of the sustained scorn to which they are subjected' (this might be what Howe means by Conrad's failure of 'self-resistance'; we are troubled by a novelist who sets up easy targets for what must prove excessive scorn). Gekoski (pp. 150–51) finds that Conrad achieves a 'technical masterpiece', but only 'at the cost of complexity of thought and emotion'. Technical masterpiece, *tour de force*, show of fictional virtuosity: the terms all raise the question of how one can relate the satiric brilliance to the fictional adequacy.

Clearly, in this novel as in the stories I have cited, indolence, self-absorption, moral obtuseness—however we wish to name them—are the faults which arouse scorn even as they serve to reduce man to mechanism, to mere matter in motion. Those who live in an habitual world that calls nothing into question are perhaps engaged in a death more than a life. Those, on the other hand, who are obsessed by an extreme view like the Professor's (and perhaps Vladimir's) can shake off the bonds of the familiar and open up to view a radically different kind of reality. Yet these obsessions are such as to make those who hold them victims as much as masters. For while these men may see what others are content to miss, they need not thereby attain to wisdom. Their vision may be the savage distortion of the insane. A perception of the intolerable is not in itself a passport to reality. Conrad, nevertheless, mocks those who are, as he suggests, too timid, too torpid, too shallow to question received truths, or, what may be the same, too lucky to have had to face the intolerable. They are the men in the ranks whom Marlow regards with some disdain (but with some sense of complicity) in *Lord Jim*. They are the counterparts of Heat or Michaelis or Ossipon in *The Secret Agent*. Everything about them is suspect because they have never reached the sense of the 'problematic' that is so critical for Conrad, as it was for Nietzsche. And yet, as we have seen, the effect of Conrad's irony is to impose a moral levelling that makes for perplexity since it includes both those who are without awareness and those who are maddened by what they take to be too much. Or if not for perplexity, perhaps at times for an easy cynicism of the kind Conrad attacks in Martin Decoud. That Conrad attacks it in *Nostromo* does not, of course, acquit him of participation in it elsewhere (or even there). But it does perhaps betray an uneasiness with those ambivalences of satiric disdain that he best surmounts in *Lord Jim*, where Marlow's mixture of sympathy and realism creates a genuinely complex irony and a complex case, if not a complex character, in Jim.

Conrad builds *The Secret Agent* upon an action that is ludicrously pointless and has been ineptly conducted. His first irony is to give the action point. A bold anarchist measure is not undertaken by the anarchists themselves but is forged, so to speak, in their name, by an autocratic power which seeks to bring other nations over to its own repressive policy. The agent of that power (clearly Russia) wishes to cure the English of their 'sentimental regard for individual liberty' (p. 29) by means of a purely destructive act. Traditional targets could not release the 'absurd ferocity' of this attack upon the new 'sacrosanct fetish', science (p. 31). The act must have 'all the shocking senselessness of gratuitous blasphemy', as if one were to 'throw a bomb into pure mathematics' (p. 33).

Vladimir, as we might suspect of so academic a conspiracy, knows little about revolutionaries or secret agents. He is appalled when he finds Adolf Verloc, the 'celebrated agent', to be merely 'vulgar, heavy, and impudently unintelligent' (p. 27). The revolutionaries of *The Secret Agent* are an unattractive, unromantic lot.

All these people [Conrad wrote to his socialist friend, Cunninghame Graham] are not revolutionaries—they are Shams. And as regards the Professor I did not intend to make him despicable. He is incorruptible at any rate. In making him say 'madness and despair—give me that for a lever and I will move the world', I wanted to give him a note of perfect sincerity. At the worst he is a megalomaniac of an extreme type. And every extremist is respectable.[21]

The others share a world that tends to obey regular laws, where contingency preserves a familiar and manageable scale. Or so it seems.

More than any other novel of Conrad's, *The Secret Agent* has a constant succession of details that are irrelevant, discordant, inexplicable, incongruous, or suspect. Verloc keeps a shop (it is, of course, in part a blind) where various 'shady wares', from patent medicines to pornography, are sold. The customers who enter are seedy and furtive, and the shop-bell mocks their stealth with its 'impudent virulence' (p. 4: the idea of impudence is the affront to reasonable expectation).

The most striking instance of the grotesque event which observes its own times and seasons is the player piano in the Silenus Café, the keys moving without hands, its jaunty, tinny tunes sounding at unpredictable intervals with a sardonic jocosity. Details carry a strangeness that remains unnoticed by the characters, and we become as a result more aware of the author. Heat finds the Assistant Commissioner in his private office, 'pen in hand, bent over a great table bestrewn with papers, as if worshipping an enormous double inkstand of bronze and crystal. Speaking tubes resembling snakes were tied by the heads to the back of the Assistant Commissioner's wooden armchair, and their gaping mouths seemed ready to bite his elbows' (p. 97). Seemed so to whom? Presumably not to Heat, who is anything but fanciful. We may think of the Assistant Commissioner's dislike of desk work, but Heat knows nothing of that. These details seem gratuitously rather than significantly violent; they awaken expectations that are neither met nor denied. They seem to be created for effect, as coercive as the floating menace of a Gothic novel. As Thomas Mann observed, the 'gaze turned upon the horrible is clear, lively, dry-eyed, almost gratified'.[22]

As an instance of the suspect detail we may take the remarks about Winnie's mother: 'She considered herself to be of French descent, which might have been true.' This suggests a narrator estimating the plausibility of remarks he has heard, but comes in fact from an author who alone can have decided whether his character's remark is truthful. And why should it not be? Pretension? A few sentences later the pretension is affirmed, but not in a way that denies the claim. 'Traces of the French descent which the widow boasted were apparent in Winnie, too. They were apparent in the extremely neat and artistic arrangement of her glossy black hair' (p. 6).

Conrad is creating a world that seems shot through with incongruity and potential violence; yet their sources are not identified and in many cases are not identifiable. Things 'seem' that way: they carry suggestions we can neither ascribe to a clear source nor comfortably ignore. The obliviousness of the characters seems heavy-lidded, lethargic, impercipient. They lack the power or the will to recognize what should at least cause a measure of disturbance. When Stevie is so moved by the 'pathos and violence' of a horse's fall as to 'shriek piercingly', it is in a crowd 'which disliked to be disturbed by sounds of distress in its quiet enjoyment of the national spectacle' (p. 9). The last phrase seems curiously contemptuous. Is their fascination with the fallen horse one of simple enjoyment, with none of the terror or shock we often find in spectators of other accidents? That Stevie's response is appropriately intense seems clear enough on this occasion. Yet shortly we are to learn of the violence he creates in turn by shooting off fireworks when two office-boys, as a practical joke, disturb him with 'tales of injustices and oppression'. The commotion Stevie creates is called an 'altruistic exploit' (p. 10). Does that dry phrase confirm the implication that Stevie is genuinely responsive to 'pathos and violence' or simply that he is more acutely disturbed by the thought of them? Is he, in short, morally superior or simply pathologically sensitive? And shall we say sensitive or irritable?

In the famous scenes of the second chapter, we see Hyde Park through Verloc's 'glances of comparative alertness'. But is it Verloc who sees 'here and there a victoria with the skin of some wild beast inside and a woman's face and hat emerging above the folded hood' (p. 11)? As Byron in *Don Juan* tells us what the court poet 'sung, or would, or could, or should have sung', so, with Conrad, we follow Verloc's eye-beam but observe what he does not. The 'bloodshot' sun turns London into a scene of 'opulence and luxury', at least this part of London, where the 'whole social order favourable to' the 'hygienic idleness' of the rich 'had to be protected against the shallow enviousness of unhygienic labour'. And while that irony evokes our sense of class differences and of the obliviousness of the idle rich, Mr Verloc, alone rusty in this scene of gold, remains an incongruous case, a man 'born of industrious parents for a life of toil' who has embraced indolence as a vocation, 'with a sort of inert fanaticism, or perhaps rather with a fanatical inertness' (p. 12).

The play with terms and witty extravagance recall Dickens, and the method is carried through: 'At the notion of a menaced social order he would perhaps have winked to himself if there had not been an effort to make in that sign of scepticism. His big, prominent eyes were not well adapted to winking. They were rather of the sort that closes solemnly in slumber with majestic effect' (p. 13). The last sentence mockingly converts indolence to solemnity, inertness to majesty. Two paragraphs later the street itself has 'the majesty of inorganic nature, of matter that never dies', the grandeur, as it were, of the lifeless and the mindless (p. 14). Matter keeps slipping out of or away from form. The mind aspires to the condition of matter. It is, once more, a satiric pattern. Verloc's mind is capable of 'moral nihilism' but is hardly energetic enough to become 'diabolic'. Indolence and inertia displace evil as well as good, for inertia is that conservative reluctance to stand outside the system of belief and social order on which one's life has been based. The desire to remain untroubled is far more powerful than the will to create or destroy.

This satiric pattern is clearest in Chief Inspector Heat. Chance and absurdity unnerve him. He can live with crime that has gain as a motive; it is a form of 'work' by which men keep themselves alive. He understands the mind of a burglar as like his own. 'Both recognize the same conventions. . . . They understand each other, which is advantageous to both, and establishes a sort of amenity in their relations' (p. 92). This is the large area of the normal, the common recognition of traditions and social institutions, however disparate the moral choices of the members. The Professor offends Heat by standing outside, by refusing to participate in the game whose rules most men obey. 'Revolution, legality—counter moves in the same game; forms of idleness at bottom identical. . . . But I don't play; I work fourteen hours a day, and go hungry sometimes' (pp. 69–70). The Professor mocks Ossipon, who has ineptly described the explosion as 'nothing short of criminal'. Ossipon angrily defends his terms: 'One must use the current words', he replies, in effect affirming his participation in the same game as Chief Inspector Heat and the rest of civil society (p. 71). Ossipon's word reveals the toughness of the social structure; it is deeply embedded in the terms by which we think.

The chief enemy of that structure is the Professor, who exhibits an 'ascetic purity' of thought 'combined with an astounding ignorance of worldly conditions'. His conviction of his own merit makes him, like his evangelical father, 'supremely confident in the privileges of his righteousness' (p. 80). But the Professor has replaced radical Protestantism with a 'frenzied puritanism of ambition', which he nurses as something 'secularly holy' (p. 81). Yet he is haunted at moments by the 'unattackable solidity of a great multitude', who are stubbornly resistant, 'numerous like locusts, industrious like ants, thoughtless like a natural force, pushing or blind and orderly and absorbed, impervious to sentiment, to logic, to terror, too, perhaps' (p. 82). With this suspicion of futility to allay, the Professor enjoys thrusting his presence on Chief Inspector Heat; he feels that he is confounding in the Chief Inspector all his enemies at once and 'affirming his superiority over all the multitude of mankind' (p. 84).

Here the satiric pattern becomes troubling, for the standard of energy is itself more repellent and destructive than the torpor it seeks to abolish. Is there a third term? The new Assistant Commissioner has a nature 'not easily accessible to illusions'. He has a healthy mistrust of men's motives, and he does not deceive himself about his own. He wants, if he can, to exculpate Michaelis in deference to an influential lady (one of his wife's valuable 'connections') who is Michaelis's patron. She is a woman of intelligence as well as generosity, 'seldom totally wrong, and almost never wrong-headed' (p. 105). There is much that is imperious about her aristocratic stance: a sympathy with Michaelis's radicalism based on their common dislike of the middle classes, and a reliance upon the status of birth that makes her irresponsibly ready to entertain the idea of the 'economic ruin of the system'. The Assistant Commissioner has an affection for the lady: 'a complex sentiment depending a little on her prestige, her personality, but most of all on the instinct of flattered gratitude. . . . Her influence upon his wife, a woman devoured by all sorts of small selfishnesses, small envies, small jealousies', was 'excellent' (pp. 111–12). He is able to recognize with 'derisive self-criticism' (p. 112) his own desire to please her. This self-awareness does not lead him to abandon his attachment to his self-interest, which is happily not in conflict with his duties. In fact, this motive releases in the Assistant Commissioner considerable administrative talent. He is not easily cajoled into believing what his subordinates think it fit he should believe so that they may conduct their affairs as they wish. He has a larger conception of the game to be played than Heat does: 'The existence of these spies amongst the revolutionary groups, which we are reproached for harbouring here, does away with all certitude' (pp. 140–41). The rules must be changed. As he says to Vladimir, 'we don't intend to let ourselves be bothered by shams under any pretext whatever' (p. 227).

Clearly the Assistant Commissioner has the fullest awareness of all these characters. He can act freely and imaginatively. By preventing Heat from victimizing Michaelis in order to conceal his use of Verloc, the Assistant Commissioner undoes Vladimir's scheme. He can abstract Heat from his London setting and see him with detachment:

> His memory evoked a certain old fat and wealthy native chief in the distant colony whom it was a tradition for the successive Colonial Governors to trust and make much of as a firm friend and supporter of the order and legality established by white men; whereas, when examined sceptically, he was found out to be principally his own good friend, and nobody else's. Not precisely a traitor, but still a man of many dangerous reservations in his fidelity, caused by a due regard for his own advantage, comfort, and safety. A fellow of some innocence in his naïve duplicity, but none the less dangerous. He was physically a big man, too, and (allowing for the difference of colour, of course) Chief Inspector Heat's appearance recalled him to the memory of his superior. (p. 118)

The Assistant Commissioner becomes a satirist himself for the moment. He is, moreover, adroit in handling the cabinet minister as well as his own subordinate. To liken him to the Professor seems to me profoundly mistaken. In a sense, the Assistant Commissioner has the degree of consciousness that might pull *The Secret Agent* from satire to novel, but he has a limited role, largely subservient to the working out of the ironic plot. He participates in the common plight in having a motive of self-interest among others, but he stands outside it in recognizing what must be done.

The other place we might look for a third term, an exception to the contrast of indolence and obsession, is in Winnie Verloc. She is presented ambiguously as a woman of reserve or of indifference; she seems, in fact, a somnambulist in all but her devotion to her retarded brother. She has chosen to marry Verloc in order to insure support for Stevie, and, that ambition realized, she walks through life somewhat as Verloc walks through the Knightsbridge streets. She refuses to take notice of 'the inside of facts' or 'the inwardness of things'. Winnie's mother, in contrast, more sensitive to Verloc's impatience, devises a means of securing Stevie's place with the Verlocs. She inveigles herself into an almshouse in order to halve the number of Winnie's dependents that Verloc must support. But here, too, illusion must play a part. In performing this 'heroic and unscrupulous' act, she assumes (rightly) that Winnie's loyalty to Stevie will endure: 'She excepted that sentiment from the rule of decay affecting all things human and some things divine. She could not help it; not to have done so would have frightened her too much' (p. 162). This movement to the very edge of endurable truth makes her an 'heroic old woman'. Typically enough, Winnie has no real perception of her mother's fears and countermeasures. Yet like her mother she has sacrificed much for the security of Stevie; her marriage to Verloc has been the form of that sacrifice. But, whatever Winnie's motives, she has pleased Verloc as a wife; she has more than lived up to the terms of her secret bargain. Her life has been 'stagnant and deep like a placid pool', only slightly stirred by the flirtation of Comrade Ossipon, 'an existence foreign to all grace and charm, without beauty and almost without decency, but admirable in the continuity of feeling and tenacity of purpose' (pp. 243–44).

Her discovery of Stevie's death is overwhelming, 'altering even the aspect of inanimate things'. All of the bonds which have held her to Verloc, or even to life, have been broken with the loss of her one purpose, her care for Stevie. Awakened at last into an independent life, she does not know 'what use to make of her freedom'. Verloc, on the other hand, has begun to divest himself of responsibility; he blames the label in Stevie's coat for his discovery. 'I don't blame you', he tells his wife, 'but it's your doing all the same' (p. 255). It was she, moreover, who kept thrusting Stevie upon his attention: 'if you will have it that I killed the boy', he concludes, 'then you've killed him as much as I' (p. 258). With that, Winnie's freedom from human ties is complete. When she stabs her husband to death she is 'a woman enjoying her complete irresponsibility and endless leisure, almost in the manner of a corpse' (p. 262).

In what follows, Winnie Verloc, who has achieved intensity and a degree of heroism, shrinks into a pathetic bur sordid hysteria. She is now overwhelmed by the fear of the gallows, desperate to find any way of escape. She turns to Ossipon for help when she comes upon him; he resumes his flirtation and finds her responsive. She tries to be deliberately seductive, perhaps even somewhat persuaded of Ossipon's affection for her. She is like her mother; not to believe in this 'would have frightened her too much'. She tries to hold Ossipon's loyalty, in spite of his horror at the sight of the corpse, by means of the large sum of money Verloc has given her. Ossipon is both foolish and vicious: he 'gazed scientifically at that woman, the sister of a degenerate, a degenerate herself—of a murdering type. He . . . invoked Lombroso, as an Italian peasant recommends himself to his favourite saint' (p. 297). There is farcical misunderstanding; he praises Stevie as 'a perfect type in a way', and Winnie replies tenderly: 'He was that indeed. . . . You took a lot of notice of him, Tom. I loved you for it.' And Ossipon reflects aloud, with new dread: 'Yes, he resembled you.' As Winnie laments, we are told, 'the truth—the very cry of truth—was found in a worn and artificial shape picked up somewhere among the phrases of sham sentiment'. Her last words are one of these phrases: 'I will live all my days for you, Tom!' (p. 298).

Winnie Verloc emerges as a moral being somewhat as Alvan Hervey does in 'The Return' or as Razumov far more powerfully does in *Under Western Eyes*. But her new existence is immediately aborted by her dread of the gallows. This fear seems arbitrary rather than necessary to Winnie's character, and it has the effect of degrading her to desperate wishfulness and a coarse pathos. She can be compared with the Verlocs' charwoman, Mrs Neale:

> She followed it with the everlasting plaint of the poor, pathetically mendacious, miserably authenticated by the horrible breath of cheap rum and soap-suds. She scrubbed hard, snuffling all the time, and talking volubly. And she was sincere. And on each side of her thin red nose her bleared, misty eyes swam in tears, because she felt really the want of some sort of stimulant in the morning. (p. 184)

In *Under Western Eyes* Conrad found an adequate 'third term' in Sophia Antonovna. She impresses Razumov by her acuteness and her dedication. He knows little of her history, but he cannot despise her as he has the others he meets in Zurich. There runs through her talk, however, an affectionate maternal impatience with the childishness of men as well as a deeper acceptance of inferiority to them: 'That's where you men have the advantage. You are inspired sometimes both in thought and action. I have always admitted that when you *are* inspired; when you manage to throw off your masculine cowardice and prudishness you are not to be equalled by us' (p. 250). The last words of the novel echo this indispensable faith: 'Peter Ivanovitch is an inspired man.' Her faith, however misdirected, is formidable. As she recalls the oppression of the Russian people, she exclaims: 'One must believe for very pity. This can't go on.' And she is ready to accept the consequences of acting upon that pity: 'You've got to trample down every particle of your own feelings: for stop you cannot. You must not' (p. 345). For Razumov this 'old revolutionary hand, the respected, trusted, and influential Sophia Antonovna', much more 'representative than the great Peter Ivanovitch', is 'the true spirit of destructive revolution' (p. 261). If she is ruthless and obsessed, if she exhibits 'the stupid subtlety of people with one idea' (p. 283), she is at least selfless and sincere. And to call here 'sincere' is not, as in the case of Mrs Neale, a further accusation.

The Secret Agent remains a troubling book. As a satire, it might be seen to assimilate all of its characters to self-absorbed blindness, whether obsessive or indolent. Yet it offers itself as a 'simple tale' and leads us at many points to accept it as a novel. The result, as we have seen from critics' comments, is to direct our attention to the virtuosity of ironic method. Yet it seems questionable to divorce such virtuosity from its thematic and dramatic uses, and it is there that one feels the presence of an author who wavers between the sardonic and the sentimental. We are not allowed the full detachment which might allow us to scorn the shams and bunglers alike. Nor are we allowed to entertain very long or far the sympathy which the more complex characters awaken. The only way we can resolve these conflicts is to move to a level of abstraction that leaves precise motives and actions behind in the search for large covering terms. If we turn instead to the author's motives, we may be troubled by an irony earned at the expense of disabled characters. *The Secret Agent* is an important book for the problems its raises. It makes us ask ourselves what we expect of a novel, at least in its traditional form, what we ask of satire beyond derision and of irony beyond denial.

NOTES

1. *The Shape of Utopia* (Chicago, 1970), pp. 110, 121. Elliott wrote entertainingly here about the literary difficulties presented by the 'new dispensation which eliminates conflict from society' and leaves little place for 'the angularities of character upon which the novel so much depends' (p. 105). He returned to the issue in 'The Costs of Utopia', *Transactions of the Fourth International Congress on the Enlightenment, Studies in Voltaire and the Eighteenth Century*, 152 (1976), 677–92.

2. I am using the terms 'novel' and 'fiction' loosely; they may be taken to refer to the tradition of mimetic fiction. As Ian Watt has recently shown with thoroughness and acuteness, Conrad's is among the earliest English fiction systematically to displace narrative sequence by thematic; it is also, with Hardy's, among the earliest to make explicit use of metaphysical concerns. Nevertheless, I believe that my rough and exploratory contrast between satire and fiction can be applied to Conrad. Compare Ian Watt, *Conrad in the Nineteenth Century* (Berkeley and Los Angeles, 1980).

3. *The Power of Satire: Magic, Ritual, Art* (Princeton, New Jersey, 1970), p. 214.

4. *Forms of Life: Character and Moral Imagination in the Novel* (New Haven, Connecticut, 1983), pp. 235–65.

5. Tony Tanner, in an article on *Under Western Eyes*, cites the relevant, if somewhat overweening, speech of the hero of T. S. Eliot's *The Family Reunion*: 'You have gone through life in a sleep, | Never woken to the nightmare. I tell you, life would be unendurable | If you were wide awake.' ('Nightmare and Complacency: Razumov and the Western Eye', *Critical Quarterly*, 4 (1962), 197–214).

6. Sylvia Bank Manning, *Dickens as Satirist* (New Haven, Connecticut, 1971), p. 9. Further citations are made by parenthetical page numbers in the text.

7. *The Secret Agent*, Uniform Edition (London, 1923), p. 179. All references to Conrad's fiction will be to this edition, by parenthetical page numbers in the text.

8. *The Return of Eva Peron* (London, 1980), p. 215.

9. *Conrad: The Moral World of the Novelist* (London, 1978). This seems to me an important book, and I regret very much that I had not seen it when I wrote on Conrad earlier (see note 4). Lawrence Graver, who draws interesting resemblances to Flaubert and Kipling, speaks of the 'ruthless belligerence' of the work in *Conrad's Short Fiction* (Berkeley and Los Angeles, 1969), p. 11.

10. Cited from *De la Division du travail social* (1893) in his own translation by Steven Lukes, in *Emile Durkheim: His Life and Work* (Harmondsworth, 1975), pp. 149–50. See also *The Division of Labor in Society*, translated by George Simpson (New York and London, 1933), pp. 129 ff.

11. Graver discusses it briefly (pp. 34–39) and supplies a short list of selected criticism before 1969 (p. 229). For Gekoski, see note 13 below.

12. On the revisions of *The Secret Agent*, see Walter F. Wright, *Romance and Tragedy in Joseph Conrad* (Lincoln, Nebraska, 1949), pp. 175–97.

13. R. A. Gekoski is very interesting on the story. I cannot follow his emphasis on religious conversion and the 'affirmation of the transcendental value of Love'; and I am, as a result, less inclined to think that Hervey's final vision might have been intended to be ironic. See his discussion in *Conrad*, pp. 51 ff. For the possible influence of this story upon *The Waste Land*, see Robert L. Morris, 'Eliot's "Game of Chess" and Conrad's "The Return"', *MLN*, 65 (1950), 422–23.

14. *Joseph Conrad: The Three Lives* (London, 1979), pp. 599, 587.

15. *Joseph Conrad: The Way of Dispossession* (London, 1977), pp. 167, 170.

16. *The Great Tradition*, Peregrine Edition (Harmondsworth, 1962), p. 237.

17. *Conrad the Novelist* (Cambridge, Massachusetts, 1958), pp. 230–31. I should say that these quotations from Guerard and others whose work I greatly admire are meant to be not representative samplings but responses to particular problems.

18. *Conrad: The Secret Agent. A Casebook*, edited by Ian Watt (London, 1973), pp. 62, 77, 80.

19. *Poets of Reality: Six Twentieth-Century Writers* (Cambridge, Massachusetts, 1966), pp. 41, 66.

20. *Politics and the Novel* (New York, 1957), p. 94.

21. *Joseph Conrad's Letters to R. B. Cunninghame Graham*, edited by C. T. Watts (Cambridge, 1969), Letter no. 60 (7 October 1907), p. 170.

22. 'Joseph Conrad's *The Secret Agent*' (1926), reprinted in the translation of H. T. Lowe-Porter in *Conrad: The Secret Agent*, edited by Ian Watt (p. 106).

ANTHONY WINNER

The Secret Agent: *The Irony of Home Truths*

The irony that blankets the London of *The Secret Agent* seems far removed from the ambiguous interplay of sheltering illusion and innate disorder in *Lord Jim* and *Nostromo*. "Regulated hatred," the quality that D. W. Harding bestows on an aspect of Jane Austen's fiction in his controversial essay, aptly describes Conrad's narrative.[1] Almost every setting, character, and action mocks and is mocked by elusive moral judgments. Language itself is out of joint: adjectives become nouns, breaking faith with their function; negatives and negative prefixes abound, casting doubt on the simplest declaration; superlatives occur so often and so ludicrously as to travesty praise and blame. The novel is rich in those parallels, analogies, and cross-references through which Conrad elsewhere expresses the ambiguities of moral understanding. But by the end, when the Professor refuses to look at the "odious" masses that refuse to look at him, we find ourselves baffled. We remember Winnie's refusal to look deep into things; Sir Ethelred's refusal to listen to complications; the inability to see human meaning that stigmatizes Mr. Verloc and Comrade Ossipon. We seem near to grasping a pattern, but the overlappings yield only the opaqueness of coincidence. And yet the novel, for all its instances of absurdity and grossness, does not appear to most readers as an unsafe, threatening, or absurd experience. If the irony cruelly represents the

From *Culture and Irony: Studies in Joseph Conrad's Major Novels*, pp. 70–91, 128–29. © 1988 by the Rector and Visitors of the University of Virginia.

deformity of value, it also works as in the previous novels to salvage a saving remnant of civilizing illusion.

Conrad's irony here has much in common with the idea of work that Marlow advocates in *Heart of Darkness*. The frequent foulness of London approximates in a sleazy, secondhand way the horrors of the Congo. Our plausible response would be to join those who avert their gaze. The irony, by holding offensiveness at bay, appears to allow us the safety of what Guerard calls an "entertainment."[2] The heavily melodramatic turns of plot are too excessive to touch us. As Schwartz puts it: "The reader shares the moral superiority, detachment, and condescension of the narrator. Conrad expects us to juxtapose the narrator's ironic redefinition of such terms as 'freedom' and 'knowledge' with definitions established by social and moral tradition."[3] The discrepancy between the spectacle of disorder and the reflexes of our moral beliefs frees us to be entertained. Just as Marlow's fidelity to his demanding work holds him safe from the Congo life all around him, so Conrad's irony seems at first to provide the support needed to endure an immersion in what Claire Rosenfield calls "this monstrous presence of stone and brick and darkness," this archetypal "world totally devoid of meaning."[4]

But the foulness is more insidious, immediate, and intimate than the distant heart of darkness. Repeatedly, the scenes and images press beyond the protection irony can offer. During the Assistant Commissioner's investigation of the Greenwich explosion in which Stevie is blown apart, he enters an Italian restaurant: "one of those traps for the hungry . . . without air, but with an atmosphere of their own" (p. 148). The irony summons up the response of stable understanding: we know that real meals and restaurants never live up to ideal expectation. Yet the next comment shocks us with its bitterness. The atmosphere is that of "fraudulent cookery mocking an abject mankind in the most pressing of its miserable necessities." Pushing beyond normative social satire, the narrative opens up a bleak perspective of human distress. Guerard sees in these lines a serious intrusion "of a different authorial consciousness and voice" from those which control the irony of the rest of the book.[5] Yet the view of the London wasteland is consistent. "Fraudulent," "abject," and "miserable" refer to the ugliness that the narrative presents as inevitably consequent on man's material necessities. The adjectives might be more appropriate to a traditional gnostic fury at the violation of spiritual integrity by the vile facts of our physical condition. Conrad, of course, is no Manichean. But the bloated flesh, ungainly needs, and offensive settings that engross *The Secret Agent* offer glimpses of a cosmic defamation quite as cruel as that which Hardy and other contemporary pessimists discover in the nakedness of the human situation.

The Secret Agent takes place in a grimly actualized version of those "mean streets" that Arthur Morrison and other observers of the London poor had been sentimentalizing. Both setting and cast correspond to the lower depths in which naturalistic fiction so often finds its case histories. However, unlike Zola's Paris, which is besotted by its lust for money, drink, or sex, Conrad's London is offensive in its very essence. The Verlocs' "domestic drama" (p. 222) illustrates a distasteful meanness that apparently expresses the city's truth. After Winnie learns of her husband's role in Stevie's death, she burrows into outraged silence. Enraged in his turn at her refusal to heed his own egocentric distress, Mr. Verloc accuses her of having shoved Stevie into his affairs and thus of being herself responsible for the young man's fate. "In sincerity of feeling and openness of statement, these words went far beyond anything that had ever been said in this home, kept up on the wages of a secret industry eked out by the sale of more or less secret wares: the poor expedients devised by a mediocre mankind for preserving an imperfect society from the dangers of moral and physical corruption, both secret, too, of their kind" (p. 258). The authorial distaste is aesthetic as well as moral. The dismal, fraudulent household is typical of the unsightly disease that afflicts most of the novel's milieus. In the manner of ironic discourse, the Verlocs' home perverts the meaning of home; the vehicle traduces the tenor. In *The Secret Agent*, moreover, as Schwartz observes, the "vehicles of a metaphor do not simply express a quality to be associated with the tenor, but replace the tenor as the essential quality of the imagined world."[6] Eclipsing instead of insinuating the truths they violate, the vehicles seem to cohere into a hermetically black vision of the way things are in London.

Yet London should be the home of the values to which Conrad's faithful seamen swear allegiance. By so grotesquely perverting these values, the city draws down some of the novel's most bitter irony. In much of his previous fiction, Conrad juggles two views of the homeland of moral service and order. Present-day Britain is both a realm of flabby and complacent lives and a source of the civilizing force that supports moral endeavor. Traveling down the Congo, Marlow fondly recalls the trimmed lawns, hygienically packaged meats, and protective policemen in far-off London. If the city is overwrapped in comforts, it is nonetheless a safe shelter in a dark world. In *Lord Jim*, Marlow evokes with wry yet almost filial irony the comforts that protect those at home from the rending realities that cause Jewel to waste her life in tears. Home is peopled by women like Kurtz's Intended, who are too good and too vulnerable to bear stark truth, and by men like Jim's clergyman father, whose useful existence is supported by ignorance and by the bulwark of cultural platitudes. Distance blurs the tension between protection and evasion into Conrad's characteristic misty ambiguity. We are not unduly perplexed to realize that Jim is condemned for betraying the code of trust that cushions the lives of the tourists Marlow so disdains. But *The Secret Agent* tells a London story. Existence in the heartland of home appears to confirm all the negative judgments that have been diffused by distance and nostalgia. Not only is the earthbound city "emblematic of the complexity which Conrad sees as the particular characteristic of . . . shore moralities";[7] it is in itself a worse betrayer of faith than a Kurtz. Where from afar one saw a flickering beacon of moral truth, now one is mired in miserable corruption. As if Conrad were a Gulliver forced to confront in Brobdingnagian closeup the ideals on which the moral action of his previous fiction rests, the warts and more damaging disfigurations of home truths prove appalling.

Conrad's sense that this irony of disenchantment may seem excessive accounts for the defensive tone at the conclusion to his 1920 Author's Note. "But still I will submit that telling Winnie Verloc's story to its anarchistic end of utter desolation, madness and despair, and telling it as I have told it here, I have not intended to commit a gratuitous outrage on the feelings of mankind" (p. xv). Certainly Conrad's intense attention to what he calls the requirements of his art belies any suggestion of the gratuitous. Yet when decent, civilized citizens such as Winnie and her mother take over from dim African natives or Arab pilgrims as innocent victims, we do feel ourselves in the presence of outrageous melodrama. Nostromo's fate, of course, arouses a similarly painful sensation. But the Capataz's vanity and materialism in part blunt identification; moreover, even in his default and death the hope invested in his "genius" continues to resound. Nostromo is in his way an exceptional man. The "mediocre mankind" of *The Secret Agent* is, in Guerard's words, "flabby, debased, eternally gullible."[8] The best that Winnie and her kin can aspire to is that heroism of the commonplace often cherished by English moral realism of the previous century. And even such aspiration is unpleasantly disallowed. When Winnie's mother gets herself admitted to the home for worthy widows so that Mr. Verloc will be burdened only by poor Stevie, the cab that takes her to her exile mocks her good intentions. "The conveyance awaiting them would have illustrated the proverb that 'truth can be more cruel than caricature,' if such a proverb existed. Crawling behind an infirm horse, a metropolitan hackney carriage drew up on wobbly wheels and with a maimed driver on the box. This last peculiarity caused some embarrassment. Catching sight of a hooked iron contrivance protruding from the left sleeve of the man's coat, Mrs. Verloc's mother lost suddenly the heroic courage of these days" (pp. 155–56). The grotesque requires ironic distancing; but the irony carries the mother's admirable act into caricature.

In the Author's Note, Conrad speaks of his "vision of . . . a monstrous town more populous than some continents and in its man-made might as if indifferent to heaven's frowns and smiles; a cruel devourer of the world's light" (p. xii). London is now a blackness into which the moral clarity and civilizing purpose associated with light disappear. Conrad's pessimism, his sense of cosmic indifference and human deficiency, is condensed into the city, which becomes the urban ground of general irony. Although the terrorist Professor, the self-styled "moral agent" (p. 80) of explosive anarchy, is shown to be as mediocre as the masses he loathes, the sick city lends plausibility to his scorn. Commenting on the words "madness and despair," used both in the Author's Note and in the newspaper report of Winnie's fate, he proclaims "doctorally": "There are no such things. All passion is lost now. The world is mediocre, limp, without force. And madness and despair are a force. And force is a crime in the eyes of the fools, the weak and the silly who rule the roost" (p. 309). Not only is conventional life in the Professor's view "open to attack at every point" (p. 68); as the novel presents it, the city's life deserves to be attacked. The Professor wants to strike "a blow fit to open the first crack in the imposing front of the great edifice of legal conceptions sheltering the atrocious injustice of society" (p. 80). The black anarchist's shabby motives ridicule this plan of vengeance; and Conrad, of course, mocks the very idea of radical action. But the fact of outrageous injustice and the odious disjunction between things as they are and as they ought to be appear to demand nothing less than revolution.

Foolish trust, debilitating misery, and blind routine dominate the life of the monstrous town. Most of the characters cannot or will not see. Were they Conrad's readers, he would have to admit failure in his ambition: "by the power of the written word to make you hear, to make you feel ... before all, to make you *see*."[9] Winnie and her mother are prototypical in their intuition that direct perception of the world around them would be catastrophic. The intuition is correct. The turning point for Winnie, the beginning of her end, comes when she is able to see, to visualize, Stevie's destruction. Only the Professor and Stevie, however blinkered by their myopias, perceive some of the truths that the others evade or pervert. The Professor's personality and ideas reduce rational scorn of the general decadence to absurdity. Though far more appealing, Stevie's "convulsive sympathy" does the same. His response to the cabman and his "steed of apocalyptic misery" (p. 167) demonstrates his ability to feel but carries his ideal sentiments into a realm more cruelly grotesque than caricature. "He could say nothing; for the tenderness to all pain and misery, the desire to make the horse happy and the cabman happy, had reached the point of a bizarre longing to take them to bed with him. And that, he knew, was impossible" (p. 167). Stevie is naked before the irony he embodies. He is vulnerable perception unaided by any possibility of acting on what he feels. His raging sense of frustration parallels the Professor's.

At the bottom of his pockets his incapable, weak hands were clinched hard into a pair of angry fists. In the face of anything which affected directly or indirectly his morbid dread of pain, Stevie ended by turning vicious. A magnanimous indignation swelled his frail chest to bursting, and caused his candid eyes to squint. Supremely wise in knowing his own powerlessness, Stevie was not wise enough to restrain his passions. The tenderness of his universal charity had two phases as indissolubly joined and connected as the reverse and obverse sides of a medal. The anguish of immoderate compassion was succeeded by the pain of an innocent but pitiless rage. (p. 169)

Stevie is the obverse of the Professor, who is not wise enough to know his own powerlessness. Both are bombs manufactured by London's reality. At issue is the need for some power to make sense of this reality. Both Stevie's judgment and the countervailing force it cries out for are movingly direct: "Poor brute, poor people," "Shame!" "Bad world for poor people" (p. 171). The episode is harrowing yet also antic. Our reaction might well resemble that suggested a few pages earlier when the grotesquely miserable cabman explains that his travail supports a "missus and four kids at 'ome." "The monstrous nature of that declaration of paternity seemed to strike the world dumb" (pp. 166–67). The irony joins two premises: that as humane people we ought to be struck dumb; that as weak people seeking protection from facts we will take refuge in dismissive amusement. Such irony enacts the defensive function of black humor: the hyperbole screens us from the pain just as the persistent wordplay—"magnanimous ... frail chest"; "candid ... squint"—blunts too naked an involvement in the action. The strategy realizes the implications of Marlow's bafflement in *Lord Jim* when Jewel's irremediable plight drives all his words into a "chaos of dark thoughts." Marlow's own extensive verbal work strives to preserve "the sheltering conception of light and order which is our refuge" (p. 313) while acknowledging the cruel facts that make this refuge a sham or an illusion. His irony compromises both the pure light of civilization and the blackness of real horror. The irony of *The Secret Agent* condenses horror into hyperbole, moral light into what Cooper calls Winnie's "amoral nobility,"[10] and the necessity for unpalatable compromise into the verbal game that civilization must by its powerless nature play.

* * *

Stevie and the Professor stand outside the game. Winnie is both the game and its stakes. Near the end, after she discovers the truth about her husband

and kills him, she is cast adrift. She tries to communicate her pain, isolation, and dread to the squalid, thick-skulled Comrade Ossipon. He has no idea what she is trying to express; she, reduced to a state much like that Stevie experiences when confronted with the cab and its "perfection of grotesque misery" (p. 170), cannot find words. But whereas Stevie elicits a tragicomic irony, Winnie calls forth one of the few clearly reliable expressions of narrative sympathy: "She lamented aloud her love of life, that life without grace or charm, and almost without decency, but of an exalted faithfulness of purpose, even unto murder. And, as so often happens in the lament of poor humanity rich in suffering but indigent in words, the truth—the very cry of truth—was found in a worn and artificial shape picked up somewhere among the phrases of sham sentiment" (p. 298). The passage recalls Flaubert's celebrated gloss on the way the jaded roué Rodolphe dismisses Emma Bovary's clichéd cry of love: "Human speech is like a cracked kettle on which we tap crude rhythms for bears to dance to, while we long to make music that will melt the stars."[11] Flaubert strives to perfect an art that will transform crude reality into enduring music. The irony that Conrad undertakes follows from the premise that the only hope of music in a universal dissonance is bound into human crudeness. Average men and women with their uncharming natures and shopworn hopes are as disenchanting a subject for art as London is a depressing setting for culture. Both as artistic and as moral material, Winnie is so minimal as to be grotesque. That the task of ironic protection has been reduced to the mean measure of Winnie, Stevie, and her mother helps account for the sense of infuriation that underlies so much of the novel. Outrage vies with pathos, each with its own irony.

The competing impulses create frustrating ambiguity in the work of irony that parallels the devious efforts of the police when their work of social protection runs up against the incomprehensible Greenwich explosion. The bomb that splatters Stevie across the park satisfies in its way the goal that Mr. Vladimir sets for Mr. Verloc. The nasty First Secretary of the foreign embassy wants to arouse the nation by "an act of destructive ferocity so absurd as to be incomprehensible, inexplicable, almost unthinkable; in fact, mad" (p. 33). And indeed, Chief Inspector Heat, the very model of a complacent, conventional policeman, is aghast. "The complexion of that case had somehow forced upon him the general idea of the absurdity of things human, which in the abstract is sufficiently annoying to an unphilosophical temperament, and in concrete instances becomes exasperating beyond endurance" (p. 91). Exasperation undermines efficiency—in policework as in ironic art. Heat's vexed bewilderment awakens in his superior, the Assistant Commissioner of police, "a special kind of interest in his work of social protection ... a sudden and alert mistrust of the weapon in his hand" (p. 103). In the passage already quoted in the Introduction, Heat, sensing that the case is about to be taken out of his hands, feels

> like a tight-rope artist might feel if suddenly, in the middle of the performance, the manager of the Music Hall were to rush out of the proper managerial seclusion and begin to shake the rope. Indignation, the sense of moral insecurity engendered by such a treacherous proceeding joined to the immediate apprehension of a broken neck, would, in the colloquial phrase, put him in a state. And there would be also some scandalized concern for his art, too, since a man must identify himself with something more tangible than his own personality, and establish his pride somewhere, either in his social position, or in the quality of the work he is obliged to do. (pp. 116–17)

Not only is Heat undone by his perception of what Conrad calls absurdity and many modernists term entropy; the entire system of protection in which the Chief Inspector finds his worthwhile meaning is cast into doubt. Like Winnie, who is equally literal-minded and equally faithful of purpose, Heat cannot grasp the unlikely nature of his service. He understands crime as a misapplied idea of industry resulting from "imperfect education" (p. 92). "Thieving was not a sheer absurdity" (p. 91). But such a view cannot comprehend the destructive ferocity of the Professor, the preposterous behavior of the mock anarchists who surround Mr. Verloc, or the bizarre inefficiency of language. As only the Assistant Commissioner will be able to see—and he quite dimly—protection cannot function except through an ironic sense of reality's treacherous proceedings.

Winnie's life suggests why. If policework echoes the way irony must function, Winnie's small art encapsulates what irony must protect. In one of those usages that undermine and then reconstitute the meaning of words, the narrative refers several times to her "philosophy," which consists in "not taking notice of the inside of facts" (p. 154). Denying all distracting complications in life, she directs the entire "ardour of [her] protecting compassion" (p. 58) on her brother. Protecting Stevie's "difficult existence," she has achieved a "life of single purpose and of a noble unity of inspiration, like those rare lives that have left their mark on the thoughts and feelings of mankind" (p. 242). Abjuring her one true love, the butcher who has money enough to support her but not Stevie, she settles on Mr. Verloc and the protection she believes he will extend to her family. Her commonplace heroism and moral art as well as her unglamorous faithfulness place her in the same tradition of nineteenth-century moral realism that is subjected to irony when her mother enters the home for widows. But Winnie is a larger subject and the irony is more intense. The reference to rare lives is countered at once: "But the visions of Mrs. Verloc lacked nobility and magnificence" (p. 242). Superlative praise dangles on a tightrope above the demeaning picture of a charmlessness so complete as to suggest a grotesquerie of being itself. Winnie purchases "seven years' security for Stevie loyally paid for on her part" (p. 243) by a marital service that seems as miserable a necessity as mankind's need for food; during these years, security grows "into confidence, into domestic feeling, stagnant and deep like a placid pool" (p. 243). Seeing Mr. Verloc at last take an interest in Stevie, whom he wants to employ in the Greenwich outrage, she believes that her work has triumphed: "And this last vision had such plastic relief, such nearness of form, such a fidelity of suggestive detail, that it wrung from Mrs. Verloc an anguished and faint murmur, reproducing the supreme illusion of her life. . . . 'Might have been father and son'" (p. 244). Fostering Stevie's destruction, Mr. Verloc ravages Winnie's illusion and her art. Her temperament, "when stripped of its philosophic reserve, was maternal and violent"; she regards her fate with the rage and dismay of a betrayed woman" (p. 241). In a novel in which only betrayal and degrading injustice—whether enforced by Mr. Vladimir on Mr. Verloc or society on the silly Michaelis—create sympathy, the betrayal of Winnie's trust is rending.

Pathos, however, does not diminish irony. Winnie's art and home rest on near-ridiculous materials: a retarded boy and a fly-blown smut shop, "a perfection of grotesque misery and weirdness of macabre detail." The idea of this stagnant, superficial wife of a bungling double agent as any kind of artist is absurd. Yet the irony rescues value of a sort. The shelter Winnie would create is no mean illusion. Throughout the sections leading to the disastrous revelation and the murder of Mr. Verloc, the narrative insinuates the kind of sad admiration that we observed in Marlow's ironic respect for the chief accountant in *Heart of Darkness*.

Repeatedly, the ironic hyperbole sets Winnie's predicament against the background of the primal state out of which civil order has emerged. When Mr. Verloc first gives evidence of duplicity, unaccountably withdrawing the family savings and bringing the cash home, Winnie suddenly distrusts the safety she has worked for. "This abode of her married life appeared to her as lonely and unsafe as though it had been situated in the midst of a forest" (p. 101). Later, having finally understood that Stevie, the "presiding genius" of this abode, is dead, "Mrs. Verloc gazed at the whitewashed wall. A blank wall—perfectly blank. A blankness to run at and dash your head against. . . . She kept still as the population of half the globe would keep still in astonishment and despair, were the sun suddenly put out in the summer sky by the perfidy of a trusted providence" (p. 244). The total eclipse releases Winnie "from all earthly ties. She had her freedom" (p. 251). But freedom demands a force commensurate to a precivilized absolutism of events. Winnie, now that her small art is undone; is as powerless as Stevie. For her, freedom is a more annihilatingly heroic challenge than it will be for Razumov in Conrad's next novel. "Her intention had been simply to get outside the door for ever. And if this feeling was correct, its mental form took an unrefined shape corresponding to her origin and station. 'I would rather walk the streets all the days of my life,' she thought. But this creature, whose moral nature had been subject to a shock of which, in the physical order, the most violent earthquake of history could be only a faint and languid rendering, was at the mercy of mere trifles, of casual contacts" (p. 255).

The conceits magnify both Winnie's plight and her insufficiency. The rhetoric aspires to the naked embattlement of truths engendered by Kurtz's bestial horror, Jim's struggle for honor in primal Patusan, and Nostromo's fall from service into a vain grasping for his ego's survival. Winnie tumbles into the darkness that Marlow once saw as extending from savage Africa to the estuary of the Thames. She puts into the knife thrust that kills her husband "all the inheritance of her immemorial and obscure descent, the simple ferocity of the age of caverns, and the unbalanced nervous fury of the age of barrooms" (p. 263). But even as a primal actor Winnie is banal and shallow. "Mrs. Verloc, who always refrained from looking deep into things, was compelled to look into the very bottom of this thing. She saw there no haunting face, no reproachful shade, no vision of remorse, no sort of ideal conception. She saw there an object. That object was the gallows. Mrs. Verloc was afraid of the gallows" (p. 267).

The resonant amplification of Winnie's fate is cut short by an almost childlike syntactic simplicity. If many of the images cast her as an exceptional victim of the cruelty meted out to average humanity by a perfidious universe, the strong ironic current reminds us that the sister is but the other side of the brother's thin coin. Unlike Zola's Gervaise or Hardy's Tess, whose predicament is similarly extreme, Winnie is not so much average as she is flat. Her betrayal is plangently evoked, but she is a mere descendant of Mrs. Micawber and Mrs. Gradgrind. After the loss of Stevie—"the salt of passion in her tasteless life" (p. 174)—and the murder of her husband, she stands on the threshold of the multidimensionality that might grant individuality and meaningful freedom. But she cannot develop; she is quite without even Nostromo's vain flair. Her single passion, her "exalted faithfulness of purpose," ratifies flatness: Stevie is her Mr. Micawber.

With Winnie, Conrad presents a supreme instance of essential simplicity interwoven with a grandly ambiguous moral action. Her fixed idea torn away, Winnie becomes flotsam. Harrowed by her terror of the gallows, she is as stricken of refuge as the friendless, solitary orphan Razumov. "The vast world created for the glory of man was only a vast blank to Mrs. Verloc. She did not know which way to turn. Murderers had friends, relations, helpers— they had knowledge. She had nothing. She was the most lonely of murderers that ever struck a mortal blow. She was alone in London: and the whole town of marvels and mud, with its maze of streets and its mass of lights, was sunk in a hopeless night, rested at the bottom of a black abyss from which no unaided woman could hope to scramble out" (pp. 270–71). Instead of a source of light, London is the abyss of general irony, a moral quicksand dragging down all meaning. Blending outrageous comedy and ironic pathos, Ossipon's hope of exploiting Winnie's plight and her destitution, the long penultimate chapter exhibits the ravages of flatness. From the novel's first paragraph, in which Mr. Verloc leaves "his shop nominally in charge of his brother-in-law," Stevie, and his wife "in charge of his brother-in-law," (p. 3), the themes of interdependence and protection have been made to seem a mocking trap. Now Winnie is freed into an entrapping nothingness. Her smallness is even further reduced. Yet it is just in this context that she receives the homage already quoted: her life, charmless and "almost without decency," has been "of an exalted faithfulness of purpose, even unto murder."

Human minimalism and the truth of Conrad's idea are now inextricable. As Cooper writes, Winnie becomes "an heroic figure in the environment of London's squalor."[12] The narrative seems to practice a diminished version of Emilia Gould's "imaginative estimate" that finds in the raw silver—and by extension in its simple foreman—"a justificative conception." As in *Nostromo*, this conception resides ironically and painfully not in the glory of principled Faction but in the stolid limitations of charmless common needs. Winnie is the principle that civilization serves pressed flat. Her thinness protects her from the often luridly scornful irony directed at the miasma in which she is found while at the same time protecting the reader from too sheer an empathy with her "anarchistic end of utter desolation."

* * *

But even this precarious affirmation is subject to irony. As Winnie's qualities are a more serviceable form of her brother's simpleminded virtues, so Mr. Verloc's omnivorous yet inert egoism is the debased but logical image of Winnie's limitations. Central among the "figures grouped about Mrs. Verloc and related directly or indirectly to her tragic suspicion that 'life doesn't stand much looking into'" (pp. xii–xiii), Mr. Verloc reduces the irony of moral realism to the status of simple delusion. He is that antimatter implied by the kind of matter Winnie embodies. He translates her stubborn

fidelity into almost archetypal inertia; his corrosive egoism is the vile implication of the moral torpor apparent in his wife, in her mother, and in the
London masses. Attuned only to his own needs, Mr. Verloc is blind to all
others. "Mr. Verloc lacked profundity. Under the mistaken impression that
the value of individuals consists in what they are in themselves, he could
not possibly comprehend the value of Stevie in the eyes of Mrs. Verloc" (p.
233). Stevie's value expresses that mixture of illusion, moral truth, and faith
that allows us to be more than our unaided personalities. Mr. Verloc is the
nemesis of such value. He exudes "the air common to men who live on the
vices, the follies, or the baser fears of mankind; the air of moral nihilism
common to keepers of gambling hells" (p. 13). He leeches out the meaning
of human community. Gloating over the comfortable protection he observes
in the wealthy district surrounding Mr. Vladimir's embassy, he

> would have rubbed his hands with satisfaction had he not been
> constitutionally averse from every superfluous exertion. . . . He was
> in a manner devoted to [idleness] with a sort of inert fanaticism,
> or perhaps rather with a fanatical inertness. Born of industrious
> parents for a life of toil, he had embraced indolence from an impulse
> as profound, as inexplicable, and as imperious as the impulse which
> directs a man's preference for one particular woman in a given
> thousand. He was too lazy even for a mere demagogue. . . . It was
> too much trouble. He required a more perfect form of ease; or it
> might have been that he was the victim of a philosophical unbelief
> in the effectiveness of every human effort. (p. 12)

Mr. Verloc's force, like Satan's, is that of negation. He strains the order of
syntax and baffles words. Not the Professor's terrorism, certainly not the
shabby revolutionism of his colleagues, but the double agent's negation of
all mankind's efforts at effective meaning—an incarnation of the Schopenhauerian Will that undoes human intentions—is the true anarchy. Since the
irony of the novel parallels Conrad's ideal of valuable work, Mr. Verloc is
the irony's archenemy.

The secret agent's parasitism recalls the way in which Lantier in Zola's
L'Assommoir saps the industrious aspirations of the families he invades. But
Lantier is spawned by what Zola sees as a decadent era, by a historical situation that may be superseded; Mr. Verloc emerges from the darkness that
Conrad sees as separating the moral illusions that give life structure from
an ever-present primal disorder. The treacherous husband not only adopts
the protective coloration of valuable illusion; he embodies the terrifying
cohabitation of the arts of meaninglessness with the works of faith. Marrying

Winnie, he transforms the sanctuary of home into the nihilism of a disorderly house. The Assistant Commissioner can tell Sir Ethelred that Mr. Verloc has a "genuine wife and a genuinely, respectably, marital relation. . . . Yes, a genuine wife. And the victim was a genuine brother-in-law. From a certain point of view we are here in the presence of a domestic drama" (pp. 221–22). With Mr. Verloc, however, "genuine" and "domestic" are stripped of meaning—as are most other words of value in the narrative he so infects. The agent performs an act of vampirism on "the sheltering conception . . . which is our refuge." His insidious subversion of order places him in the company, not of the obviously evil Kurtz and Gentlemen Brown, but of James Wait and the faithless pilgrims of the Eldorado Exploring Expedition.

Since civilization relies upon the interdependent integrity of all its components, the threat Mr. Verloc incarnates is a matter of public as well as domestic drama. He undermines the protective structure that holds Mr. Vladimir and the Professor at bay. Carrying out the former's plan for a gratuitous blasphemy to be directed at learning—at the moral education central to Victorian culture—he plays into the hands of the alien ambitions that would overturn all Western civilization. The bomb that kills Stevie awakens the fear of foreign intentions common to the period: the kind of apprehension that underlies Erskine Childers's celebrated spy novel, *The Secret of the Sands* (1903). The suspicion that something more than "barefaced audacity amounting to childishness of a peculiar sort" (p. 138) may be involved in the affair brings first the Assistant Commissioner and then the Home Minister, Sir Ethelred, into the investigation. Both men fear that home in its largest meaning may be in jeopardy.

Public protection is, however, just as involved in irony as the shelter Winnie tries futilely to create for Stevie. The Assistant Commissioner seems at first a more efficient enforcer of the values of the home service than the credulous wife. Straddling the gap between London truths and the bright illusions of moral empire, keenly aware of the ironic ambiguities of the game civil order must play, the Assistant Commissioner appears to carry something of the glamour of Conradian high drama into the entropic settings appropriate to Mr. Verloc.[13] Not only does the Assistant Commissioner solve the mystery of the Greenwich outrage; he generates the sole instant resembling moral satisfaction that the novel allows: the expulsion of Mr. Vladimir from the civilized precincts of the Explorers Club, that "building of noble proportions and hospitable aspect" (p. 228). The gifts of this "born detective" (p. 117) have been developed by policework in the colonies, where issues are straightforward and possibilities for action still bright. The colonies nurture the clue to effective detection, which is also the key to the work of irony: mistrust. But the colonies have been left behind.

The Assistant Commissioner's socially ambitious wife, unable to abide life abroad, badgers him into returning home. The town galls him; he resents "the necessity of taking so much on trust" (p. 114). Even worse, he himself is forced to become the subject of his own mistrust. On the one hand, the Greenwich "affair, which, in one way or another, disgusted Chief Inspector Heat, seemed to him a providentially given starting-point for a crusade" (p. 222) against foreign meddling. Yet on the other hand, the high cause conceals a selfish motive. His wife's wealthy and influential patron has taken up the defense of the idealistic anarchist Michaelis. Chief Inspector Heat suspects Michaelis and wants to arrest him. Should Heat have his way and the "ticket-of-leave apostle" be sent back to prison, the Assistant Commissioner believes that "the distinguished and good friend of his wife, and himself" would never forgive him.

> The frankness of such a secretly outspoken thought could not go without some derisive self-criticism. No man engaged in a work he does not like can preserve many saving illusions about himself. The distaste, the absence of glamour, extend from the occupation to the personality. It is only when our appointed activities seem by a lucky accident to obey the particular earnestness of our temperament that we can taste the comfort of complete self-deception. The Assistant Commissioner did not like his work at home. The police work he had been engaged on in a distant part of the globe had the saving character of an irregular sort of warfare or at least the risk and excitement of an open-air sport. . . . Chained to a desk in the thick of four millions of men, he considered himself the victim of an ironic fate—the same, no doubt, which had brought about his marriage. (pp. 112–13)

In his distaste for domestication, for hole-and-corner action, for a world swaddled in secrecies and galling compromises, the Assistant Commissioner reflects the tone of the novel as a whole. In Guerard's words, this "may well be the author in a succinct if unconscious self-portrait. Yet the Assistant Commissioner evokes none of the major emotional involvement . . . we feel in the portrait of Razumov."[14] The Assistant Commissioner unravels the case and gets rid of Mr. Vladimir. But the corrosive irony that London represents becalms the possibility of sympathy as it swallows the meaning of successful detection. However appealing this man with his "long, meagre face with the accentuated features of an energetic Don Quixote" (p. 115), he simply disappears from the final quarter of the novel, apparently carrying with him what few saving illusions the narrative offers.

Winnie can kill her husband; the Assistant Commissioner can solve the mystery. Neither can counteract the banal, anonymous horror for which Mr. Verloc stands. Winnie is freed and forced from home into the mean streets. Seeking succor, she puts her trust in the unsavory Ossipon, one of her husband's cabal. He robs and then deserts her, leaving her on the boat train while he strolls home. "And again Comrade Ossipon walked. His robust form was seen that night in distant parts of the enormous town slumbering monstrously on a carpet of mud under a veil of raw mist. It was seen crossing the streets without life and sound.... He walked through Squares, Places, Ovals, Commons, through monotonous streets with unknown names where the dust of humanity settles inert and hopeless out of the stream of life" (p. 300). The perpetrator of the last of the novel's betrayals blends into the ugly murk that has obscured Winnie and the Assistant Commissioner. Reaching his "small grimy house" with its "mangy grassplot" (p. 300), Ossipon ratifies the general inertia by falling asleep in the daylight.

Mr. Verloc's qualities seem to spread from his corpse over the town. His inheritance funds the brief final chapter that recounts a conversation between Ossipon and the Professor. The description of the latter's lodgings presses unpleasantness into odium. "The room was large, clean, respectable, and poor with that poverty suggesting the starvation of every human need except mere bread. There was nothing on the walls but the paper, an expanse of arsenical green, soiled with indelible smudges here and there, and with stains resembling faded maps of uninhabited continents" (p. 302). The initial adjectives recall the home that Winnie worked for; the poisonous poverty brings to mind Stevie's reaction to the cabman and his nag; the reference to the violence done to human need echoes the comment on the Italian restaurant. But just as the maplike stains suggest no known region, so the cross-references suggest no interpretation that can sustain analysis.

Both in itself and as a conclusion to the narrative, the scene balks any meaning other than its offensiveness. Yet we are aware that some stronger value must be nearby. The irony, for all its variousness, continually summons up a context of evaluation that we all share. Meanwhile, the Professor rants on, and his spite still seems a plausible reaction to the omnipresent bleakness. He would rid the world of "the weak, the flabby, the silly, the cowardly, the faint of heart, and the slavish of mind. They have power. They are the multitude. Theirs is the kingdom of the earth. Exterminate, exterminate! ... First the blind, then the deaf and the dumb, then the halt and the lame—and so on. Every taint, every vice, every prejudice, every convention must meet its doom" (p. 303). We remember Kurtz's gloss on his report to the International Society for the Suppression of Savage Customs: "Exterminate all the brutes!" This new version, concocted of black anarchism and perverted

Nietzscheanism, is equally outrageous. Imperialism must civilize; civilization must protect. But the Professor's wrath hardly understates the depravities that the city exhibits. Faith and fact, fiction and falsity, meaning and absurdity have been subject to so many doublings, overlappings, and contortions that one might well wish to wipe the slate clean and begin anew. Push the almost inert, stubborn decency of Winnie and her mother a fraction farther and we arrive at her husband's horror; press merited distaste to its conclusion and we join the Professor's loathing.

Indeed, the Professor is the bomb in the grip of the novel's irony. He is the barely human point at which horror and ugliness collapse into a moral standoff: into the perilous ambiguity that may conceal the mere possibility of something better. His capsule biography much earlier in the narrative predicts his function. His "considerable natural abilities" having been unrewarded by his teachers, his ambitions frustrated, his eyes were opened as a young man "to the true nature of the world, whose morality was artificial, corrupt, and blasphemous" (pp. 80–81). He became a rebel.

> The way of even the most justifiable revolutions is prepared by personal impulses disguised into creeds. The Professor's indignation found in itself a final cause that absolved him from the sin of turning to destruction as the agent of his ambition.... He was a moral agent—that was settled in his mind. By exercising his agency with ruthless defiance he procured for himself the appearances of power and personal prestige. That was undeniable to his vengeful bitterness. It pacified its unrest; and in their own way the most ardent of revolutionaries are perhaps doing no more but seeking for peace in common with the rest of mankind—the peace of soothed vanity, of satisfied appetites, or perhaps of appeased conscience. (p. 81)

Although the Professor is the only ardent revolutionary in the novel, the passage diffuses his uniqueness. Sharing the insufficiency of flat mankind, he is in his frightful way fulfilling a common, miserable human need. The explosive and detonator that he always carries close to hand conform absurdly to the common rule: "a man must identify with something more tangible than his own personality." The Professor's goal reduces the formula to madness; but the maddened instance underscores the formula's truth.

Revolution here is a gross aberration of man's need to buttress selfhood in some larger meaning. The Professor's creed is in line with all other illusions. The terrorist is a fearsome horror. But his fearful loathing of other men expresses his awareness that he cannot escape the common denominator of human fact. His cringing and demeaning hatred is at the same time the irreducible remnant of Conrad's faith in civil order. The city's millions defame dreams and ideal conceptions; but they also defuse the nightmare the Professor promises. He "felt the mass of mankind mighty in its numbers. They swarmed numerous like locusts, industrious like ants, thoughtless like a natural force, pushing on blind and orderly and absorbed, impervious to sentiment, to logic, to terror, too, perhaps. This was the form of doubt he feared most.... What if nothing could move them? Such moments come to all men whose ambition aims at a direct grasp upon humanity—to artists, politicians, thinkers, reformers, or saints" (pp. 81–82). If as Guerard observes "the obsessed Professor pushes certain ideas of the author to a dangerous extreme,"[15] the mass of men embody the hope at the farthest reach of the author's irony.

Conrad has followed the mutation of moral exceptionalism into a bizarre shelter in a seeming dead end. Jim's imagination of self-creation based on popular tales is a first stage toward this end; Nostromo's unlikely potential for moral service goes even farther in the direction of diminished glory. The cast of *The Secret Agent* carries the reduction as far as it will go. In the last paragraph the Professor disappears, swallowed like Winnie and her kin, like Mr. Verloc, like the Assistant Commissioner, by the inert natural force that is the only antidote to the force of scorn. "And the incorruptible Professor walked, too, averting his eyes from the odious multitude of mankind. He had no future. He disdained it. He was a force. His thoughts caressed the images of ruin and destruction. He walked frail, insignificant, shabby, miserable—and terrible in the simplicity of his idea calling madness and despair to the regeneration of the world. Nobody looked at him. He passed on unsuspected and deadly, like a pest in the street full of men" (p. 311).

Again, Conrad's image becomes clearer if compared to Zola's treatment of a similar scene. The last glimpse of the Professor echoes the parting evocation of the black anarchist Souvarine in *Germinal*. After destroying the mine that sustains good workers and bad capitalists alike, Souvarine heads "yonder, somewhere into the unknown." "It would be he, no doubt, whom the expiring bourgeoisie would hear beneath them as the very paving stones exploded under their feet."[16] Zola, while portraying Souvarine as terrifying and abhorrent, stands behind the vision of decadence and injustice crying out for destruction. No individual, he believes, but a vengeful burgeoning of the masses will accomplish the inevitable regeneration. By contrast, the quality of Conrad's natural force has no clear meaning at all. Its value is an ironic parallel to Mr. Verloc's vampirism. Madness and despair, the key words flowing from Winnie's fate, are stifled in unsightly dust; the Professor is reduced to a pest. Like "the sound of exploding bombs," he will be lost in the "immensity of passive grains without an echo. For instance, this Verloc affair. Who thought of it now?" (p. 306). Zola sees the moral order that English moral realism associates with the best values of culture as a mystical attribute of the anonymous masses. The "people" will seed a germinal rebirth of value. Conrad's irony conveys only a flatness. The force, "blind and orderly and absorbed," that thwarts the Professor casts its pall as well on art and all other illusions of human aspiration. This almost entropic leveling of the protective virtue of culture gives weight to Stevie's judgment: "Bad world for poor people. Shame."

All value in *The Secret Agent* is grotesquely disadvantaged. It is true, as Schwartz argues, that the "*control* and *discipline* of [Conrad's] language, as opposed to the language of London, create an alternative to the world observed."[17] But the tone of the novel's ironic discourse conforms to the description of the Assistant Commissioner's work: "No man engaged in a work he does not like can preserve many saving illusions about himself. The distaste, the absence of glamour, extend from the occupation to the personality." In passage after passage, the language of irony has seemed to many readers an inhuman game with human needs. There are no saving illusions. The novel almost grudgingly permits the minimal illusion that protects a minimal achievement. But the self-consciousness that signals Conrad's version of romanic irony—his complex playing with the idea of civilization as fiction—now seems directed as much at the offensiveness of the fiction's raw materials as at the fictionality of true shelter. The strain of control, art, and irony is painfully apparent. Yet the flat faith and stolid order do finally hold meaninglessness and the horror of primal disorder at a remove. Language can still perform a protective work. We are not yet confronted with the utter cynicism that will betray all mankind's works in *Under Western Eyes*.

NOTES

1. D. W. Harding, "Regulated Hatred: An Aspect of the Work of Jane Austen," *Scrutiny* 8 (1940): pp. 346–62.

2. Guerard, p. 222.

3. Schwartz, p. 167.

4. Claire Rosenfield, *Paradise of Snakes* (Chicago: Univ. of Chicago Press, 1967) p. 90.

5. Guerard, p. 228.

6. Schwartz, p. 162.

7. Christopher Cooper, *Conrad and the Human Dilemma* (London: Chatto & Windus, 1970), p. 20.

8. Guerard, p. 225.

9. Preface to *The Nigger of the "Narcissus,"* p. xiv.

10. Cooper, p. 19.

11. Gustave Flaubert, *Madame Bovary*, trans. Francis Steegmuller (New York: Random House, 1957), p. 216.

12. Cooper, p. 49.

13. Both in himself and in his relation to Conrad, the Assistant Commissioner has been much discussed. For example, Schwartz, rejecting Avrom Fleishman's view of the official as "a moral ideal," argues that the Assistant Commissioner "is mocked by the selfish motives of his quest" to unravel the mystery (Schwartz, p. 163).

14. Guerard, p. 223.

15. Ibid., p. 224.

16. Emile Zola, *Germinal* (Baltimore: Penguin Books, 1954), p. 453. I have emended L. W. Tancock's translation.

17. Schwartz, p. 167.

MARK A. WOLLAEGER

"Heart of Darkness": Visionary Skepticism

"Inconceivable," "impenetrable," and "inscrutable": Marlow's favorite adjectives in "Heart of Darkness" fill out the lexicon of negative theology discussed in the previous chapter. The argument advanced there, that Conrad's attitude toward the irrational can be understood as a version of the Schopenhauerian will *and* as a covert quest for the divine, brings us now to consideration of two literary modes associated with the sacred: the Gothic and the melodramatic. Between them these modes reproduce the divided attitude toward the noumenal I have been tracing in Conrad and Schopenhauer: the Gothic tradition brings out a sense of the lurking malevolence of Schopenhauer's metaphysical will, and melodrama attempts to recover the consolation of morality in a world losing touch with the assurance of an ethical order. The Gothicism of Marlow's path toward Kurtz culminates in paired scenes of melodrama: the climactic encounter with Kurtz and the interview with the Intended.

The urgency of Marlow's narration on board the *Nellie*—he plunges into it without warning, "the speech that cannot be silenced" (*HD* 97)—bespeaks his need to be purged of thoughts he still finds disturbing: "... No, it is impossible; it is impossible to convey the life-sensation of any given epoch of one's existence—that which makes its truth, its meaning—its subtle and penetrating essence. It is impossible. We live, as we dream—alone...." (*HD* 82).[1] The

From *Joseph Conrad and the Fictions of Skepticism*, pp. 57–77, 211–16. © 1990 by the Board of Trustees of the Leland Stanford Junior University.

skeptical implications of this passage reverberate throughout Conrad's canon. Marlow earlier gives voice to a more measured skepticism in his subversion of the frame narrator's naïve celebration of "the great spirit of the past" on the Thames (*HD* 47); but from "Heart of Darkness" forward until the affirmations of the later romances, skepticism continually threatens to become more radical and inclusive. Since *Lord Jim* will introduce more complex instances of the skeptical crises that both generate and threaten Marlow's discourse, I will defer full discussion of radical skepticism to later chapters and focus here on the problematics of transcendence that elicit the countervailing operations of skepticism characteristic of the later fiction.

Melodrama, Gothic, and the Numinous

Conrad's melodramatic tendencies have often been singled out for criticism, less so his Gothic.[2] Yet, given the relative optimism and pessimism of the two traditions, we can see that Conrad criticism itself has developed along broadly melodramatic and Gothic lines. Although Hillis Miller recognizes that man's confrontation with "a spiritual power external to himself . . . offers the possibility of an escape from subjectivism," his emphasis falls on the darker vision of what he considers Conrad's nihilism.[3] Thus the characteristically Gothic description of Conrad's art: "By a return, through language, to the heart of darkness, the writer affirms himself as the power which breaks down the frontier between man and the darkness, and makes the darkness enter for a moment the daylight world. Writing is a dangerous hovering between two realms which are incompatible."[4] For readings more inclined to focus on the triumphant drama of morality one turns to Ian Watt, who recognizes the potential nihilism of Conrad's vision, yet emphasizes his effort to respond: "Alienation, of course, but how do we get out of it?"[5]

The analogy with Schopenhauer allows us to define a middle ground, for the irrationality of the metaphysical will may be considered a melodramatic-philosophical ground for a Conradian Gothic. The melodrama of Schopenhauer's philosophy lies in the relation between his ethics and his theory of the will. Although virtue generally overcomes evil in melodrama, in Schopenhauer the amorality of the metaphysical will always triumphs, for the will has only itself to battle. Yet by introducing the possibility that the individual somehow can cease to will through an act of will—the achievement of resignation—Schopenhauer, against all odds, restores the possibility of a marginally happy ending, not to mention an ethical system cognate with the stoic resignation of Christian humanism.[6] The question of spiritual value and the sacred in the Gothic and melodramatic traditions thus provides a logical point of departure for my reading of skepticism and the numinous in "Heart of Darkness."

The Gothic revival of the 1790s has long been recognized as a response in part to the loss of the sacred in an age dominated by scientific rationalism.[7] With the decline of religion, humankind's primitive fear of a divine power greater than itself found expression in the ghosts, demons, and supernatural grotesqueries of Gothic fiction. "Gothic novels arose out of a quest for the numinous," according to Devendra Varma. "They are characterized by an awestruck apprehension of Divine immanence penetrating diurnal reality."[8] Yet the evident romanticism of the Gothic resurgence of irrational energies did not reveal a reassuring immanence of the divine in nature as much as the demonic within the apparently angelic. Hence the tales of sexual abandon and perversion within monasteries and the preoccupation with the crumbling walls of ruined abbeys—objective correlatives for the decay of religious order.[9] But the decadence also betokened a nostalgia for the other-worldly experience of the sacred. Varma continues:

> The consequent "renaissance of wonder" created a world of imaginative conjurings in which the Divine was not a theorem but a mystery filled with dread. The phantoms that prowl along the corridors of the haunted castle would have no more power to awe than the rats behind fluttering tapestries, did they not bear token of a realm that is revealed only to man's mystical apperception, his source of all absolute spiritual values.[10]

This is Otto's *mysterium tremendum*, the felt presence of the *origin* of spiritual value without the rational apprehension of the values themselves.[11]

The melodramatic tradition, according to Peter Brooks, also seeks to resacralize the world but is "less directly interested in the reassertion of the numinous for its own sake than in its ethical corollaries." "Melodrama starts from and expresses the anxiety brought by a frightening new world in which the traditional patterns of moral order no longer provide the necessary social glue. It plays out the force of that anxiety with the apparent triumph of villainy, and it dissipates it with the eventual victory of virtue."[12] Just as Gothic writers seek to rediscover what Varma calls the "source of all absolute spiritual values," so authors of melodrama aim to pierce to "the moral occult": "the domain of spiritual forces and imperatives that is not clearly visible within reality, but which they believe . . . demands to be uncovered, registered, articulated." Looking back at the momentary "disturbance" of being in "The Lagoon," or Hollis's more sustained vision in "Karain," we can identify versions of the moral occult Brooks locates in melodrama. Melodrama, Brooks continues, tends "to diverge from the Gothic novel in its optimism, its claim that the moral imagination can open up the angelic spheres as well as the demonic depths and can allay the threat of moral chaos." Thus, in Otto's terms the melodramatic restores to the numinous the traditional ethical value of the holy.

The ghosts that emerge in Conrad with the sudden intuition of a world beyond conventional perception suggest an immediate link to the Gothic. One book on the Gothic tradition even begins with a reference to the frame narrator's description of Marlow's mode of narration in "Heart of Darkness":[13] "to him the meaning of an episode was not inside like a kernel but outside, enveloping the tale which brought it out only as a glow brings out a haze, in the likeness of one of these misty halos that sometimes are made visible by the spectral illumination of moonshine" (*HD* 48).[14] Effectively evoking the story's ambiguity, the description nevertheless misleads to the extent that it fails to acknowledge the narrative investment in penetrating to a truth Marlow imagines *within* the heart of darkness, and Marlow's conflicted impatience with surface phenomena on his journey to the "Inner Station" can be assimilated to the melodramatic mode. Describing melodrama as "a mode of excess" typical of the moral imagination, Brooks deepens and broadens the concept to include a characteristic pressure placed on the surface of reality in order to penetrate to a more spiritual realm.[15] For Marlow the defeat of all human intentions in the heart of darkness intensifies the desire to pierce to occulted moral values. But when Marlow's sense that a veil has been lifted offers him visions he would prefer not to have, we are returned again to the divided attitude toward the transcendent in *Tales of Unrest*.

Description and the Surface of Truth

The language of Conrad's descriptions in "Heart of Darkness" frequently seems to refer beyond the immediate scene, though it is not clear to what. The more florid of these passages have been condemned in the well-known critique of F. R. Leavis, who complained about Conrad's "adjectival insistence" in "Heart of Darkness": "The insistence betrays the absence, the willed 'intensity' the nullity. He is intent on making a virtue out of not knowing what he means."[16] No doubt Conrad is sometimes guilty of rhetorical excess, and not every passage in "Heart of Darkness" can be defended. But here he stands accused (and for Leavis, at least, convicted) of knowing no more than Marlow, whose words Leavis quotes in order to demonstrate Conrad's epistemological shortcomings. Separating the perspectives of Conrad and his narrators is usually a complicated affair, but the failure even to try prevents Leavis from seeing that in Marlow Conrad dramatizes a gradual recognition and acceptance of the limits of human knowledge and, consequently, of what can be represented in Marlow's discourse.[17]

But Leavis is right to call our attention to the verbal excess that characterizes "Heart of Darkness." As Marlow's language strains toward definitive meanings, his words sometimes accumulate without effect; hence Leavis's irritated awareness of the stream of adjectives such as "inconceivable," "unspeakable," "inscrutable." But the effort to evoke the ineffable by describing what it is not sometimes amounts to more than an acknowledgment that language is an imperfect tool. Like the language of mysticism, Marlow's discourse often finds rapture in its inadequacy and consummation in the release into silence. Words become gestures, and they gesture toward a presence that resists verbal articulation.[18] They constitute, in short, a negative theology. The desire to overcome verbal limitations by gesturing even more emphatically derives from a conviction analogous to Schopenhauer's motive for positing the world as will: the belief that the world as representation—whether it be a hippo sunning itself on a riverbank or the "pale plumpness" shaking hands with Marlow in Brussels—does not encompass the whole of reality. Beyond representation lies the Gothic threat of the numinous and the melodramatic appeal of the moral occult.

These dimly perceived realms are usually expressed through variations of the trope of the container and the thing contained: the surface conceals depths; the outside, an inside. While backed against his beached steamer by the garrulous brickmaker, Marlow wonders "whether the stillness on the face of the immensity looking at us two were meant as an appeal or as a menace": "The moon had spread over everything a thin layer of silver—over the rank grass, over the mud, upon the wall of matted vegetation standing higher than the wall of a temple, over the great river I could see through a sombre gap glittering, glittering, as it flowed broadly by without a murmur. All this was great, expectant, mute" (*HD* 81). Nature overshadows the temple, and Marlow responds to the sinister hint of the wholly other by trying to put a face on it. But the projection only refigures his alienation from the inhuman scene as an incomplete humanity: "I felt how big, how confoundedly big, was that thing that couldn't talk, and perhaps was deaf as well. What was in there?" The oppositions of inner/outer and surface/depth continue throughout the narrative, and Marlow's occasional glimpses beyond the enigmas and opacities of outer or surface reality only intensify the ambiguity about what is concealed.

Marlow distinguishes explicitly between a "surface-truth" and "an inner truth." The former he associates most directly with the immediate tasks of preserving the security of one's existence: "I had to watch the steering, and circumvent those snags, and get the tin-pot along by hook or by crook. There was surface-truth enough in these things to save a wiser man" (*HD* 97). The wiser man is apparently endangered by his own wisdom, which hinders him from finding solace in the distraction offered by Marlow's "superficial" duties: "when you have to attend . . . to the mere incidents of the surface, the real-ity—the reality, I tell you—fades. The inner truth is hidden—luckily, luckily"

(*HD* 93). One needs to shield oneself in work, here defined as part of surface reality, in order to escape from the vague threat of a hidden, second-order reality. Viewed from this angle, the workaday business of "mere incidents" appears to be the domain of timid functionaries, those without the courage to endure the grim secrets of the world.[19]

Although Marlow attributes a higher value to work elsewhere in "Heart of Darkness," he does so only after implicitly redefining it as constituting the inner reality of the *individual*: "I don't like work ... but I like what is in the work,—the chance to find yourself. Your own reality—for yourself, not for others—what no other man can ever know. They can only see the mere show, and never can tell what it really means" (*HD* 85). Such reversals in Marlow's rhetoric can be disorienting. He sometimes disdains work as merely a necessary distraction from something unbearable; he sometimes describes it as a locus of value.[20] His inside/outside opposition always privileges the former as being more real; but that inner reality can be either the Gothic suggestion of an unknown threat, as in the malevolence seemingly concealed within the jungle, or the private domain of personal values, which, like Prince Roman's "needs" and "aspirations," must remain "secret" and "unexpressed" (*TH* 48). The trope of the privileged yet vulnerable inside will recur in an ironic form in *Nostromo*, where Charles Gould's refusal to divulge his thoughts fails to preserve what he imagines to be the purity of his intentions; he becomes instead a more complex version of the Kurtz-like hollow man.

In "Heart of Darkness" the conflicting interpretations of the hidden inside represent two perspectives on the same problem. Often figured as an eerie stillness or silence, the Gothic menace of the forest suggests to Marlow that reality must be elsewhere—in the concealed inside—and in consequence his own sense of reality must be an illusion, part of the surface truth. But if the blankness of nature overawes consciousness by its utter indifference to human meaning and value, that recognition also triggers what Gillian Beer has described as "a massive compensatory activity within the psyche" that is characteristic of the post-Darwinian mind. Evolutionary theory, Beer argues, fostered a heightened awareness of the "*incongruence* between mind and world" such that the human image-making faculty was forced to struggle to restore man's sense of belonging in the world.[21] The sole source of signification, the inner reality of the individual also becomes the sole locus of value.[22]

Yet the privileged sanctum of Marlow's inner reality is nearly turned inside out by his "remote kinship with this wild and passionate uproar" of the natives on the banks of the river (*HD* 96). Thus it is not surprising that the undermining of distinctions between Marlow's inner reality and the outer reality of the forest is literalized in the presence of "restrained" cannibals on board the steamer. Here, as in "Karain," the collision of cultures triggers an acute sense of cultural relativity that threatens to deepen into a full-blown skeptical crisis. If the cannibals on shore seem to Marlow to represent something inhuman in human form, those on board are humans whose "inhumanity" can be overlooked: "after all, they did not eat each other before my face" (*HD* 94). If pursued, such observations inevitably undermine the very distinctions Marlow would like to preserve, and he soon takes refuge in his articulation of the necessity of surface truths, which safely push less tolerable truths out of sight.

The crucial term Marlow uses to define his essential difference from his environment is "intention," along with other examples of a strongly teleological vocabulary: "idea," "force," and—the concrete token and symbolic representative of British efficiency—the "rivet." Veiled threats may secure the rivets required to repair the steamboat, but intentions require the shelter of consciousness. When consciousness is endangered, Marlow's saving sense of the purposive and pragmatic begins to ebb, and he derides his dangerous maneuvering up the river to save a human life as mere "monkey tricks" (*HD* 94). With mindless movement threatening to supplant ethical action, Marlow's self-description barely safeguards his intuitive apprehension of the privileged duality presupposed by man as the symbol-making animal. "Man's animality is in the realm of sheer matter, sheer motion," writes Kenneth Burke. "But his 'symbolicity' adds a dimension of action not reducible to the non-symbolic—for by its very nature as symbolic it cannot be identical with the non-symbolic."[23] Inclined by skepticism to subvert his own claims to meaning and so to collapse the very difference Burke articulates, Marlow is troubled by the *ease* with which the constructions of consciousness are defeated. He will neither cede his uniquely human difference from blank nature nor admit that all meaning derives from the symbol-making activity of his mind. Throughout the story Marlow remains suspended between the suspicion that all values and meaning are projections and his desire to "see through" to a moral occult.

Though he is intensely aware of an intention hidden within the "impenetrable forest," Marlow's efforts at interpreting it are completely frustrated until his discovery of actual writing in the wilderness. Finding on a "stack of firewood . . . a flat piece of board with some faded pencil-writing on it" (*HD* 98), Marlow feels as if the forest has suddenly rendered itself legible. Stepping inside an adjacent hut Marlow then comes upon a book, *An Inquiry into some Points of Seamanship*, which exemplifies what he most desires to find—"a singleness of intention,"—and instantly feels "a delicious sensation of having come upon something unmistakably real" (*HD* 99). Yet even this avatar of intelligibility is marked by the mystery of the wilderness, for the book is filled with marginalia that to Marlow look like "cipher." Although he realizes that the writing is "plainly referring to the text" and thus is intended as commentary or explanation, the affair remains "an extravagant mystery."[24] The mystery later vanishes with the discovery of the book's Russian owner, but it is this sort of deadlocked dialogue between meaning promised and meaning denied that pushes Marlow into an uneasy rhetoric of the unknowable. An unambiguously human connection would momentarily banish anxieties about what makes such connections possible (or impossible), and the desire for the consolations of reading anticipates Marlow's increasingly intense desire to talk with Kurtz: "I assure you to leave off reading was like tearing myself away from the shelter of an old and solid friendship" (*HD* 99–100).

The deepest fear here is that the mysterious intentions housed in the wilderness will overpower his own, and when Marlow reads nature rather than the abandoned book, the wilderness offers him visions he is not eager to have: "suddenly, as though a veil had been removed from my eyes, I made out, deep in the tangled gloom, naked breasts, arms, legs, glaring eyes,—the bush was swarming with human limbs in movement" (*HD* 110). The "amazing reality of . . . concealed life" here suggests both figurative dismemberment and a troubling confusion of the human and the natural (*HD* 80). Where in Schopenhauer the common ground of the will tends to connect diverse phenomena like a current of electricity ("the powerful, irresistible impulse with which masses of water rush downwards, the persistence and determination with which the magnet always turns back to the North Pole" [*WWR* I: 117–18]), in Conrad the emphasis falls on a potential loss of the capacity to differentiate between what normally are highly particularized phenomena. The thought that behind every representation lies the same will threatens to level fundamental hierarchies, even to the extent that the human, the animal, and the organic begin to blend into one another. Conrad thus extends the subversive effect of Schopenhauer's implicit claim that "the absolute unity at the root of our essence . . . is the expression or reflection of that homogeneity which results from the lack of a definitive and difference-producing purpose for life."[25] Marlow accordingly finds little comfort in the suggestion by the manager's uncle that he put his trust in the wilderness:

> I saw him extend his short flipper of an arm for a gesture that took in the forest, the creek, the mud, the river,—seemed to beckon with a dishonouring flourish before the sunlit face of the land a treacherous appeal to the lurking death, to the hidden evil, to the profound darkness of its heart. It was so startling that I leaped to my feet and looked back at the edge of the forest, as though I had expected an answer of some sort to that black display of confidence. (*HD* 92)

The man gestures inarticulately with a flipper; Marlow senses the possibility of an articulate response from the forest. By the time Marlow intercepts Kurtz crawling toward his "unspeakable rites," the conflation of the human and the animal has entered the narrative as a direct threat: "A black figure stood up, strode on long black legs, waving long black arms, across the glow. It had horns—antelope horns, I think—on its head" (*HD* 143). If the limbs Marlow sees swarming in the bush do not seem completely human either, their dismemberment becomes literal when Marlow finally reaches the Inner Station and sees the human transformed into the grotesquely ornamental in the form of the heads on pikes around Kurtz's shack. The reader never learns whether Kurtz's "unspeakable rites" involve cannibalism—they remain part of the inaccessible "inside"—yet cannibalism would be an appropriate metaphor for the breakdown of boundaries the story obsessively investigates.[26]

The fantasy of an undifferentiated vision projected in Marlow's descriptive language represents a nightmarish version of his naïve response to Kurtz's report on the "Suppression of Savage Customs": "It gave me the notion of an exotic Immensity ruled by an august Benevolence" (*HD* 118). Marlow would like to resolve the confusing multiplicity of the forest into the consoling vision of a benign will—a kindly monarch, apparently—rather than the frightening force of Schopenhauer's will. The quest for a benevolent principle of harmony and hierarchy must be understood in the context of the ironic pilgrimage Marlow finds himself enacting, and following this path will lead us, with Marlow, to Kurtz.

Searching for the God in Man

Literature has registered God's disappearance in a variety of ways.[27] In Dickens, God's presence remains accessible beyond the human labyrinth of the city for those who have eyes to see. George Eliot, in the well-known anecdote of her conversation with F. W. H. Myers, showed greater equanimity in accepting a world whose transcendental sanctions had not receded but vanished. Of God, immortality, and duty she "pronounced, with terrible earnestness, how inconceivable was the *first*, how unbelievable the *second*, and yet how peremptory and absolute the *third*." Beyond equanimity, Lawrence exhibits almost complete indifference when Birkin heralds the new secularism in a dependent clause.[28]

There is a certain belatedness in Conrad's response to the *deus absconditus*, and in this respect he is closer to Dickens than to George Eliot or Lawrence. The shock that reverberates through his work is immediate, emotional, and anguished—like Marlow's when he discovers that Kurtz has escaped:

> The fact is I was completely unnerved by a sheer blank fright, pure
> abstract terror, unconnected with any distinct shape of physical
> danger. What made this emotion so overpowering was—how shall
> I define it?—the moral shock I received, as if something altogether
> monstrous, intolerable to thought and odious to the soul, had been
> thrust upon me unexpectedly. (*HD* 141)

I take Marlow's anxiety and terror as a synecdoche for Conrad's own
response to finding the heavens empty. But well before Marlow's shock over
Kurtz's absence, the departure of God in "Heart of Darkness" is closely
linked to Marlow's journey toward Kurtz.

When Marlow begins his narration with a rather weak attempt to distinguish between British colonialism and the more brutally rapacious Belgian
variety in the Congo Free State, his argument suggests the need for what
sounds like a form of primitive religion: "What redeems it is the idea only. An
idea at the back of it; not a sentimental pretence but an idea; and an unselfish
belief in the idea—something you can set up, and bow down before, and offer
a sacrifice to . . ." (*HD* 51). Kurtz, who comes to be seen as a supernatural
being by the natives, practices only a selfish religion, perhaps even a religion
of the self. Nevertheless, from the amoral hypocrisy of the company manager
Marlow turns "mentally to Kurtz for relief—positively for relief" (*HD* 138).
Although Kurtz has plummeted from the culmination of European Liberal-
ism to atavistic savagery, Marlow still prefers the assertion of some form of
conviction to a skeptical emptying out of all beliefs.

The extent to which conviction in "Heart of Darkness" is shadowed by a
hunger for spiritual value has often been underestimated owing to the distracting ferocity of Conrad's ironic treatment of simpletons like the stave-bearing
pilgrims of the Eldorado Exploring Expedition.[29] But irony in Conrad does
not always suggest self-righteous indignation. "True irony," says Burke, "is
based upon a sense of fundamental kinship with the enemy, as one *needs* him,
is *indebted* to him, is not merely outside him as an observer but contains him
within, being consubstantial with him."[30] Fatuous as they are, the pilgrims
are important insofar as Marlow feels *impelled* to cast them away. Kurtz, more
obviously one of Marlow's secret sharers, seeks ivory, but Marlow recognizes
that the ivory is as much an idol as a commodity: "The word . . . rang in the
air, was whispered, was sighed. You would think they were praying to it" (*HD*
76). The substitution signifies a spiritual void, a hollowness like that of the
accountant or the brickmaker, and Kurtz hungers to fill that emptiness as
much as his coffers. It is this displaced religious impulse that draws to Conrad admirers such as T. S. Eliot and Graham Greene, a High Anglican and a
Roman Catholic.

Before discovering Kurtz's emptiness, Marlow fixates on the desire to hear his voice as a defense, like the shelter afforded by the book of seamanship, against the frightening blankness and silence of the wilderness. Unsettled, at one point Marlow suddenly breaks from his monologue to address his audience more directly, as if challenging them to respond. The rhetorical gesture instantly conjures the social connection whose absence he feared in the wilderness: "how can you imagine what particular region of the first ages a man's untrammelled feet may take him into by the way of solitude—utter solitude without a policeman—by the way of silence—utter silence, where no warning voice of a kind neighbour can be heard whispering of public opinion?" (*HD* 116). The passage assumes that an investment in authority, whether the disciplinary effect of the police or of language, acts as a defense against a kind of "natural" atavism. It also brings out the extent to which Conrad's work is suffused with the fear of loneliness.[31] The narrator of *Under Western Eyes* remarks of Razumov: "Who knows what true loneliness is—not the conventional word, but the naked terror? . . . No human being could bear a steady view of moral solitude without going mad" (*UWE* 39). Such fear is basic to the psychology of skepticism: "As long as God exists, I am not alone. And couldn't the other suffer the fate of God?" This train of thought leads to the hypothesis that "the philosophical problem of the other [is] the trace or scar of the departure of God."[32] Descending from the divine to the human, the problem of the other plays out our anxieties about knowing and being known. For Marlow, Kurtz becomes that other, yet he occupies an unsettling position between the human and something beyond "the threshold of the invisible" (*HD* 151).

Marlow first becomes obsessed with the consolation of Kurtz's voice when his native helmsman is killed by a spear thrown from the riverbank. Whatever his deficiencies, the helmsman had carried out one of the most valuable duties a character in Conrad can perform—like Singleton, he had steered. His death persuades Marlow that Kurtz also must have died in the attack: "I couldn't have felt more of lonely desolation somehow, had I been robbed of a belief or had missed my destiny in life" (*HD* 114). A potential substitution for the helmsman ("And couldn't the other suffer the fate of God?"), Kurtz presents himself to Marlow only as a voice, and the promise of this voice comes to represent the sheltering and sheltered intention he so desires. But before experiencing the deep duplicity of Kurtz's "gift of expression . . . the pulsating stream of light, or the deceitful flow from the heart of an impenetrable darkness" (*HD* 113–14), Marlow comes face to face with a parody of his own desire to believe in Kurtz in the figure of the Russian harlequin, who babbles with the enthusiasm of a disciple of Reverend Moon: "'I tell you,' he cried, 'this man has enlarged my mind.' He opened his arms wide, staring at me with his little blue eyes that were perfectly round" (*HD* 125). Although his own loyalty will run deeper, at this moment Marlow "does not envy him his devotion to Kurtz" (*HD* 127).

Marlow's preference for the nightmare of Kurtz over that of the trading company eventually assumes the form of an ambivalent discipleship. Like a priest presiding over the relics of a saint, Marlow takes care to alter the text that will perpetuate an idealized version of Kurtz by tearing off the savage postscript to the "Suppression of Savage Customs." Lying to the Intended, Marlow continues to protect an ideal image of Kurtz, again by paying tribute only to what Kurtz originally intended. The anxious effort to suppress publicity about Kurtz's savage customs is of a piece with Marlow's lame defense of English colonialism in expressing a longing for the sort of certainty once provided by religion.

Hoping for something human in the wilderness, Marlow finds the Russian—a blithering zealot—and Kurtz. But Kurtz has withdrawn into a world of his own creation. From the Russian Marlow learns that "'you don't talk with that man—you listen to him'" (*HD* 123). Even before meeting him Marlow remarks, "I had never imagined him as doing, you know, but as discoursing" (*HD* 113). Yet when Marlow hears about Kurtz's "monologues," he considers that the Russian's devotion may be "about the most dangerous thing in every way he had come upon so far" (*HD* 127). In his climactic showdown with Kurtz just beyond the circle of his worshipers, Marlow understands these monologues as the expression of a man whose "intelligence," though "perfectly clear," was "concentrated . . . upon himself with horrible intensity" (*HD* 144). Bracketed within Marlow's first encounters with the Russian and Kurtz is his horrified discovery that what seemed "round carved balls" ornamenting fence posts are actually "symbolic" heads on stakes with all of the faces but one turned in toward Kurtz's house. The heads literalize the potential violence of moral skepticism; the human other has become purely instrumental. Those gazing inward reflect Kurtz's own self-absorption while the one turned outward beckons, like the forest, to Marlow, who ultimately manages to establish the connection he has been seeking all along.

The Russian only listens to Kurtz (and consequently is "filled" and "occupied" by him); Marlow, when faced with the necessity of preventing Kurtz's return to the midnight rites, *talks* him back to the hut. Dialogue emerges here as an antidote to the self-enclosure of monologue. Yet in narrating his story to the audience on the *Nellie*, Marlow reexperiences the danger to which Kurtz has succumbed. To his auditors Marlow had "for a long time" already become, as Kurtz was to Marlow, "no more to us than a voice" (*HD* 83). Marlow himself underlines the problem when, in the passage that begins this chapter, he declares the impossibility of ever communicating "the life-sensation" of his experience in Africa: "We live, as we dream—alone." Providing Marlow with an audience to shape his utterance, Conrad aims to transform a potential prison house of language into what Henry James called "a noble sociability of vision."[33] The breadth of this society, however, is quite limited. "Be civil," someone interrupts: to the extent that dialogue between Englishmen becomes a synecdoche for all civilized discourse, Marlow is.

Although dialogue holds the potential to undo the solipsism of monologue, the fear that language may inevitably fail to communicate whatever is most important runs deep in Conrad. "Your own reality," Marlow claims in his praise of work, is inaccessible to others: "they only see the mere show, and never can tell what it really means" (*HD* 85). For Bakhtin true dialogic structure emerges from what Keats called "negative capability," the capacity to understand all points of view from the inside out and the willingness to accord each an equal say. The monologic is associated with the Romantic cult of the personality and its tendency to objectify whatever cannot be absorbed into its own perspective.[34] Kurtz has long been recognized as the epitome of Romantic individualism,[35] and in "Heart of Darkness" Conrad dramatizes, in the relationships between Kurtz and Marlow and between Marlow and the inscribed audience, the danger of the collapse of the dialogic into the monologic. Marlow, by withdrawing his hesitating foot, preserves the capacity to maintain a dialogue with his audience—though admittedly (if we exclude the chorus of critical response) a rather one-sided one. In *Nostromo* the collapse into monological authority will be associated with political and physical violence, the ferocious imposition of a single will. Although Kurtz's savagery anticipates this theme, in "Heart of Darkness" Conrad ultimately seems less concerned with the political critique of colonialism that dominates the first section of the novella than with the more narrowly social and literary problem that Marlow's narration may become purely self-reflexive.

By its very nature, however, language cannot become a wholly private set of dream symbols. If, as Wittgenstein asserted, a word's meaning is its use, "use" also implies the history of its use: maverick usage does not necessarily assign a new (and possibly private) meaning to a word.[36] "The fantasy of a private language," according to Cavell, "can be understood as an attempt to account for, and protect, our separateness, our unknowingness, our unwillingness or incapacity either to know or to be known."[37] Marlow's rather defensive outbursts against his audience are suggestive of a conflicted attempt to confront his own sense of isolation. In *Lord Jim*, where Jim reaches "the secret fount of [Marlow's] egotism," the ambivalent desire to share and withhold through narration is played out in the disruptions and dislocations of narrative chronology. Here the emphasis falls less on the problem of other minds per se than on the capacity of Marlow's narration to rescue "the shade of the original Kurtz," the one committed to humanitarian ideals, from the encompassing darkness (*HD* 147).

Watching Kurtz die, Marlow feels "as though a veil had been rent" (*HD* 149), but the unveiling only leads to an undecidable question. Kurtz may or may not have been able to reaffirm the validity of ethical categories in his dying words: he whispers, "at some image, at some vision"—an image from memory or a vision of certitudes beyond the human? Deathbed scenes in Victorian literature, one critic has suggested, may function in part to suppress such uncertainties: "When the heart is so strongly moved, the skeptical intellect is silenced."[38] The absence of the sentimental response to skepticism in Kurtz's last moments only heightens the indeterminacy of what we are to make of his experience ("the horror, the horror"?) and so intensifies the skeptical confusion inspired in Marlow and the reader. Has Kurtz pierced to the moral occult, or is Marlow again turning to him for relief where none is warranted?

Absent in the moment of Kurtz's death, sentimentality more frequently characterizes Conrad's representation of women. In Marlow's meeting with Kurtz's fiancée, then, we might expect to find a resurgence of the sentimentality resisted earlier.

Marlow's Narration: Toward the Shelter of the Aesthetic

In "the shade of the original Kurtz" Conrad refashions the "tender ghosts of ideals" found in Karain. The doubleness of what lies beyond the threshold of the visible—the ghost of Kurtz's original intentions or an "initiated wraith from the back of Nowhere" (*HD* 117)—recalls the contrast between the unseen that threatens Karain and what the narrator sees as the "charming shades of loved women." In that story imagination is ambiguously linked to a mode of perception capable of penetrating to a realm of absolute value. In the figure of Kurtz's Intended, Conrad again associates the shadowy realm of the ideal with women, but in so doing he cannot fully accept the imagination as an adequate repository for the ideals of civilization.

In the melodrama of Marlow's interview with the Intended, imagery of the ghostly becomes insistent.[39] Although the encounter is often criticized for its melodrama, it is important to understand why the characteristic excess of the melodramatic imagination comes into play, even when the resulting scene is not as accomplished as many others in Conrad. The extravagant representation—the insistence on the enveloping gloom of the darkness, the cries of the wilderness reverberating through the house—provides a gauge for the intensity of Conrad's desire to make legible signs of the absolute ethical values that Marlow could not read on the face of the African jungle. The representation is, as usual, equivocal: although the darkness absorbs almost everything, Marlow preserves what light remains in the Intended's idealized vision of Kurtz by refusing to destroy it with the one fact she would not have been able to bear. The characteristic optimism of melodrama resists but cannot overcome the Gothic threat of Conrad's darker vision.

A context for Marlow's lie evolves from his occasional outbursts of misogyny earlier in the narrative. In each he claims that women live in an ideal realm divorced from reality: their world is "too beautiful altogether, and if they were to set it up it would go to pieces before the first sunset. Some confounded fact we men have been living contentedly with ever since the day of creation would start up and knock the whole thing over" (*HD* 59). The ideals Kurtz bore into the wilderness ultimately survive only in the illusions of—a rare bit of wordplay for Conrad—his Intended.[40] Better there than nowhere, perhaps, but the tone of the scene wavers uneasily, suggesting at one moment Marlow's ironic awareness of the Intended's severely limited understanding, at another a breathless idealization of futile feminine nobility. As Howard Felperin has remarked, "when Marlow finally meets Kurtz's lady, that presiding figure of his romantic questing, the scene is far from one of unmitigated irony but one of irony itself ironized to maintain the spell of romance."[41] The logic of the narrative does not offer woman's capacity to believe as a symbolic resolution of Marlow's impasse, for the inclination to idealize the female imagination essentially recovers the vanishing ethical value of the holy only to transform it into the fundamental otherness of woman.[42] By the time he came to write *Under Western Eyes*, Conrad was able to indulge in parody of his own tendency to idealize female spirituality in the ridiculously extravagant "feminism" of Peter Ivanovitch, whose sycophantic attentions to the wealthy Madame de S—— are unmasked as symbolic violence in his brutal treatment of Tekla. In "Heart of Darkness" the narrative suspends Marlow between the suspicion that civilized ideals survive only in the pathetic naïveté of Kurtz's fiancée and the thwarted attempt to pierce to a moral occult. The novella ends inconclusively by returning us to the narrative frame and the impossibility of knowing whether any of Marlow's immediate listeners learned anything from the story, let alone understood what Conrad called its "secondary notions."[43]

Conrad cannot easily accept the pessimistic implications of Marlow's failure to discover transcendental sanctions for ethical values. Faced with the diabolical specter of Kurtz, Marlow reacts with the anger shown in "The Idiots" by Jean-Pierre, who pounds furiously on the doors of a church that is, predictably, empty. Just as Jean-Pierre rages against futility, Marlow resents "bitterly the absurd danger of our situation, as if to be at the mercy of that atrocious phantom had been a dishonouring necessity" (*HD* 133). Resentment at feeling dependent may cover a deeper fear. Though dramatized as an active presence, evil is defined as a vacancy, and fear of vacancy haunts the novella.[44] The absence of God in "Heart of Darkness" strips man's honor by leaving him prey to the nightmarish assaults of the numinous as sheer power—ghosts of the Gothic, "atrocious phantoms" lacking the ethical value of the holy.

Conrad's fantasy of the knitting machine, cited in Chapter One, was written a few years before "Heart of Darkness," and it is deeply engaged in the indignity of God's departure:

> There is a—let us say—a machine. It evolved itself (I am severely scientific) out of a chaos of scraps of iron and behold!—it knits. I am horrified at the horrible work and stand appalled. I feel it ought to embroider—but it goes on knitting. . . . And the most withering thought is that the infamous thing has made itself; made itself without thought, without conscience, without foresight, without eyes, without heart. It is a tragic accident—and it has happened. You can't interfere with it. The last drop of bitterness is in the suspicion that you can't even smash it. . . .
>
> It knits us in and it knits us out. It has knitted time space, pain, death, corruption, despair and all the illusions—and nothing matters.[45]

Taken one way, the machine can be read as a technological version of Schopenhauer's blind will: it stands beyond the warp and woof of the reality it determines. Or, as I argued in the first chapter, the operation of the machine represents a fiction of skepticism cognate with Descartes's *malin génie*. In the context of the present discussion, the machine represents not a metaphysical postulate but, rather, Conrad's anxious attempt to fill with his imagination the vacancy left by God. (Compare Marlow's impulsive attraction as a child to "the most blank" space on the map—*HD* 52.) After a glance toward science in the claim that the machine "evolved itself," the passage betrays Conrad's feeling that the "accident" was actually a malicious joke played by God, who absconded after building the machine only as an affront to man's desire for autonomy. "The machine is thinner than air," Conrad continued, a few weeks later, "and as evanescent as a flash of lightning."[46] The resentment Conrad directs at the paradoxically immaterial machine disguises his fear of an absence he cannot face, and the extravagant displacement reinstates God through negation as an absent cause presiding over man's humiliation.

The religious note in Conrad's lamentations sounds quite clearly after the brutal death of Winnie's brother, Stevie, in *The Secret Agent*: "She kept still as the population of half the globe would keep still in astonishment and despair, were the sun suddenly put out in the summer sky by the perfidy of a trusted providence" (*SA* 244). Unlike Winnie, however, Marlow does not believe that the darkness is all. "We live," says Marlow, "in the flicker—may it last as long as the old earth keeps rolling!" (*HD* 49). In "Heart of Darkness" the possibility of "an unselfish belief in the idea" persists in ghosts of the ideal. But Conrad reserves a place for the flicker of belief only in what Marlow presents as the deluded imagination of women.

Although Marlow's lie to the Intended imposes the false closure of popular romance on a radically inconclusive story—"The last word he pronounced," Marlow tells the Intended, "was—your name" (*HD* 161)—the act of narration that constitutes the greatest part of the novella issues as a response to the lie he once told.[47] Retelling his own story within Kurtz's, Marlow rescues what meaning he can from the corruption of Kurtz's idealism. In *Nostromo* Emilia Gould will be forced to conclude that "there was something inherent in the necessities of successful action which carried with it the moral degradation of the idea" (*N* 521). The words, of course, could be cited as a summary of Kurtz's decline. As for Marlow, the possible success of his act of narration may lie in its own failure.[48]

Universal truths, such as those hidden within the shadowy realm of the ideal, can only be compromised by their fall into the particularity of language. A skeptical refusal to commit idealized conceptions to linguistic expression may end, like Charles Gould, in silence and passivity or, like Jim, who dies with his hand over his mouth, in resignation. Marlow's intensely skeptical expression of the limitations of language in "Heart of Darkness" permits the belief that beyond language may lie a realm of value barely detectable in the spectral signs of its absence. As empiricism shades into mysticism, Marlow, like Conrad, becomes more verbose, straining to make words gesture beyond themselves. Paradoxically, the skeptical probing of Marlow's narration may ultimately shelter the metaphysical significance it simultaneously puts in question by shying away from an absence Marlow cannot face. Although Marlow may not fully understand the significance of his own narration, and although the events he describes are notably bereft of consolation, the compulsion to establish a dialogue with the men on the *Nellie* both mitigates the danger of skeptical self-enclosure and attempts to reinvest, in the words of the Preface, "the commonplace surface of words" with the "magic suggestiveness" of the ideal.

"Heart of Darkness" clears space for a more sustained investigation of the sheltering power of the aesthetic in *Lord Jim.* Moral skepticism, the sense that values may be purely arbitrary inventions, reappears with renewed intensity in Marlow's meditations on "a sovereign power," and skeptical reflections on what "inside," if any, is concealed by the "outside" are also reworked, again with greater urgency, in Conrad's narrative projection of the problem of other minds. Picking up these and related issues from "Heart of Darkness," *Lord Jim* ultimately recasts them within the context of fiction making itself.

NOTES

1. Quoting Marlow, I will include quotation marks only when the context does not make clear who is speaking. "Heart of Darkness" appears in the Doubleday volume entitled *Youth and Two Other Stories*, but for the sake of clarity I will cite it as *HD*.

2. Leavis, *The Great Tradition*, is the *locus classicus* for complaints about Conrad's melodrama. Although Wilt, *Ghosts of the Gothic*, xi, quotes the well-known description of Marlow's mode of narration in "Heart of Darkness" as an exemplary account of Gothic conventions, the citation is used only to legitimate the wanderings of her own narrative. Wilt eventually returns to "Heart of Darkness," but only to introduce her treatment of the Gothic in Lawrence. Brooks, who writes brilliantly about melodrama in *The Melodramatic Imagination* and about Conrad in *Reading for the Plot*, does *not* discuss melodrama when analyzing "Heart of Darkness." Conrad himself described *The Secret Agent* as an attempt to sustain an ironic melodrama. See To Poradowska, June 20, 1912, in Gee and Sturm, eds., *Letters to Poradowska*, 116. Although Conrad never characterized his writing as Gothic, much of his fiction participates in the tradition. *The Secret Agent* clearly picks up Gothic elements from Dickens—particularly from *Bleak House*—in the sordid vision of London. The shared symbolism of exploding a character in the middle of a novel may be considered a form of Gothic melodrama, though the explosion in Dickens is far more mysterious than the bombing in Conrad. In *Lord Jim* one can detect the Gothic in Stein's dark, mysterious house, where Marlow is met by "an elderly, grim Javanese servant," who, before vanishing like "a ghost only momentarily embodied for that particular purpose," guides him through the shadowy interior, where Stein awaits him, oracular, in a circle of light. The pure evil of Gentleman Brown and the spectral intensity of Jones in *Victory* also draw on Gothic conventions.

3. Miller, *Poets of Reality*, 7.

4. Ibid., 37.

5. Watt, *Conrad in the Nineteenth Century*, 33.

6. Schopenhauer is quick to point out that his largely traditional ethical system is also consonant with Indian theology. Although Schopenhauer never accepted any of the radical ethical transvaluations that his metaphysics might imply, he inscribes within *The World as Will and Representation*, as Karsten Harries pointed out in a Yale lecture (February 20, 1983), the possibility of a Nietzschean response to his metaphysical pessimism. See *WWR*, I: 273. Lee M. Whitehead, in "Conrad's 'Pessimism' Re-examined" (1969–70), makes some perceptive remarks about Schopenhauer's concept of aesthetic contemplation but then argues unpersuasively that Conrad exhibits a Nietzschean response to Schopenhauer.

7. I am aware that this is only one dimension of a complex literary phenomenon, for the Gothic tradition can also be traced back through Gray and Collins to Richardson. To explain the Gothic revival is to account for the development of the Romantic movement itself. On the connection between Otto's concept of the holy and Gothic fiction, see Varnado, "The Idea of the Numinous in Gothic Literature," in Thompson, ed., *The Gothic Imagination*. For a more historically minded treatment

of Gothic terror as "a genuine expression of religious malaise" rooted in Protestant theology, see in the same volume Porte, "In the Hands of an Angry God."

8. Varma, *The Gothic Flame*, 211.

9. Ruins were also seen as the mysterious work of great forces or eternal processes. For a useful compendium of Gothic conventions which locates them in various Romantic traditions, see Railo, *The Haunted Castle*.

10. Varma, *The Gothic Flame*, 211.

11. See Otto, *The Idea of the Holy*, 12–24.

12. Brooks, *The Melodramatic Imagination*, 20. Succeeding quotations are from pages 20–21. Although Brooks does not mean to assert that the moral occult constitutes a metaphysical reality, for Conrad it does, and I will adapt the concept accordingly.

13. Wilt, *Ghosts of the Gothic*, xi. Wilt analyzes the incorporation of Gothic elements and procedures into what F. R. Leavis canonized as "the great tradition."

14. The *Ms.* reads "not inside like a kernel but outside *in the unseen*" (emphasis added). *Heart of Darkness*, Norton Critical Edition, 9. For the symbolist and impressionist background of this well-known passage, see Watt, *Conrad in the Nineteenth Century*, 169–200. For a rhetorical reading, see Miller, *Heart of Darkness Revisited* (1985).

15. Brooks, *The Melodramatic Imagination*, 4.

16. Leavis, *The Great Tradition*, 180. And from the same passage: "Conrad must . . . stand convicted of borrowing the arts of the magazine-writer . . . in order to impose on his readers and on himself, for thrilled response, a 'significance,' that is merely an emotional insistence on the presence of what he can't produce."

17. Guetti, *The Limits of Metaphor*, has argued that "the emphasis shifts in 'Heart of Darkness' from the idea of a 'reality' beyond language to the limitations within language that were seen as evidence for the existence of such a reality" (p. 3). Although I am largely in agreement with Guetti's critique of Leavis (pp. 4–6), I cannot wholly accept his interpretation of the problem of the ineffable in exclusively linguistic terms, for this approach underestimates Conrad's investment in an absolute realm beyond language.

18. Compare Brooks, *The Melodramatic Imagination*, 77. He argues that gestural signification in the nineteenth-century novel represents a transformation of the hyperbolic gestures of theatrical melodrama: "Gesture appears as a way to make available certain occulted perceptions and relationships, to render, with the audacity of an as-if proposition, a world of significant shadows."

19. Compare Conrad's essay on Anatole France, in Wright, ed., *Conrad on Fiction*, 63: "only in the continuity of effort there is a refuge from danger for minds less clear-seeing and philosophic than his own." In Lord Jim Marlow defines "the wisdom of life" more explicitly as a kind of repression: the "putting out of sight all the reminders of our folly, of our weakness, of our mortality" (*LJ* 174).

20. For a lucid new historical critique of the ideology of work in *Heart of Darkness*, see Thomas, "Preserving and Keeping Order by Killing Time in *Heart of Darkness*," in Murfin, ed., *Joseph Conrad: "Heart of Darkness,"* esp. 252–55.

21. Beer, *Darwin's Plots*, 74–76. See also pp. 53–62 on metaphor as an expression of man's need to tame the "thisness" of a reality that resists interpretation.

22. Compare Levenson, *A Genealogy of Modernism*, discussing Pater's legacy to English modernism as promoting "a bifurcation into a realm of fact and a realm of subjective consciousness. Value was to reside within consciousness, and all other value became derivative" (p. 18).

23. Burke, *The Rhetoric of Religion*, 16. Conrad will later insist on the symbol-body duality in his satiric treatment of Peter Ivanovitch's escape from prison in *Under Western Eyes*.

24. Gilliam, "Undeciphered Hieroglyphs" (1980), is very interesting on this scene, and her conclusion essentially accords with my understanding of the metaphysical in "Heart of Darkness": Conrad's "complex ambivalence anticipates a full-blown modern attitude toward language, but despite his intense scepticism he does not foreclose on the possibility of linguistic signification, as a post-modernist might. . . . He hoped for and feared both possibilities—that the paleography of Russian character might indicate either that language is ultimately empty or that it bears a profound metaphysical meaningfulness" (p. 49).

25. Simmel, *Schopenhauer and Nietzsche*, 9–10.

26. For a surprisingly persuasive attempt to write out the unspeakable, see Reid, "The 'Unspeakable Rites' in *Heart of Darkness*" (1963–64). Reid uses *The Golden Bough* to argue for the hidden presence of human sacrifice and cannibalism.

27. The classic treatment of this theme is Miller's *The Disappearance of God*, which analyzes "heroic attempts to recover immanence in a world of transcendence" (p. 15).

28. In *Bleak House*, Tulkinghorn, much to his misfortune, does not have eyes to see. As he walks out on the leads, Tulkinghorn's absorption in the futile legal documents on his writing table blinds him to the signs that portend his own death: "The time was when men as knowing as Mr Tulkinghorn would walk on turret-tops in the starlight, and look up into the sky to read their fortunes there." *Bleak House*, 631. The Eliot anecdote is quoted in Haight, *George Eliot*, 464. In *Women in Love*, Gerald asks, " . . . you mean if there isn't the woman, there's nothing?", to which Birkin replies, "Pretty well that—seeing there's no God" (p. 51).

29. Watt, *Conrad in the Nineteenth Century*, 222, compares "Marlow's persistent description of the company agents as 'pilgrims'" with Eliot's ironic echoing of the Grail legend in *The Waste Land* and Joyce's use of the *Odyssey* in *Ulysses*. The Moslem passengers of the *Patna* are also called "pilgrims," and it is their "exacting faith" and "unconscious belief" that seem to carry them safely to port in a leaking ship. Watt's discussion recalls Brooks's theory of melodrama as a response to the loss of "social glue."

30. Burke, "Four Master Tropes," Appendix D in *A Grammar of Motives*, 514.

31. For a sustained treatment of this theme, see Gillon, *The Eternal Solitary*.

32. Cavell, *The Claim of Reason*, 470.

33. James, *Notes on Novelists*, 351.

34. Bakhtin, *Problems of Dostoevsky's Poetics*, 9–13, 27.

35. For the classic reading of "Heart of Darkness" as an expression of "the disenchantment of our culture with culture itself," see Trilling, "On the Teaching of Modern Literature," in his *Beyond Culture*. He elaborates the argument, now cast as the rebellion of the Romantic self against the inauthenticity of society, in *Sincerity and Authenticity*, 106–11, 133.

36. On the mind's resistance to the private redefinition of language, see Quigley, "Wittgenstein's Philosophizing and Literary Philosophizing" (1988), esp. 220–21.

37. Cavell, *The Claim of Reason*, 369.

38. Houghton, *The Victorian Frame of Mind*, 277.

39. The scene has been one of the most widely discussed in Conrad. For a concise review of the critical controversy, see Martin, "The Function of the Intended in Conrad's *Heart of Darkness*" (1974). Stark, "Kurtz's Intended" (1974), offers a more comprehensive survey, but his own reading is very odd. For a more recent and critically sophisticated meditation on "the taint of mortality" Marlow finds in lies, see Stewart, "Lying as Dying in *Heart of Darkness*" (1980). The essay has since been revised and expanded in his *Death Sentences*.

40. A standard joke about oral examinations: What is the name of Kurtz's fiancée? The horror. Like most jokes, this one works on a variety of levels, and the comic conjunction of the (ideal) Intended and the horrifying fits nicely with my argument. The ambivalence registers also as a sexual one: "the whore" resonates in "the horror."

41. Felperin, "Romance and Romanticism" (1980), 704.

42. On this dimension of women in Conrad, see Bross, "The Unextinguishable Light of Belief" (1969–70). For a very rich discussion of the novelistic appropriation of the traditional iconography of truth as a woman, including a few pages on "Heart of Darkness," see Welsh, "The Allegory of Truth in English Fiction" (1965).

43. See Chapter One, pp. 8–9, n. 21.

44. See Guerard on evil, *Conrad*, 37.

45. To Graham, December 20, 1897, in Watts, ed., *Letters to Graham*, 56–57. The letter is frequently read as expression of proto-existentialism, though Said devotes a more interesting chapter to the machine in *The Fiction of Autobiography*. The letter also recalls Pip's dream near the end of *Great Expectations*, when he imagines himself as "a steel beam of a vast engine, clashing and whirling over a gulf" and begs to have his part hammered off (471–72). Pip wakes from his dream to forgive Magwitch for placing him where he does not belong. Marlow, in contrast, cannot escape his nightmare, nor will Conrad extend his forgiveness to God.

46. To Graham, January 14, 1898, in Watts, ed., *Letters to Graham*, 65.

47. Brooks, *Reading for the Plot*, 255: "Marlow's narrative has revealed the central motive that compelled his act of narration. . . . He must retell a story, that of Kurtz, mistold the first time."

48. Raval, "Narrative and Authority in *Lord Jim*" (1981), advances a similar argument. The essay is revised and expanded in Raval's *The Art of Failure*.

CEDRIC WATTS

Conrad and the Myth of the Monstrous Town

I wander thro' each charter'd street,
Near where the charter'd Thames does flow,
And mark in every face I meet
Marks of weakness, marks of woe . . .
   (Blake, "London")

Oh, blank confusion! true epitome
Of what the mighty City is herself,
To thousands upon thousands of her sons,
Living amid the same perpetual whirl
Of trivial objects, melted and reduced
To one identity, by differences
That have no law, no meaning, and no end—
Oppression, under which even highest minds
Must labour, whence the strongest are not free.
   (Wordsworth, "The Prelude")

A crowd passed over London Bridge, so many
I had not thought death had undone so many.
   (Eliot, "The Waste Land")

From *Conrad's Cities: Essays for Hans van Marle*, edited by Gene M. Moore, pp. 17–30. ©
1992 by Editions Rodopi B.V.

1

"God made the country and man made the town", said Willlam Cowper in *The Task* (1784). From ancient times to the present, a familiar cultural dichotomy has been the contrast between the town or city, seen as relatively bad, and the countryside, coast or ocean, seen as relatively good. A. O. Lovejoy and George Boas, in *Primitivism and Related Ideas in Antiquity*, have shown the venerable ancestry of this aspect of cultural primitivism; the tradition has been established and maintained by the Bible, Homer, the Gilgamesh epic, Hesiod, Plato, Ovid, and many others. (By "primitivism" Lovejoy and Boas meant, of course, not "primitiveness" but "the commendation of the relatively primitive".)[1] Strongly challenged in the Augustan Age, particularly by Samuel Johnson with his belief that "when a man is tired of London he is tired of life", this dichotomy was reinforced in the Romantic and the Victorian eras: Blake and Wordsworth, cited above, gave it memorable expression. In the following pages, I discuss critically Conrad's versions of it; and, for brevity, I concentrate on his depiction of London in *The Nigger of the "Narcissus"*, "Karain", *Heart of Darkness* and *The Secret Agent*. In my title, "Monstrous Town"—Conrad's phrase in *Heart of Darkness*—reminds us that London can be termed monstrous not only because it is immense but also because it may appear unnatural, voracious, actively oppressive. We may note that in general, in the case of Conrad and other writers, a "myth" of the monstrous town emerges to the extent that the city is anthropomorphised as wilfully oppressive or given a totalising, apparently unqualified, negativity. (Thus, Blake sees the masses as trapped in "mind-forg'd manacles"; Wordsworth sees ubiquitous uniformity; Eliot sees the citizens as the living dead.) In all these cases, a form of negative mystification or "antipathetic fallacy" is at work.[2] In so far as the representation of the city is diversified and complicated, however, it modulates away from the mythical towards the realistic.

2

Texts of cultural primitivism commend a state of being which is far simpler than that of their authors or their assumed readers. Lovejoy and Boas distinguished between "soft" and "hard" primitivism.[3] The former extols a state of hedonistic ease, as in the mythical Land of Cockayne (where wine flows in streams, cooked fowls fall from trees, and the men can live idly); Tennyson's "The Lotos Eaters" is a famous version. "Hard" primitivism extols dutiful labour, and suggests that a life of austere toil promotes human virtue, dignity and order, taming egotism and checking introspection. The strength of the pastoral tradition lies partly in the fact that it can move between the two: to the extent that the pastoral life is seen as one of ease (shepherds playing their pipes in the shade on a sunny day), it offers a soft primitivist idyll; to the extent that it is seen as one of toil (shepherds building a fold or seeking lost sheep in winter) it becomes hard primitivism: Wordsworth's "Michael" constitutes a celebrated example. In this poem, Michael's son, Luke, is morally good when helping his industrious father in the countryside but becomes corrupted after taking residence in "the dissolute city". Conrad's *The Nigger of the "Narcissus"* is, in its basis, a maritime "hard primitivist" text: a maritime pastoral exploiting the familiar contrast between a salutary closeness to nature and an oppressive entrapment by the urban. I emphasise the phrase "in its basis", for the basis is not the totality; but the dichotomy in which the maritime life is seen as relatively good and the urban life as relatively bad exerts an unmistakable, and partly reductive, force.

> The true peace of God begins at any spot a thousand miles from the nearest land; and when He sends there the messengers of His might it is not in terrible wrath against crime, presumption, and folly, but paternally, to chasten simple hearts—ignorant hearts that know nothing of life, and beat undisturbed by envy or greed.[4]

Celebrated rhetoric, and largely contradicted by the narrative that follows. This passage serves reasonably well as a fanfare for Singleton, but Donkin certainly represents crime, presumption, envy and greed, and he will be influential on the others. But then, of course, Donkin is a product of London: his natural habitat is the urban. When the seamen are eventually being paid, the clerk regards Donkin as "an intelligent man" but Singleton as "a disgusting old brute." Donkin will gain work ashore, while Singleton is expected to die amid the ocean: "Let the earth and the sea each have its own", remarks the elegiac narrator. At sea, the *Narcissus* had been depicted not only as an object of beauty, like a great bird with white wings, but as an active entity in the moral struggle between authority and subversion, a live entity hampered by the symbolic weight of Wait, so that when Wait was buried at sea, she "rolled as if relieved of an unfair burden". As the *Narcissus* enters the dock at London, the myth of the monstrous town dominates the narrator's imagination:

> The stony shores ran away right and left in straight lines, enclosing a sombre and rectangular pool. Brick walls rose high above the water—soulless walls, staring through hundreds of windows as troubled and dull as the eyes of over-fed brutes. At their base monstrous iron cranes crouched, with chains hanging from their long necks, balancing cruel-looking hooks over the decks of lifeless

ships. A noise of wheels rolling over stones, the thump of heavy
things falling, the racket of feverish winches, the grinding of
strained chains, floated on the air. [...] The *Narcissus* came gently
into her berth; the shadows of soulless walls fell upon her, the dust
of all the continents leaped upon her deck, and a swarm of strange
men, clambering up her sides, took possession of her in the name
of the sordid earth. She had ceased to live. (122f.)

Within this rhetoric resides a valid aesthetic claim: a sailing ship at sea
often looks beautiful; the same ship, when docked, immobile and being emptied of its cargo, lacks that beauty. Descriptively, though, this passage is evidently marred by what F. R. Leavis, in reference to a different Conradian text,
termed "adjectival insistence": we are offered "soulless" walls, windows "troubled and dull as the eyes of over-fed brutes", cranes like rapacious predators,
oppressive noise, "feverish" winches, "strained" chains, and—again—"soulless"
walls.[5] (What would a soulful wall look like?) The ship, a centre of virtue, is
being captured and killed by the urban dockland, anthropomorphised as the
location of monstrous oppression. The prose protests too much: the myth
emerges in stark and questionable form. If pastoral poetry is sentimental to
the extent that it veils the economic dependence of the rural world on the
requirements of the urban world, so Conrad's maritime version of pastoral
is sentimental to the extent that it veils the dependence of maritime life on
the commercial activities of the city. If there were no cranes and warehouses,
there would be no ship either: each is as soulless as the other. Conrad's emo-
tive prose has rigged the argument so blatantly that the reader is thus goaded
into arguing back.

In the concluding paragraphs of *The Nigger of the "Narcissus"*, the totalising tendency, though voiced, is then checked and questioned. On Tower Hill,
the seamen from the *Narcissus* seem "discomposed", "deafened and distracted
by the roar of the busy earth"; they resemble "castaways", "lost, alone, forgetful, and doomed", upon "an insecure ledge of a treacherous rock." Yet, while
"the roar of the town" remains "merciless and strong", a flood of sunshine
irradiates the grimy houses and falls like a benediction on the men, the trees,
and the walls of the Tower:

The sunshine of heaven fell like a gift of grace on the mud of the
earth, on the remembering and mute stones, on greed, selfishness;
on the anxious faces of forgetful men. And to the right of the dark
group the stained front of the Mint, cleansed by the flood of light,
stood out for a moment, dazzling and white, like a marble palace in
a fairy tale. The crew of the *Narcissus* drifted out of sight. (128)

Even here, the sun can shine; even here, the stained front of the Royal Mint, symbol of economic power, can be momentarily cleansed and transformed. In a novel which has employed a metaphysical or supernatural "covert plot", a brief heavenly benediction is invoked by the imagery here to counter the facile myth of the monstrous city.[6] As in earlier Conradian texts, however, a combination of personification and rhythmically alliterative rhetoric can still overpower the narrator's intelligence: for instance, the phrase "the remembering and mute stones" sounds fine but does not bear scrutiny. "Mute" the stones must be; "remembering" they are not.

In the conclusion of "Karain", the sunshine had been far less robust:

A watery gleam of sunshine flashed from the west and went out between two long lines of walls; and then the broken confusion of roofs, the chimney-stacks, the gold letters sprawling over the fronts of houses, the sombre polish of windows, stood resigned and sullen under the falling gloom.[7]

In fact, the last two pages of "Karain" offer an interestingly complex rendering of the myth, with descriptive irony working strongly against the anonymous character who is the narrator. This character meets Jackson in the Strand, and Jackson wonders whether the "charm" given to Karain by the Europeans was actually efficacious in exorcising Karain's fears; indeed, Jackson asks whether the haunting (of Karain by the ghost of the friend he had shot) "really happened to him". The anonymous character is at once reproachful: "My dear chap [. . .] you have been too long away from home. What a question to ask! Only look at all this" (88). He thus invokes the city, implying that all around them is a solid guarantee of familiar realities. So, in response to a questioner who is tempted by the "absurd" notion that a real ghost might have been exorcised by a charm, the narrator seeks to exorcise this regression into superstition by invoking everyday urban reality. The descriptive paragraphs which follow are not entirely negative: the narrator sees two young women "talking vivaciously and with shining ayes" and "a fine old fellow" who struts proudly along; but predominantly the negative prevails:

Innumerable eyes stared straight in front, feet moved hurriedly, blank faces flowed, arms swung. Over all, a narrow ragged strip of smoky sky wound about between the high roofs, extended and motionless, like a soiled streamer flying above the rout of a mob. [. . .]
A clumsy string of red, yellow, and green omnibuses rolled swaying, monstrous and gaudy; two shabby children ran across the road; a

knot of dirty men with red neckerchiefs round their bare throats
lurched along, discussing filthily; a ragged old man with a face of
despair yelled horribly in the mud the name of a paper [...]

"Yes; I see it," said Jackson, slowly. "It is there; it pants, it runs,
it rolls; it is strong and alive; it would smash you if you didn't look
out; but I'll be hanged if it is yet as real to me as . . . as the other
thing . . . say, Karain's story."

I think that, decidedly, he had been too long away from home.
(88f.)

It is evident that the predominant effect of the description of the crowded city
is to undercut ironically the narrator's confidence and to support Jackson's
doubts. Against the turbulence, overcrowding, noise, ugliness, confusion
and squalor associated with the city, Karain's picturesquely tropical world
with its archaic values (simple heroism and leadership, passionate actions
and betrayals, superstitious credulities) seems "more real": aesthetically,
ontologically and morally better. Karain's salvation, of course, depended on
his trust in the gentlemen-sailors from England and in the prestige of the
great white queen, Victoria; so an element of historical condescension (as the
Europeans patronise their Malay client) has been strong in this tale; but the
concluding paragraphs usefully check and question that element. Here the
predominantly pejorative notion of the "monstrous town" can be deployed
in a way that usefully complicates a familiar Victorian colonialist view of
exotic races.

Naturally, *Heart of Darkness*, that most richly janiform or paradoxical
of Conrad's texts, characteristically extends the paradoxical view of the city
by juxtaposing two contrasting stereotypes. The "monstrous town" is also the
"greatest town"—"greatest" connoting "most impressive in its historical and
even moral achievements". This latter connotation is elaborated by the character who is the anonymous primary narrator, a qualification being that here
London is seen mainly in its maritime aspects: the tidal Thames, rather than
its urban hinterland, evokes the nostalgic patriotic tribute.

The tidal current runs to and fro in its unceasing service, crowded
with memories of men and ships it had borne to the rest of home
or to the battles of the sea. It had known and served all the men
of whom the nation is proud, from Sir Francis Drake to Sir John
Franklin, knights all, titled and untitled—the great knights-errant
of the sea. [...] Hunters for gold or pursuers of fame, they all had
gone out on that stream, bearing the sword, and often the torch,
messengers of the might within the land, bearers of a spark from

the sacred fire. What greatness had not floated on the ebb of that river into the mystery of an unknown earth! . . . The dreams of men, the seed of commonwealths, the germs of empires. (137)

Yet the same narrator repeatedly notes a malignant feature in the landscape: over London the air "seemed condensed into a mournful gloom, brooding motionless"; the Director's work is done "within the brooding gloom". The sun may shine on the waters of the Thames, but:

> the gloom to the west, brooding over the upper reaches, became more sombre every minute, as if angered by the approach of the sun.
> And at last, in its curved and imperceptible fall, the sun sank low, and from glowing white changed to a dull red without rays and without heat, as if about to go out suddenly, stricken to death by the touch of that gloom brooding over a crowd of men. (136)

At dusk,

> the place of the monstrous town was still marked ominously on the sky, a brooding gloom in sunshine, a lurid glare under the stars. (138)

In the "Author's Note" to *The Secret Agent*, Conrad was to define explicitly the following dichotomy: the ocean is "the reflector of the world's light", whereas the "monstrous town", London, is "a cruel devourer of the world's light".[8] As we have seen, the conclusion of *The Nigger* lets the sunlight flood down momentarily on Tower Hill, as though in brief heavenly blessing on the crew at the completion of their voyage; at the conclusion of "Karain", a "watery gleam" of sunshine is quickly banished by the "falling gloom"; and, at the opening of *Heart of Darkness*, there is repeated invocation of the idea that while light has gone forth on the Thames ("the torch", "a spark from the sacred fire"), the city is a devourer and destroyer of sunlight, as though it possessed the capacity to render the very sun "stricken to death by the touch of that gloom". Thus, even before Marlow enters with his celebrated challenge, "And this also [. . .] has been one of the dark places of the earth", the primary narrator has already established a central ambiguity of this tale. If the title, *Heart of Darkness*, evokes and explicitly refers to the darkness of equatorial Africa, its range of connotations has very systematically and paradoxically been extended in the opening paragraphs. As the primary narrator observes and records it, London itself is one ominous heart of darkness. Thus, before Kurtz has been described or even mentioned, the reader is being alerted to the possibility that the standard opposition—"light", "enlighten-ment", "civilisation" and "virtue" being opposed to "darkness", "benighted-ness", "barbarism" and "evil"—may be strongly challenged and intermittently subverted. Conrad's inauguration of proleptic ironies and paradoxes is here superbly assured, fluent and dextrous. His method is to interlink and confuse stereotypical dichotomies of contrasting kinds. Thus, London is depicted as both a source of light and a devourer of light; both a source of greatness and a sender of destruction.

Later in the tale, Marlow's contrast between Roman imperialism ("robbery with violence") and modern imperialism is first established and then demolished by his narrative; similarly, the contrast between Britain (whose empire is where "some real work is done") and supposedly inferior nations is first established and then eroded by the information that Kurtz "was educated partly in England"; "his mother was half-English, his father was half-French"; so that Britain is indeed part of that Europe, all of which "contributed to the making of Kurtz". The notion of torch-bearers going forth on the Thames bearing "a spark from the sacred fire" may at first sound very positive; but the later reference to the woman who, carrying a torch, is blindfolded, and to the conflagration in the wilderness which is like "an avenging fire" to consume the "trash" of the colonialists, lend retrospective ironies to the imagery. Even the fact that the accountant on the yawl *Nellie* was "toying architecturally with the bones" (i.e., with dominoes made of ivory) acquires, in retrospect, a sinister resonance. Throughout the tale, familiar certitudes and prejudices are evoked and then, in varying and prob-lematic degrees, questioned and undermined. That the vista of London and her river evokes a patriotic historic tribute and yet is associated with the defeat of light by gloom is utterly appropriate to the method of paradoxical connotations which Conrad exploits so intensively.

3

The myth of the monstrous town receives its most elaborate Conradian exposition in *The Secret Agent*, which, according to the "Author's Note", began when

> the vision of an enormous town presented itself, of a monstrous town more populous than some continents and in its man-made might as if indifferent to heaven's frowns and smiles; a cruel devourer of the world's light. There was room enough there to place any story, depth enough for any passions, variety enough there for any setting, darkness enough to bury five millions of lives. (10)

The British Empire, as the novel reminds us, was famed as "the Empire on which the sun never sets"; yet, at the heart of this empire is the murky city, and in the heart of the city is Verloc's seedy home, "nestling in a shady street behind a shop where the sun never shone" (174, 209).

There is, of course, an idyllic sunlit prelude to the murk of the main action. In Chapter 2, as Verloc strolls across the city to Vladimir's embassy, it is a pleasant morning of early spring:

> And a peculiarly London sun—against which nothing could be said except that it looked bloodshot—glorified all this by its stare. It hung at a moderate elevation above Hyde Park Corner with an air of punctual and benign vigilance. The very pavement under Mr Verloc's feet had an old-gold tinge in that diffused light, in which neither wall, nor tree, nor beast, nor man cast a shadow. Mr Verloc was going westwards through a town without shadows in an atmosphere of powdered old gold. (19)

The sun may be "bloodshot" and a subject of stylishly ironic condescension ("moderate elevation", "punctual and benign vigilance"), but the later phrasing here, "old-gold tinge" and "powdered old gold", does give a positively attractive glow to the scene. London, in and around Hyde Park, could (and can) indeed look so aureate on some fine spring days; but the description is more functional than may initially appear. First, during this walk Verloc contemplates approvingly the "opulence and luxury" of the city: in Hyde Park the fashionable and well-to-do gentry customarily displayed themselves on horseback and in their carriages, so there prevails some harmony between the aureate scene and the aureate stratum of society. Secondly, Verloc is feeling complacently at ease, so his mood may tinge the narrator's account; but his walk will take him to the embassy at which Vladimir gives him a fateful ultimatum, after which Verloc's mood becomes gloomy—and the weather too becomes appropriately sombre. As Vladimir's destructive plan gradually yields its horrible consequences, the depiction of London becomes increasingly negative. Thirdly, this description helps to establish a chronological and thematic contrast between this day of good weather, when Verloc meets Vladimir, and that fatal murky day a month later, when Stevie is killed and Verloc consequently is murdered.

At the centre of moral darkness is the literal murk in which Verloc's shop seems to be permanently situated. There, "the sun never shone" (209); his household is "hidden in the shades of the sordid street" (40); and though at night a brightly-lit public house glows nearby,

[t]his barrier of blazing lights, opposing the shadows gathered about the humble abode of Mr Verloc's domestic happiness, seemed to drive the obscurity of the street back upon itself, make it more sullen, brooding, and sinister. (127)

London itself, as the plot unfolds, becomes murky, wet, stagnant and muddy. On the very night after talking to Vladimir, the depressed Verloc leans his forehead against his bedroom window-pane:

a fragile film of glass stretched between him and the enormity of cold, black, wet, muddy, inhospitable accumulation of bricks, slates, and stones, things in themselves unlovely and unfriendly to man. (54)

Investigating the bomb-explosion, the Assistant Commissioner "walked along a short and narrow street like a wet, muddy trench"; and, later:

His descent into the street was like the descent into a slimy aquarium from which the water had been run off. A murky, gloomy dampness enveloped him. The walls of the houses were wet, the mud of the roadway gleamed with an effect of phosphorescence. (124)

The descriptive insistence on the wet muddiness of London has various functions. One, as has been suggested, is to offer a metaphorical correlation of increasing moral murk with the meteorologically murky. Another is a less specific association of sombre plot-materials with a London regarded in its more sombre climatic aspects. There is, in addition, a kind of sardonic relish with which the narrator evokes the murk, just as there is a certain sardonic relish in his depiction of the various grotesque and unsavoury revolutionaries. The Assistant Commissioner, we are told,

advanced at once into an immensity of greasy slime and damp plaster interspersed with lamps, and enveloped, oppressed, penetrated, choked, and suffocated by the blackness of a wet London night, which is composed of soot and drops of water. (126)

Lastly, there is a proleptic quality. Winnie Verloc will eventually suffer death by drowning; and the association of London with murky wetness seems imaginatively to herald her watery death in the Channel. The following proleptic lines blend the narratorial vision with tacit reportage of Winnie's emotions:

[A]nother wave of faintness overtook her like a great sea [...]
She was alone in London: and the whole town of marvels and
mud, with its maze of streets and its mass of lights, was sunk in a
hopeless night, rested at the bottom of a black abyss from which no
unaided woman could hope to scramble out. (218)

One of the features of London which made it a uniquely enabling
location for writers was that within a few square miles there were the most
striking contrasts: Soho and Buckingham Palace; sordid squalor and majestic opulence; working-class tenements and the Houses of Parliament; down-
trodden masses and the centre of imperial power. Conrad (prompted in part
by Dickens' creative achievement in *Bleak House*) exploits the contrasts to
the full in *The Secret Agent*.[9] In one evening, the Assistant Commissioner
can walk from police headquarters in Scotland Yard to the Home Secretary's
office, can take a cab to Soho, walk to Verloc's home nearby, take Verloc to the
Continental Hotel for a forty-minute conversation, take a cab to the House
of Commons to report again to the Home Secretary, "walk slowly home" to
change his clothes, visit the fashionable mansion of an aristocratic lady, and
walk from there with Vladimir to the Explorers' Club: all before 10.30 p.m.

As has been often recognised, the remarkable chronological precision
of *The Secret Agent* has thematic force. The novel contrasts the regular pro-
gression of clock-time with the fluctuating subjective experience of time:
for example, Verloc's thought-processes as Winnie moves to stab him are
elaborated as though they took minutes, when by the clock they take a few
seconds. And the central action of the novel is the abortive attempt to assail
the Greenwich Observatory and its first meridian, the co-ordinator of the
world's time. Conrad was always interested in different aspects of imperialism: martial, economic, national, international, individualistic; and, in *The
Secret Agent*, he is fascinated and partly amused by the recognition that in the
late nineteenth century, Great Britain practised chronological imperialism:
the London suburb, Greenwich, ruled the world's clocks. Vladimir is more
logical than he may at first seem when he declares:

"The whole civilized world has heard of Greenwich. [...]
the blowing up of the first meridian is bound to raise a howl
of execration [...] Go for the first meridian [...] The first
meridian." (37, 39)

The earth rotates from west to east; it was customary to regard noon as the
time when the sun is overhead, or most nearly overhead; so different places

even within the same country frequently had their clocks set at different times. The development of railways, and the consequent need for reliable time-tables, were among the factors which led the British Government to decree in 1880 that British clocks should adopt the time established at the Greenwich Observatory. In subsequent international conferences (particularly the Washington Conference of 1884), the different nations of the world agreed that the basis for the co-ordination of international time-zones would be the meridian passing through Greenwich, the so-called "zero meridian"; thus, a person travelling 180 degrees east of Greenwich would have to advance his or her clock by 12 hours, and a person travelling 180 degrees west of Greenwich would have to put his or her clock back 12 hours. In *The Secret Agent*, with its plot set in the year 1886, Vladimir is annoyed not only by Britain's democratic institutions (and her tradition of sanctuary for political refugees) but also by London's newly-established centrality as coordinator of the world's time.[10]

Thus, Vladimir's plan for an attack on the first meridian signals this novel's complex depiction of time and in particular its ironic interplay of clock-time and subjective time. Chief Inspector Heat, for instance, "rose by the force of sympathy, which is a form of fear, above the vulgar conception of time": he feels that "ages of atrocious pain" (78f.) could exist in an instant. London, with Greenwich as its suburb and with Big Ben surmounting the Palace of Westminster, the Mother of Parliaments, was the ideal setting for such a novel.

It was ideal in another respect, too. *The Secret Agent* exploits to ironic effect the sheer immensity, the sheer vastness of population, of London. Conrad tried (not very convincingly) to persuade Cunninghame Graham that among the revolutionaries the Professor is not despicable: "He is incorruptible at any rate"; he sounds "a note of perfect sincerity."[11] Yet the Professor fears defeat by both time ("The time! Give me time!" he cries in impatience) and the multitude:

> "Ah! that multitude, too stupid to feel either pity or fear. Sometimes I think they have everything on their side. Everything—even death—my own weapon." [...] The contemplation of the multitudes thronging the pavements extinguished his assurance under a load of doubt and uneasiness [...] (243f.)

> The resisting power of numbers, the unattackable solidity of a great multitude, was the haunting fear of his sinister loneliness. (85)

Inspector Heat, on the other hand, can feel that "All the inhabitants of the immense town [...] were with him" (85) in the battle against the revolutionaries and anarchists. Heat's view is qualified by the narrator, who gives some mild support to Winnie's cynical opinion that the police exist "so that them as has nothing shouldn't take anything away from them who have" (144). The forces of law and order in the city may prevail, but often the right thing is done for dubious motives: Heat hopes to arrest Michaelis in order to protect Verloc, his informant; the Assistant Commissioner pursues Verloc (and thus Vladimir) partly in order to protect Michaelis, the protégé of his wife's wealthy friend.

In *The Secret Agent*, the myth of the monstrous town has provided a strong imaginative basis. The city is depicted as dauntingly vast and densely-populated, as frequently murky and oppressive, and, in some areas, as morally murky too. The dominant impression is of gloom and of incommunication or misunderstanding between people. Nevertheless, when allowance has been made for much satiric stylisation, there are sufficient discriminations and qualifications to enmesh the myth adequately with realism. The authorities are, on the whole, sane and decent; Winnie and her mother have a selfless loyalty to Stevie. The ironic narrator imparts drily comic, blackly comic, mock-heroic and absurd qualities to the sometimes drably sordid saga. The novel's main weakness is one endemic in Conrad's fictions: the villains (here mostly lazy, grotesque, and parasitic on women) are depicted in terms too starkly caricatural. The weakness is partly redeemed by the markedly satiric conception of the whole, which also has the effect of licensing the emphasis on urban murk. The city, though depicted predominantly in its depressing aspects (as befits the sombre themes), therefore emerges as possibly the most memorably potent entity of the text.

NOTES

1. A. O. Lovejoy and George Boas, *Primitivism and Related Ideas in Antiquity* [1935] (New York: Octagon Books, 1973).

2. The antipathetic fallacy occurs when feelings antipathetic to humans are attributed to non-human nature. See Cedric Watts, *Conrad's "Heart of Darkness": A Critical and Contextual Discussion* (Milan: Mursia, 1977), 21.

3. Lovejoy and Boas, 7–11.

4. *The Nigger of the "Narcissus"*, edited by Cedric Watts (Harmondsworth: Penguin, 1988), 22.

5. F. R. Leavis, *The Great Tradition* (Harmondsworth: Penguin, 1962), 196.

6. See Cedric Watts, *The Deceptive Text: An Introduction to Covert Plots* (Brighton: Harvester, 1984), 54–74

7. *"Heart of Darkness" and Other Tales*, edited by Cedric Watts (Oxford: Oxford University Press, 1990), 88.

8. *The Secret Agent* (Harmondsworth: Penguin, 1963), 10.

9. In *A Personal Record* (London: Dent, 1946), 124, Conrad records his "intense and unreasoning affection" for *Bleak House*.

10. This paragraph is indebted to a paper on *The Secret Agent* given by Professor D. L. Higdon at the Conrad Conference at Canterbury in 1990.

11. *Joseph Conrad's Letters to R. B. Cunninghame Graham*, ed. Cedric Watts (London: Cambridge University Press, 1969), 170.

CHRISTOPHER GOGWILT

Subversive Plots:
From Under Western Eyes *to* The Secret Agent

It is no coincidence that *Nostromo, The Secret Agent,* and *Under Western Eyes,* the three most powerful novels of what Norman Sherry calls Conrad's "Western world," are also often distinguished as Conrad's "political" novels. Irving Howe suggestively pinpoints this distinction by considering a "curious paradox of [Conrad's] creative life": "he repeatedly abandoned his established subjects and turned, with a visible shudder of disgust, to the world of London anarchists, Russian émigrés, Latin revolutionaries."[1] All three novels might be read as attempts to plot revolutionary politics to contain their ideological content, and read this way the writing of *Nostromo* (1902–4), *The Secret Agent* (1906–7), and *Under Western Eyes* (1907–11) charts a course for Conrad's political evolution that parallels the formation of a reactionary idea of the West which was consolidated following and in reaction to the Russian revolution of 1917.

Yet the way these novels plot an oppressive world of revolutionary politics more successfully subverts than affirms the invention of the West as political, cultural, and historical identity. *Under Western Eyes* does seem to reproduce a characteristic feature of twentieth-century formulations of "the West" not only as the expression of a long, coherent political history, but as the only coherent version of political history, all others constituting either failed models of political development, caricatures of the "Western" model,

From *The Invention of the West: Joseph Conrad and the Double-Mapping of Europe and Empire,* pp. 159–89, 254–57. © 1995 by the Board of Trustees of the Leland Stanford Junior University.

or systems of political organization essentially mythic or ahistorical. Even as *Under Western Eyes* reproduces this construction of "the West" as the closure of political history, however, its aesthetic power depends on dramatizing the confusion of European political identity that this idea implies. Insofar as the novel argues against the complacency of European responses to Russia, such an argument depends on showing how the complacent "Westerners" are profoundly unconscious of their own political heritage. The statue of Rousseau in *Under Western Eyes* presides, as I have already argued, over a mistaken legacy of revolution which includes *both* Russian *and* Western European political traditions. It is this general sense of a profoundly mistaken European political identity which links *Under Western Eyes* and *The Secret Agent* as novels of prewar Europe. Reading back from *Under Western Eyes* to *The Secret Agent*, Conrad's fiction emerges more clearly as a far-reaching genealogy of the political discourses which become consolidated in the twentieth-century idea of "the West."

The vexed struggle informing the double-writing of *A Personal Record* and *Under Western Eyes* to correct the mistaken "Slavic" identity of Russian and Polish political traditions suggests how Conrad's *Under Western Eyes* uses the term "Western" to make its reader "see" the set of mistaken political legacies it articulates. I shall explore this point in examining how the novel produces the term as cliché, and creates a problem of reading by means of the cliché construct of the "Western reader." Simultaneously part of the ideological containment of the novel's plotting and part of its subversive effect, Conrad's fiction of political genealogy depends not on providing a corrected version of tradition—tracing, for example, an authentic Polish lineage of European political tradition—but on insisting on the mistaken identity of all legacies of European political tradition. The axiomatic principle of the Conradian genealogy, so to speak, is that all heirs of revolution must necessarily be illegitimate.

Conrad's interest in mistaken political legacies defines a new engagement with the rhetoric of political revolution which in fact begins with *Nostromo*, perhaps the fullest example of what I am calling Conrad's genealogy of political discourses. But that sense of a departure from established subjects, which Irving Howe invokes to attempt to explain the paradox of Conrad's attraction to revolution and revolutionaries, might better be located with the publication of *The Secret Agent*, which appeared at the time much more a break from Conrad's established subjects than *Nostromo* and which, moreover, drew more critical attention to Conrad's Polish origins than ever before.[2] *The Secret Agent* is clearly informed by Conrad's increasing attention to Russian politics, and the later addition of chapter 10 to the serialized version of *The Secret Agent* underscores the connection to the later novel, by seeming to crystallize the formalism of foreign intrigue and domestic drama in the standoff between opposed Russian and English views of Europe, Europe's political order, and what constitutes (in the terms of Vladimir's appeal for solidarity with the Assistant Commissioner of police) a "good European" (*TSA*, 227).

The stereotyping of revolutionaries, anarchists, and terrorists through foreign names and a marked attention to physiognomic features does suggest that *The Secret Agent* is built on an embedded allegory of a racialized European otherness threatening the "good European" social, political, and cultural order. When read in terms of a stage in the evolution of Conrad's politics from *The Secret Agent* to *Under Western Eyes*, *The Secret Agent* might offer evidence of an early version of the contrast between Russia and the West, projecting a political vision of Manichean struggle between two political traditions: a "Western" tradition of national identity against a politics of racial identity peculiar to Eastern Europe and the specifically Slavophile strains of Russian Pan-Slavism. Yet what makes the connection between *Under Western Eyes* and *The Secret Agent* so revealing in tracing the discursive shift from "good European" to "Western" identity is the manner in which "the West" is shown to be a later invention, part of an intensified struggle to separate the confused racial, national, and cultural origins of contested European political traditions.

Producing "the West" as Cliché in *Under Western Eyes*

When Conrad was compelled, in 1908, to abandon "Razumov" as the working title for his Russian novel because of its resemblance to "Rezanov," the title of a novel by Gertrude Atherton published in 1906, he complained that "my title has a significance whereas hers probably has not."[3] The complaint lends some credence to the argument that the final title *Under Western Eyes* misses the "significance" of Conrad's choice of names for his Russian hero, and by extension obscures the significance of the novel. The name "Razumov"—"son of reason," as one might translate the Russian—indicates that struggle between reasoning intellect and mysticism with which the novel makes Razumov's predicament Russia's. Moreover, Razumov's full name, Kirylo Sidorovitch Razumov, sets the allusion to "reason" in suggestive contrast to the series of associations built into the patronymic, "Cyril son of Isidor," as the narrator insists on translating the name in the first paragraph (*UWE*, 3): associations of the Cyrillic script in Kirylo, and of Egyptian religion in Isidor ("gift of Isis"). Thus the significance of Razumov's name seems carefully embedded in traits of Russian history and intellectual debate which Razumov's story is bound to reiterate. In particular, it seems to encode a complex dialectical relation between "Western" and "Eastern" influences on Russian history, capturing, among other things, the opposed ideals of a purely Slavonic orthodoxy and ideals of enlightenment reason that formed part of the Slavophile–Westerner controversy.

Yet the title *Under Western Eyes* is after all more appropriate and powerful precisely because it disrupts the complex dialectic abbreviated in Razumov's name, reproducing a specifically Russian sense of "the West" as a cliché which distances and distorts the Russian debates from which it is drawn. Insofar as Conrad's novel plots those Russian debates to contain them ideologically, the final title fully exemplifies that complex personal struggle we have already traced in the double-writing of *A Personal Record* and *Under Western Eyes*: the struggle to disentangle the Polish and Russian histories that were conflated in the stereotype of the Slav. By erasing all trace of the Slav, which indeed never surfaces in the novel, Conrad successfully plots, contains, and distances the Slavophile–Westerner debates informing the novel. In this sense, we might see how *Under Western Eyes* produces "the West" as cliché because the novel reiterates the crucial reversal that informs the rhetorical invention of the twentieth-century idea of the West: a reversing of nineteenth-century Russian views of Europe, so that what designates the *superficial* manifestation of nineteenth-century European history and culture—Herzen's "the modern Western system"—is then taken to figure the historical and cultural *foundation* for Europe. Yet Conrad's novel does not simply reflect this ideological transformation. What gives such power to its emplotment of Russian debates (particularly those embodied in Russian novels, Dostoyevsky's above all) is the manner in which the novel works to produce the uneasy ambiguities of "the West" as the governing cliché of debates about Russia.

The term "Western" acquires a resonance suggestive of a word inadequately translated. This emerges even at the moment in the novel where the idea of the West appears to come into sharpest focus as a political definition of European democratic forms of "liberty" at odds with a Russian populist-revolutionary idea of "liberty." Such a focus is provided by the ongoing dialogue of part 2 between Nathalie Haldin and the narrator, her former teacher, over the nature of political struggle and the meaning of "liberty." This dialogue might be seen to frame the entire novel, since it is from these debates that the epigraph of the novel is drawn, in the form of Nathalie's riposte to the narrator's definition of revolution as inevitable failure: "I would take liberty from any hand as a hungry man would snatch at a piece of bread" (*UWE*, 135). This dialogue, inaugurated like the events of part 1 by the news of Mr de P___'s assassination, is premised, however, on the narrator's acceptance of his imperfect understanding of the Russian political predicament. This complacent acceptance crucially qualifies the terms of the dialogue between "Western" and "Russian" views of liberty, revolution, and political struggle, which in certain respects appears to frame the novel as a novel of political ideas.

In the first exchange of this dialogue, we read:

Nathalie Haldin surprised me by saying, as if she had thought very much on the subject, that the occidentals did not understand the situation. She was very calm and youthfully superior.

"You think it is a class conflict, or a conflict of interests, as social contests are with you in Europe. But it is not that at all. It is something very different."

"It is quite possible that I don't understand," I admitted. (*UWE*, 104)

In adopting the identity of Nathalie's "occidentals," translating it a moment later to define himself in the character of a "dense westerner" (*UWE*, 105), the narrator reinforces a subtle but crucial confusion over the terms of their debate: over whether the "better form of national freedom" Nathalie is convinced "we Russians shall find" (*UWE*, 106) is a matter for debate only about the nature of Russia's political struggle, or is a matter also for debate about the nature of all political struggle, including the "social contests" of Europe.[4] This confusion has a direct bearing on the terms "occidental" and "western" which conflate two different political ideas: the sense of "the West" as an already established political identity, and the sense of "the West" as an artificial, superficial grasp of what constitutes political identity. The importance of this confusion in determining the way Russian debates are refracted through an inadequate translation of the term "western" is suggested at the conclusion of this first dialogue, when Nathalie warns the narrator he will not understand her brother: "'Don't expect to understand him quite,' she said a little maliciously. 'He is not at all—at all—western at bottom.' And on this unnecessary warning I left the room with a bow to Mrs Haldin in her armchair by the window" (*UWE*, 107). The warning is "unnecessary" not only for reasons of plot, because Haldin will not appear in Geneva, but also because the terms of the preceding dialogue have rehearsed a subtle but dramatic mistranslation of the sense of the term "western" to apply to a Russian intellectual's Westernizing sympathies. For the narrator, it is not at all necessary to explain the relation of this term to Russian polemical debates.[5]

This studied indifference to the complex resonance of the term within Russian debates informs its repeated use from the outset of the novel. Indeed the subtle ambiguities of the narrator's rehearsal of Russian debates with Nathalie Haldin in the "little Russia" quarter of Geneva have already been displaced by the formalism with which part 1 plots Razumov's predicament as the predicament of all Russia. Part 2 plots those debates—most notably the dialogue between Nathalie's brother and Razumov—through the formalist problem of reading an English narrative based on a Russian text.

The narrator's early recourse to the construct of "the Western reader" (the novel's first use of the term "Western") calls attention to this formal problem of reading and translation. This first stage in the production of "the West" as cliché occurs, significantly, immediately before the account of Razumov's evening walk and the conversion to autocracy which will decide his betrayal of Haldin to the police—that moment of conversion precipitated by the encounter with the immensity of the snow-covered land like "a monstrous blank page awaiting the record of an inconceivable history" (*UWE*, 33).

Before giving an account of Razumov's evening walk and the moment of conversion to autocracy, the English teacher of languages attempts to explain the difficulty of reading what might be described as one of the most stereotyped moments in any Russian novel by constructing a hypothetical "Western reader": "If to the Western reader they [Razumov's 'rush of thoughts'] appear shocking, inappropriate, or even improper, it must be remembered that as to the first this may be the effect of my crude statement. For the rest I will only remark here that this is not a story of the West of Europe" (*UWE*, 25). The emphasis placed on "the Western reader's" difficulty in grasping the quality of Razumov's train of thought foregrounds the way the novel contains and distances its imitation of characteristic features of Russian novels, Dostoyevsky's in particular. It is significant that the passage framed by this address to "the Western reader" reproduces two characteristic, already stereotyped features of Russian novels: the hero's spiritual conversion through identification with the vital consciousness of the religious soul of the Russian (or Slavic) people; and also that "habit of thinking aloud," as Peter Kropotkin puts it in *Memoirs of a Revolutionist*, "which astounds Western European readers."[6]

This second quality is a key element in Dostoyevsky's work. One thinks, for example, of the opening pages of *Crime and Punishment*, where the narrator comments on Raskalnikov's "habit of talking to himself, to which he had just confessed"[7]—a characteristic whose narrative significance Mikhail Bakhtin identifies as "dialogized interior monologue" and "open-ended interior dialogue."[8a] The construct of the "Western reader" seems to function both to confine, as a specifically Russian phenomenon, the significance of Razumov's conversion, and to close, in advance, the "open-ended dialogue" that Bakhtin finds in Dostoyevsky's narrative discourse.

Yet the very formalism of this containment—clearly linked to the novel's overall parody of Russian novelistic discourse—in turn subverts the seemingly stable construct of "Western reader" encountering a "Russian" text. That construct does indeed fit the projected order of interpretation governed by the relation between an experience and its transcription, an original document and its paraphrase, or a Russian text and its English translation. What such a hierarchical ordering of textual levels enforces, however, is a reading that must glimpse the original experience through discrepancies in the narrative, in the biases of the narrator's asides, and in all those "marks" by which, as the narrator has claimed on the first page, "the readers of these pages" will be able to "detect" the story's "documentary evidence" (*UWE*, 3).

The construct of "the Western reader" in fact compels a reading at an oblique angle to the obvious distinction it appears to imply: to understand Razumov's experience, the reader must read in other than "Western" ways. And indeed there is good reason to note that the "Western reader" is converted in precisely the moment of Razumov's conversion, when the hierarchical ordering of textual levels collapses in the trope of the "monstrous blank page awaiting the record of an inconceivable history" (*UWE*, 33). Around this image, Razumov's experience and the experience of reading turn to reproduce the effect of a traumatic immediacy of experience.

The identification set up between Razumov's experience of conversion and the reader's experience produces a problematic confirmation of the narrator's construction of the "Western reader" who can only find Russian history "inconceivable." In one sense the novel is a successful resolution of Conrad's antipathy toward sympathetic enthusiasm for things Russian. With each reiteration and consolidation of this sense of what is "inconceivable" to the "dense westerner," however, the novel's obsession with a purely Russian experience becomes much more precisely an experience of European preoccupation with an "inconceivable" immediacy of political experience. In the alternating perspectives of a distanced "Western" interpretation of Razumov's dilemma and the conversion of that inevitable misunderstanding into an immediacy of identification, Razumov's trial of conscience figures the unstable standpoint of the reader, or reading experience, and it is this that determines the aesthetic power of the novel. As the narrator puts it in part 2, unable to respond adequately to the Haldins' receipt of the news of Victor's arrest, "I confess that my very real sympathy had no standpoint. The Western readers for whom this story is written will understand what I mean" (*UWE*, 112).

The instability of the construct of "Western reader" might be seen to emerge from Conrad's condensation and displacement of a struggle between Russian Slavophile and Russian Western sympathies. Not only does the novel efface the "Slavic"—and Pan-Slavic—elements of Haldin's "Russian soul that lives in us all" (*UWE*, 22); it also creates a studied indifference to the figure of the Russian intellectual with "Western" sympathies. The introduction of the construct of the "Western reader" in chapter 2 in fact displaces the manner in which Haldin's dialogue with Razumov in chapter 1 reproduces a complex fusion of Slavophile and Westerner positions. In his first appearance, Haldin's judgment of the "solidity" of Razumov's character (a judgment at odds with the narrator's) reveals a prejudice, perhaps not entirely unfavorable, toward certain *English* traits in that character. Twice Haldin refers to such English traits, the second time in relation to that touchstone for Haldin's messianism, "the soul": "To be sure, I cannot expect you with your frigid English manner to embrace me" (*UWE*, 16), and "Ah! You are a fellow! Collected—cool as a cucumber. A regular Englishman. Where did you get your soul from?" (*UWE*, 21–22).

This contrast between English manners and the Russian soul informs many of the complex effects of identification and secret sharer motifs produced by Razumov's betrayal of Haldin. Their dialogue—Razumov's secret—provides a model for the sense of a hidden dialogue informing each articulation of the term "the West"—surfacing, for example, in Nathalie's warning to the narrator that Haldin "is not at all—at all—western" (*UWE*, 107).

The narrator's first articulation of the "Western reader," however, pointedly refuses the English identification that Haldin invites in suggesting Razumov's "Western" sympathies:

> It is unthinkable that any young Englishman should find himself in Razumov's situation. This being so it would be a vain enterprise to imagine what he would think. The only safe surmise to make is that he would not think as Mr. Razumov thought at this crisis of his fate. He would not have an hereditary and personal knowledge of the means by which a historical autocracy represses ideas, guards its power, and defends its existence. By an act of mental extravagance he might imagine himself arbitrarily thrown into prison, but it would never occur to him unless he were delirious (and perhaps not even then) that he could be beaten with whips as a practical measure either of investigation or of punishment.
>
> This is but a crude and obvious example of the different conditions of Western thought. (*UWE*, 25)

The narrator's exaggerated attempt to distinguish "Western thought" from that "rush of thoughts" associated with Razumov's interior monologue (or dialogized interior monologue) establishes the terms of the narrator's displacement of Razumov's early "Westerner" sympathies, and suggestively demonstrates the role of "Western thought" in effecting a closure of the Russian dialogue, its enclosure as the "dialogized interior monologue" of Razumov's document.

Thus the novel's framing devices, while splitting Razumov's "Russian" experience from its "Western" interpretation, insist on a reading oblique to the supposed subject of the narrative. This oblique relation is reproduced in the topographical details and sensory effects that sustain Razumov's experience of betrayal even through th Genevan sections. Haldin's departure from Razumov, for instance, is described with striking effects of synaesthesia: "He was gone—almost as noiseless as a vision"—

> Razumov ran forward unsteadily, with parted, voiceless lips. The outer door stood open. Staggering out on the landing, he leaned far over the banister. Gazing down into the deep black shaft with a tiny glimmering flame at the bottom, he traced by ear the rapid spiral descent of somebody running down the stairs on tiptoe. It was a light, swift, pattering sound, which sank away from him into the depths: a fleeting shadow passed over the glimmer—a wink of the tiny flame. Then stillness. (*UWE*, 63)

The displacements of sight and sound convey the power of Razumov's traumatic experience, incorporated into the remarkable bodily gesture of his running forward "with parted, voiceless lips."

What is remarkable about that gesture is its repetition, the repetition of Haldin's earlier gesture: "Haldin, already at the door, tall and straight as an arrow, with his pale face and a hand raised attentively, might have posed for the statue of a daring youth listening to an inner voice" (*UWE*, 63). This repeats, in turn, the peculiar detail of the statue in General T__'s rooms, described in the tense moment of Razumov's awaited intelligence concerning the assassin: "Filling a corner, on a black pedestal, stood a quarter-life-size smooth-limbed bronze of an adolescent figure, running. The Prince observed in an undertone—'Spontini's. "Flight of Youth." Exquisite'" (*UWE*, 43). This series of repetitions[8b] clearly registers the way Razumov, despite himself, comes to identify with Haldin as his secret sharer. He reiterates the same gesture in Geneva, attempting to conceal his betrayal of Haldin from the revolutionary Sophia Antonovna: "'I took that notebook, and ran down the stairs on tiptoe. Have you ever listened to the pit-pat of a man running round and round the shaft of a deep staircase? They have a gaslight at the bottom burning night and day. I suppose it's gleaming down there now . . . The sound dies out—the flame winks'" (*UWE*, 257). Easily incorporating the new detail of the notebook (of Sophia Antonovna's suspicions) into his story, and substituting Haldin's position for his own, he nevertheless betrays his original position in the redoubling of the strange aesthetic impression of the combined sights and sounds of observing another man's descent.

Razumov is compelled to repeat these gestures in the set of recurrent betrayals and confessions that perpetuate his psychological trauma. The narrative, moreover, registers the effects of these repetitions, displacements, and distortions as the very suspense of plotting, by which each betrayal solicits a false reading, a further displacement of seeing and hearing, as in Sophia Antonovna's surprise: "He noticed the vacillation of surprise passing over the steady curiosity of the black eyes fastened on his face as if the woman revolutionist received the sound of his voice into her pupils instead of her ears" (*UWE*, 257). Razumov's ability to read Sophia's mistaken response in the exaggerated physical description of her eyes captures succinctly the extent to which Sophia mistakes the meaning of what Razumov has betrayed. But this itself doubles the strange process of reading, whereby the readers can register a difference between the reaction of each character, without themselves knowing the nature of Razumov's own awareness. The multiplication of such displacements and substitutions makes Razumov's experience the secret of the text. Only the readers who have "listened" to the experience Razumov relates can interpret it as a confession. But it also makes the "voice" of Razumov an effect of reading that can only be a misreading, mistaking the repetitions for a continuum of psychological experience reproduced in every strange detail of the narrative.[9]

Controlled by the conceit of the English translator's version of a Russian text, this oblique reading is defined both against the imaginary model of a Russian reading of Razumov's experience (whether Mikulin's or Nathalie's; whether that of a "good" or "bad" Russian reader) and against a reading of Razumov's story by the "Western reader" posited in the opening pages of the novel. Conrad's own Author's Note reproduces this curious displacement of readership in the extraordinary claim that, while "its first appearance in England was a failure with the public," "I obtained my reward some six years later when I first heard that the book had found *universal recognition* in Russia and had been re-published there in many editions" (*UWE*, xxxi; emphasis mine). The suggestion that Razumov's experience is only fully to be understood from a Russian perspective may be read here, as in the novel itself, as a rhetorical strategy for situating the problem of reading somewhere between "the Western reader's" inevitable misunderstanding and the Russian reader's supposedly immediate identification.

Like "the heart of darkness," "under Western eyes" becomes a cliché even in the text it designates.[10] In both cases the labor of explaining its specifically literary power is easily subsumed in the range of political instances to which the cliché might apply. The title's metaphor of Western vision, though a simplistic abstraction, is on without which the tortured political experience of Conrad's Razumov could not be represented, and in a related sense the literary power of *Under Western Eyes* depends upon the very success with which "under Western eyes" is made to sound a cliché.[11] Characteristically, clichés conceal their complications. "Under Western eyes" means more than its implied gesture of indicating the limitations of a rather broadly defined worldview. A world seen "through" Western eyes is one grasped from a biased angle of vision, but the bias in the preposition "under" encapsulates two seemingly opposite meanings: the sense of *overlooking* something, and the sense of rigorous *supervision*. These opposing senses seem to define the political argument of the novel's concluding sections, in which the narrator's emphasis on "what my Western eyes had failed to see" (i.e., overlooked) is linked to the unfolding stories of agents and double agents in that "general police supervision over Europe" (*UWE*, 307) which twins autocrats and revolutionaries in the supervision of a politics the "Westerner" has overlooked.

The constitutive ambiguity in the title, however, makes the relation of the geographic designation "Western" incongruous to whatever lies "under" inspection—in this case "Europe." The preposition subverts the many possible social and political frames of reference presupposed in the geographical designation of "Western," by rendering its geographically partial qualification of "eyes" entirely contingent on a radically uncertain topography.

Raymond Williams talks of the "gesture" of the title towards a "fantastic 'Eastern' distance."[12] Yet the designation "Western" stands neither in geographic opposition to "Eastern," nor within a geometry of relations between the four cardinal compass points. It is reduced to the instability of relative distances between up and down. This reduction of geography to topography allows one to apply the cliché of the title, beyond the context of the novel, to any number of social and political relations. Conrad's attempt to extricate his work from the blot of "Sclavonism" is thus successful in displaying the stereotype of "the Slav" from its significance in opposition to "Westerner." It is successful, however, only to the extent that the sense of "Westerner" is measured not so much against "Russian," but rather against the tautology with which the novel shows how "Russian" the Russian character is.

In the conclusion to Conrad's 1929 Author's Note this tautology is grasped in a cluster of clichés: "The oppressors and the oppressed are all Russians together; and the world is brought once more face to face with the truth of the saying that the tiger cannot change his stripes nor the leopard his spots" (*UWE*, xxxii). An extreme reduction of the novel's more complex plotting of an identity between Russian autocrats and Russian revolutionaries, this nonetheless captures the problematic nature of the novel's ethnographic reduction of the Russian character, which generalizes "Russia" and "Russians" to produce a peculiarly unstable political allegory. The cliché "truth" to which Conrad appeals at the end of the Author's Note suggests a world made up of recognizably distinct national identities. It is, however, precisely this allegory of immediately recognizable national, racial, or ethnic identity which *Under Western Eyes* subverts. What is revealing is the extent to which the instability of such a view emerges not from the threats of Russian messianism, or revolutionary internationalism, but from the problematic limitations of the novel's "Western eyes."

Reading *Under Western Eyes* and the Subversive Effect of Cliché

The ethnographic reduction implicit in the repetitious talk of "things Russian" is matched by an elision of ethnographic or racial characteristics that is instrumental in producing the peculiar resonance of the novel's "Western" vision which anxiously escapes ethnographic or racial self-reference. This is enforced by the connection between images of writing and faces which makes the "Russian" character itself unreadable both as physiognomy and as text.[13] The narrator's sympathies only redouble the increasing anxiety of reference in the novel, as illustrated in this description of himself obliquely sizing up Razumov:

> He shrugged his shoulders so violently that he tottered again. I saw it out of the corner of my eye as I moved on, with him at my elbow. He had fallen back a little and was practically out of my sight, unless I turned my head to look at him. I did not wish to indispose him still further by an appearance of marked curiosity. It might have been distasteful to such a young and secret refugee from under the pestilential shadow hiding the true, kindly face of his land. And the shadow, the attendant of his countrymen, stretching across the middle of Europe, was lying on him too, darkening his figure to my mental vision. (*UWE*, 184)

The narrative shifts here from physical description—the exaggerated gesture of the narrator's avoiding looking at Razumov's face—to metaphysical speculation, as the narrator gestures toward the larger issue of the novel: "the shadow" indicating Russian autocracy. Through the qualification imposed on the realistic description, the gestures of looking and overlooking assume an extreme form of pantomimic gesticulation, so characteristic of the effects of displacement described above. What follows the strange syntax of the connective "from under" is a particular kind of misreading that balances the sympathy and antipathy of response to Razumov. Opposing the "pestilential shadow" of autocracy to the "true, kindly face" of Russia, the narrator splits the good from the bad Russian "face"—a peculiar, but again entirely characteristic, exaggeration of the distortion of the different senses of "face" in the novel. The description of Razumov's face in the beginning of the novel might be reread in this respect, in terms of the narrator's fundamental inability to explain whether he is describing a racial or a personal characteristic:

"His good looks would have been unquestionable if it had not been for a peculiar lack of fineness in his features. It was as if a face modelled vigorously in wax (with some approach even to a classical correctness of type) had been held close to a fire till all sharpness of line had been lost in the softening of the material" (*UWE*, 5).

As we have seen, this sort of effacement reflects the personal story of Conrad's containment of the political significance of the particular ethnographic designation of "Slav." But the uncertainty of ethnographic or racial reference that this then reflects in the sympathetic face of the "Western reader" is not limited to the specificity of the Slavic physiognomy and its association with other Slavic traits. The effect of the novel's production of "the West" as cliché is to make the novel's "Western eyes" constitutively unstable in relation to any ethnographic description. The aesthetic power of the passage—heightened in the transition from the controlling metaphor of English translation and interpretation of a Russian text to the dramatic appearance of Razumov side by side with the narrator—confirms the political argument that the "shadow" of Russian autocracy presents a threat to Europe. The shadow is cast across "the middle of Europe," recalling Razumov's dream vision of "an immense, wintry Russia which, somehow, his view could embrace in all its enormous expanse as if it were a map" (*UWE*, 66), and also prefiguring the map of the Baltic provinces in the final scenes of the novel. Yet this condensation of metaphors of mapping, face, vision, and political identity encodes that political distortion as one produced by the narrative's limited perspective. The narrator's anxiety not to "indispose" Razumov reproduces a sort of enforced detachment from the politics of race.

The significance of this for the novel's oblique redefinition of "the West" emerges in the narrator's attempt to explain the anti-Semitic remark that escapes in the moment when one of the revolutionary exiles urges Razumov to write:

> Razumov backed against the low wall, looked after him, spat violently, and went on his way with an angry mutter—
>
> "Cursed Jew!"
>
> He did not know anything about it. Julius Laspara might have been a Transylvanian, a Turk, an Andalusian, or a citizen of one of the Hanse towns for anything he could tell to the contrary. But this is not a story of the West, and this exclamation must be recorded, accompanied by the comment that it was merely an expression of hate and contempt, best adapted to the nature of the feelings Razumov suffered from at the time. (*UWE*, 287–88)

The narrator's editorial comments appear as a gloss on the nature of Russian anti-Semitism. Yet in explaining Razumov's interjection as "merely an expression of hate and contempt," the narrator seeks to explain away the significance of anti-Semitism in reshaping European politics in general. The overall effect serves to reinforce the translation-effect of the narrator's role. It emphasizes a difference between Russian and Western European attitudes, here grasped in a distinction between the meaning of anti-Semitism in Russia and in Western Europe; a difference, however, whose function is not to comprehend Russian politics, but to show how Russian attitudes lie beyond comprehension. Intruding the remark that Razumov "did not know anything about it," however, the narrator momentarily reveals what motivates the narrative's enforced detachment from the politics of racial difference. For not only is the narrator explaining away Russian anti-Semitism, he is also explaining away Western European anti-Semitism.

It is possible to grasp the whole passage as a complex register of the shift from early-nineteenth-century debates on "the Jewish question" in terms of the freedom of religious belief in the State to the increasing articulation of "the Jewish question" as a matter of race and not religion. Thus the English narrator considers anti-Semitism as a matter of religious persecution. Laspara's status of Jew would have to be defined in relation to the religious practices of the country in question—Austro-Hungary (Transylvania), where religious freedoms were officially sanctioned; Turkey, where both Christians and Jews formed a minority; Spain (Andalusia), well-known for an inquisitorial persecution of non-Catholics; or one of the Hanse towns, emblematic of mercantile freedom and religious toleration.

But this older liberal, "enlightened" anti-Semitism, which saw freedom of religion as a stage in the assimilation of the Jew into an emancipated society, depends on the racialized anti-Semitism of Razumov which the narrator momentarily seeks to distance. Beneath the contrast between Western European and Russian anti-Semitisms lies a distinction between the increasingly charged stereotype of the ghetto Jew, or "Ostjude" (Eastern Jew), of Eastern Europe, and the assimilated Jew of Western Europe ("Western Jew" in the terminology of Zionist debates of 1908).[14] As Steven Aschheim has discussed at length, with the post-1880 migrations from Russian pogroms, these contrasts fused to form a linchpin of pre–World War I German anti-Semitism, placing the Jew "in an inescapable double bind":

> If he maintained his traditional characteristics he could be labeled a "ghetto" Jew; if on the other hand he tried to assimilate, this could be construed as a duplicitous exercise in camouflage and proof of a flawed character.... The Ostjude was regarded as a potential

German Jew. Franz Rosenzweig saw this quite clearly [in June 1916]: " . . . the whole German fear of the East European Jew does not refer to him as such, but to him as a potential Western Jew."[15]

What is striking in the passage from *Under Western Eyes* is the extent to which the narrative displaces and condenses the distinction between ghetto Jew and assimilated Jew through the English narrator's comments on Razumov's anti-Semitic remark. What the English narrator deflects is the significance of Russian anti-Semitism in defining Western European attitudes toward "the Jewish question." Yet the English narrator simultaneously reveals the key role of that stereotype, linked to an unspecified chain of stereotypes (such as that of the Slav), in producing an idea of "the West" based on the refusal to comprehend the political significance of racism. The narrator's belabored sympathy and detachment accurately pinpoint the overall effect of the cliché use of "the West" as an impartial identification that seeks desperately to escape the web of racial resentments from which it is spun.

It is possible thus to read the construction of "the West" as cliché in *Under Western Eyes* as the study of an assumed but highly unstable impartiality of political perspective. Impartiality, detachment, neutrality, indeed, are words that have a rather peculiar resonance in late Conrad. Most striking, perhaps, is Conrad's famous claim in the 1920 Author's Note to *Under Western Eyes*:

> My greatest anxiety was in being able to strike and sustain the note of scrupulous impartiality. The obligation of absolute fairness was imposed on me historically and hereditarily, by the peculiar experience of race and family, in addition to my primary conviction that truth alone is the justification of any fiction which makes the least claim to the quality of art or may hope to take its place in the culture of men and women of its time. (*UWE*, viii)

"Scrupulous impartiality" is an interesting formulation for the difficulty of his own Polish background, as it bears on his story of Russian politics. Holding in reserve that "peculiar experience of race and family," the Note is an elaborate justification for the novel's political comment: "I had never been called before to a greater effort of detachment: detachment from all passions, prejudices, and even from personal memories." Detachment is just what marks the narrative's most peculiar construction of its Russian subject, the willed oversight of the narrator wishing not to "indispose" Razumov. In the process, a peculiar sort of effacement occurs, by which "historical" and "hereditary" influences are constructed in the absence of their immediate "appearance."

This "impartiality" surfaces also in the Note to *Victory*, written during World War I, where he applies a similar reduction to the "Teutonic character": "I don't pretend to say that this [the portrait of Schomberg] is the entire Teutonic psychology; but it is indubitably the psychology of a Teuton. My object in mentioning him here is to bring out the fact that, far from being the incarnation of recent animosities, he is the creature of my old, deep-seated and, as it were, impartial conviction" (*V*, viii).

This Note shows Conrad working to extricate "deep-seated . . . convictions" from, as it were, deep-seated prejudices. "Impartiality" and "detachment" are terms that connect Conrad's political fiction to the nonfictional political writings from the time of "Autocracy and War." What they signal is the effort to create a standpoint from which to argue for convictions against prejudices. It is revealing that, surfacing from this effort, the rhetoric of "Westernism" in Conrad's later writings fails to articulate what is "deep-seated" about his convictions. Far from consolidating the "common conservative principle" (*NLL*, 111) for which Conrad had argued in "Autocracy and War," the term "the West" is itself "an incarnation of recent animosities." Thus the success of *Under Western Eyes* is not, after all, to quarantine Russian prejudices from long-standing European convictions. Rather, its success is to refract the racialization of European discourses through the subversive effect of unstable cliché.

What makes the governing cliché of the novel's title so effective is its relation to Conrad's abiding novelistic concern for the connection between naming and cultural and political identity. Conrad's poetics of naming, or deliberate misnaming, draws attention to the highly ironic claim from the Author's Note to *Under Western Eyes*: "These people are unable to see that all they can effect is merely a change of names" (*UWE*, x). The importance of Conrad's own change of names is something he had recently emphasized in the unique signature of JCK to A Familiar Preface to *A Personal Record*. Its significance, too, for the elaborate process of rectifying the blot of "Slavonism" is something Conrad confirms in the 1924 letter to Charles Chassé, where he reflects back on his decision to change his own name to that "*neutral* pseudonym of 'Joseph Conrad.'"[16]

There is, moreover, that strange order of clichés with which the Author's Note of *Under Western Eyes* ends: "The oppressors and the oppressed are all Russians together; and the world is brought once more face to face with the truth of the saying that the tiger cannot change his stripes nor the leopard his spots." The second part of the saying, "nor the leopard his spots," is well-established from the Bible (Jeremiah 13:23, "Can the Ethiopian change his skin, or the leopard his spots?") and from Shakespeare's *King Richard II* (act I, scene 1). Taken alone, it emphasizes the saying's ethnographic reduction of

"Russians." But the first part of the saying might be glossed by a letter Conrad wrote in December 1899 apologizing to his cousin Aniela Zagórska for not responding to her letters: "In reality I am not [ungrateful]—I am only a man with a weak will—and full of good intentions, with which—as they say—hell is paved. What would you have, my dear? The Malays say: 'The tiger cannot change his stripes'—and I—my ultra-Slav nature."[17] The "truth" of the composite saying "the tiger cannot change his stripes nor the leopard his spots" must then be refracted through the range of different cultural perspectives from which the reductive essentialism of national, racial, or ethnic identity is drawn. Particularly in light of the imagery of faces in *Under Western Eyes*, the cliché "face to face" emphasizes the peculiarity of this composite "saying" and unearths the multiplicity of ethnic and political contexts which make up the "truth" of that other cliché, "the West." Working back through Conrad's writing with a view to grasping its articulation of a "Western" political identity, it is possible to discern the structure of a fictive "Western" impartiality which can only ever be the mirror of an anxiously imagined order of racial or ethnographic political identifications.

The Secret Agent and the Formalism of Political Plot

Like *Under Western Eyes*, *The Secret Agent* insists on a sort of formalist misreading of European politics. Without the controlling construct of "the Western reader," however, the earlier novel multiplies the difficulties of locating national, racial, or ethnic origins for political identity. Its plot is premised on a whole set of political misrepresentations, including Conrad's own self-conscious plotting of the Greenwich bomb outrage, the newspaper sensation of 1894. *The Secret Agent* encapsulates that new formalism of plotting which might be seen to define the distinctively "political" register of the series of novels from *Nostromo* to *Under Western Eyes* and to distinguish it from the politics of his Malay novels and his Marlow tales.

Conrad himself wrote to his literary agent Pinker on May 6, 1907, that *The Secret Agent* represented "a distinctly new departure in my work," anticipating it would be "criticised with some severity no doubt—*scrutinized* rather, I should say."[18] Critical scrutiny is a suggestive formulation for a novel about the politics of spying and surveillance. It suggests, in particular, an important link between the new political subject matter, a new sense of relation to his readership, as well as anxious anticipation of the way critics might read the author's own political affiliations. All of these do seem in some respect to revolve around Conrad's about-face on the designation of the Slav. The theme of spying and surveillance in *The Secret Agent* is structured by an almost obsessive attention to (and displacement from) ethnic and racial origins, ranging from physiognomic descriptions to the formalism of the novel's double-plotting of foreign intrigue and domestic drama. The "new departure" of *The Secret Agent* is related, too, to the rhetoric of xenophobia and racism that surfaced, in October of 1907, in his essay "The Censor of Plays" protesting the censorship of Edward Garnett's play *The Breaking Point*. The exaggerated style of foreignisms with which that article quarantines un-English phrases from and within Conrad's English reflects a new sense of both political engagement and novelistic style that marks a shift from the controlled ironies of Marlow's "English" abroad to the subversive accentuation of "English" debates at home.

Greenwich Observatory seems a more than fitting symbol for that impartial view of the world projected by the political designation of "the West" in *Under Western Eyes*. The plot to blow it up in *The Secret Agent* is thus in many respects Conrad's most successful imaginative subversion of the emerging twentieth-century idea of the West. The very embodiment of enlightenment principles of order, rationality, science, and technology, its symbolic associations inform a host of Conradian ironies. These range from the protection of Greenwich mean time in "Karain: A Memory" to Razumov's stopped watch in *Under Western Eyes*, not to mention that underlying principle of geography, the measurement of longitude. The "prime meridian," Greenwich is the universal standard for temporal and spatial measurement. It is, moreover, entirely in keeping with the novel's ironies that this had only recently been decided—in 1884, when representatives from 25 countries met at the International Meridian Conference in Washington, D.C.[19] As Mr. Vladimir reminds the reader of *The Secret Agent*, "The whole civilized world has heard of Greenwich" (*TSA*, 35).

The difficulty of containing the proliferating ironies of symbolic association provides the novel with its underlying principle of plotting. Mr. Vladimir, the First Secretary of a Foreign Embassy, imagines the attack on Greenwich Observatory will be the perfect plot to subvert the subversives: absurd, outrageous, and lacking any reasonable political meaning: "'There could be nothing better. Such an outrage combines the greatest possible regard for humanity with the most alarming display of ferocious imbecility. I defy the ingenuity of journalists to persuade their public that any given member of the proletariat can have a personal grievance against astronomy'" (*TSA*, 34). Based on an ideal conception of anarchist activity, deeply mistaken about the anarchist, revolutionary, or terrorist principles of those Vladimir intends to carry out the attack, this plot becomes the very simulacrum for political action in *The Secret Agent*. In following its failure, Conrad charts the sequence of mistaken representations which makes the novel an extended meditation on politics. Vladimir's mistake lies in a failure to realize that the members of Verloc's F.P. are ardent adherents to "the fetish of the day" which Vladimir so accurately pinpoints as science. This will compel Verloc to bypass the "Future of the Proletariat" in order to execute Vladimir's plot, leading to Verloc's mistake in choosing Stevie to carry the bomb, abetted by Winnie's mistake in pressing Stevie upon her husband, and issuing in Stevie's mistake in blowing himself to pieces instead of Greenwich Observatory.

Conrad's rewriting of the Greenwich bomb outrage makes his plot the mirror image of Vladimir's ambition to simulate an anarchist plot. Each seeks to expose the political subject his plot strives to imitate: the politics of anarchism and revolution and the politics of British domestic policy with regard to political agitators.[20] Insofar as each attempts to attract the attention of "the British public," both are engaged in the production of political rhetoric—as, too, are Michaelis, Yundt, and Ossipon. Not only is *The Secret Agent* in fact an intervention in the production of the political "text" on which it is based; it is a study, too, of the way events come to be read as political. What is revealing about the difference between *The Secret Agent* and *Under Western Eyes* is the way the earlier novel shows how the instability of the later novel's impartial fiction of a "Western reader" is produced by a multiplicity of overlapping (and always mistaken, incomplete, and partial) readings. It is through such mistakes of reading that *The Secret Agent* divulges its astonishment and outrage at not being able to define the origin, let alone the original place, of politics.

While transforming the serialized version of *The Secret Agent* into the final book, Conrad brought these mistakes of representation and reading one step closer to *Under Western Eyes* with its vision of an old European order eclipsed by the double-mapping of Russia's shadow and a "Western" indifference. With the inclusion of an entirely new chapter,[21] chapter 10, devoted to the Assistant Commissioner's exposure of the "sham" plot, Conrad tightened the submerged national allegory of opposed Russian and British diplomatic positions into something more like the opposition between Russia and the West in *Under Western Eyes*. When the Assistant Commissioner confronts Vladimir with his full discovery of the simulated anarchist plot, Conrad makes explicit the plot's veiled diplomatic war of position between two nations: "'My sentiments for my own country cannot be doubted; but I've always felt that we ought to be good Europeans besides—I mean governments and men.' 'Yes,' said the Assistant Commissioner simply. 'Only you look at Europe from its other end'" (*TSA*, 227). This veiled struggle to define the "good European" perspective hardly resolves the novel's plotting of politics. By the time the Assistant Commissioner has successfully solved the "crime," Vladimir's political "joke" has already claimed its first victim and the stage is set for the eruption of domestic violence, the lengthy description of how Winnie disposes of the "secret agent."

Nevertheless, the set of distinctions that inform the Assistant Commissioner's self-confidence illuminates the difficulty the novel poses as a formalist riddle, the difficulty of locating the site of politics itself. His claim to be able to distinguish between "the genuine article" and "shams"—"we don't let ourselves be bothered by shams under any pretext whatever" (*TSA*, 227)—echoes ironically with his previously self-satisfied conclusion to Secretary of State Sir Ethelred: "Yes, a genuine wife. And the victim was a genuine brother-in-law. From a certain point of view we are here in the presence of a domestic drama" (*TSA*, 222). The set of implied distinctions upon which the Assistant Commissioner bases his work of detection suggestively frames the novel's formalism of politics, in which the distinction between genuine and sham political acts becomes eclipsed in a bewildering game of simulated political gestures.

Rehearsing the success of his detective work, the Assistant Commissioner reiterates the distinctions between "domestic" and "foreign" to present that formalism as a sort of riddle:

> "Look at this outrage; a case specially difficult to trace inasmuch as it was a sham. In less than twelve hours we have established the identity of a man literally blown to shreds, have found the organizer of the attempt, and have had a glimpse of the inciter behind him. And we could have gone further; only we stopped at the limits of our territory."
>
> "So this instructive crime was planned abroad," Mr. Vladimir said, quickly. "You admit it was planned abroad?"
>
> "Theoretically. Theoretically only, on foreign territory; abroad only by a fiction," said the Assistant Commissioner, alluding to the character of Embassies which are supposed to be part and parcel of the country to which they belong. (*TSA*, 227–28)

The limit to which the Assistant Commissioner has taken his inquiry is in effect a double limit. His veiled hints stop just short of the international game of diplomacy, and his clever riddle about the character of Embassies underscores the limit of his interest in the possible "domestic" consequences of an event that is neither foreign, nor domestic, but merely a sham.

By emphasizing the novel's double plot of foreign intrigue and domestic tragedy, the addition of chapter 10 seems at first to clarify the novel's political satire by explaining the Greenwich bomb outrage in terms of a foreign "agent provocateur" and a domestic victim, in an embedded allegory of national interests: the threatened Russian subversion of a British order. Yet the additional chapter only emphasizes the novel's inability to crystallize such an allegory, presenting instead an interpretive riddle, the riddle of "the limits of our territory," where "territory" is suspended in an impossible relation of "domestic" to "foreign"—a double-crossing of territorial loyalties which seems the very definition of a "secret agent."

Political Agency and the Subversions of Reading

The alignment of family relations with national interests provides the plot with one of its more important misrepresentations of the origins of political identity and human society. just as Vladimir's political plot is a simulated plot, so too the family plot is a simulated plot, which depends upon the mistaken familial identity in Winnie's fantasy of a familiar triangle—mother, father, son:

> She watched the two figures down the squalid street, one tall and burly, the other slight and short. . . . The material of their overcoats was the same, their hats were black and round in shape. Inspired by the similarity of wearing apparel, Mrs. Verloc gave rein to her fancy.
>
> "Might be father and son," she said to herself. She thought also that Mr. Verloc was as much of a father as poor Stevie ever had in his life. She was aware also that it was her work. And with peaceful pride she congratulated herself on a certain resolution she had taken a few years before. It had cost her some effort, and even a few tears. (*TSA*, 187)

This awareness of "her work" will turn to the tragic recognition of how she has conspired to embroil Stevie in the Greenwich bombing.

Moreover, in the protracted description of Winnie's decision to murder her husband, her recognition of the consequences of mistaken familial identity is not the recognition of a loss of familial identity. "Family" as such, and the organization of "domestic happiness" in particular, are seen as strategic ruses, a "cover" for a protracted political struggle, a war of position like the diplomatic standoff between the Assistant Commissioner and Vladimir: "The protection she had extended over her brother had been in its origin of a fierce and indignant complexion. She had to love him with a militant love. She had battled for him—even against herself" (*TSA*, 246). This "militant love" suggests a loyalty and devotion, a territorial imperative or instinct stronger than allegiance to country, to family or some abstract vision of a "good European" perspective.

But the representation of that political instinct, too, becomes occluded in the riddle of territorial double-crossing. The deathblow delivered to Verloc is described in terms that complicate the strange emergence of this new political subject which Conrad, with deliberate antifeminist irony, repeatedly calls a "free woman": "Into that plunging blow, delivered over the side of the couch, Mrs. Verloc had put all the inheritance of her immemorial and obscure descent, the simple ferocity of the age of caverns, and the unbalanced nervous fury of the age of bar-rooms" (*TSA*, 263). Simultaneously, Winnie expels the foreign agent, destroys the covert plot of domestic drama, and severs the link between foreign and domestic on which secret agency depends. The secret of this doubling and redoubling, of domestic and foreign agents, however, exposes as illusion the kind of allegiance of loyalties supposed by the momentum of that "immemorial and obscure descent" controlling her actions. Her "descent" becomes obscure to the precise extent that one cannot ascribe an origin to the implied national, racial, and ethnic traits her act of murder manifests.

A parody of Zolaesque naturalism, the account of Winnie's act of criminal revolt epitomizes the narrative's satirical subversion of a whole range of scientific attempts to classify human types and explain human agency. The novel's direct allusions to Lombroso and to Alfred Russel Wallace's *The Malay Archipelago* single out the two nascent "sciences" of the natural laws governing human behavior: psychiatry and ethnography (Lombroso's psychiatric criminology and Wallace's evolutionary ethnography). Both are recalled in the fleeting "resemblance of her face with that of her brother" as Winnie commits the murder. This might be read in terms of the psychiatric classification with which Ossipon has defined Stevie's "typical form of degeneracy" (*TSA*, 76), or in terms of an ethnographic classification of racial origins of "descent." Origins, however, are displaced and obscured in a way that situates the novel in relation to that general crisis of historical representation over the turn of the century which Michel Foucault delineates by pinpointing psychiatry and ethnography as the crucial fault lines in the order of the "human sciences."[22]

Conrad's novel has, indeed, much more in common with Nietzsche's suspicion of origins and of "Nature's conformity to law"[23] than with the grand evolutionary narratives of the nineteenth century: Darwin's *On the Origin of Species*, or Engels's *The Origin of the Family, Private Property, and the State*. The novel's trenchant satire of socialist politics might in fact be better classified as a satire of the various social Darwinisms informing a codification of socialist visions of the future into the "science" of sociology—a codification which brought socialists and reactionaries together (particularly in Britain) in the shared pursuit of science ("the fetish of the hour"). When Conrad dedicates "this simple tale of the XIXth Century to H. G. Wells, 'The Historian of Ages to Come,'" the gesture of friendship is underwritten by a marked difference of historical perspective. Wells might also be invoked by Conrad as the Fabian socialist and champion of sociology.[24]

To classify Conrad's novel in counterpoint to the discursive formation of sociology as a discipline not only indicates the critical leverage of Conrad's thoroughgoing skepticism. It also places the novel in counterpoint to the specific, eccentric reformulation of "civilization" as "our Western civilization" that emerges in the grafting of social evolutionary thinking onto philosophical idealism in the work of Benjamin Kidd, a now little-known sociologist who, though profoundly antisocialist, became, together with H. G. Wells, a founding figure of the Sociological Society in Britain. His *Social Evolution*, published in 1894, transformed the social Darwinism of Herbert Spencer's "struggle for existence" from the struggle between individuals within society to the struggle between biopolitical entities within world history, anticipating, as mentioned earlier, Spengler's life cycles of civilizations and Toynbee's justifications of "Western civilization" as an intelligible field of study.

The thoroughness with which *The Secret Agent* exposes the mistaken grounds for representing political community situates the novel not only against the assumptions in Kidd's revealing early formulation of Europe's place in an organically evolving "Western" history, but also against the better-known lineage of organicist thinking, such as the "organicist tradition" that Avrom Fleishman discovers in aligning Conrad with the theories of Weber and Tönnies.[25] In the presumed scientific character of psychological and ethnographic description, *The Secret Agent* undermines the various abstract systems of human classification it constantly posits as possible horizons for a full reading, or interpretation. Indeed, the thoroughness of Stevie's bodily mutilation destroys all trace of that anatomical mark that might explain, in physiognomic, biological, and psychological detail, the reason for his act. Between the symbolic ordering of the universe impartially viewed by Greenwich Observatory and the symbolic violence of Stevie's dismemberment, the possibility for defining the political nature of agency disappears, even as a desire for real political expression comes to be inscribed in the event that makes Stevie the victim of a "sham."

The narrative detail of *The Secret Agent* that is most effective in suggesting a vision of alienation and anomie close to a Weberian critique of "Gesellschaft" over "Gemeinschaft" is a square piece of calico which Winnie sews into Stevie's coat and which the novel produces in the form of the triangular piece of broadcloth following the explosion. Yet this clue, leading back to the origins of the narrative's plot, unhinges fictions of national and racial origin, exposing a contingency of plotting which subverts organicist models. Conrad's unraveling of the police bureaucracy in *The Secret Agent* unravels more than the alienation of a modern, bureaucratic, "Western" society. It unravels also the possibility of separating the mistaken grounds of inauthentic modern society from "genuine" social formations.

Any assurance that one might locate where the old fabric of society first began to unravel is visibly shaken, for example, with Chief Inspector Heat, whose estrangement from his job in the course of events following the Greenwich bombing presents a classic example of alienated labor. Confronted with the clue of the triangular piece of broadcloth, Heat misrepresents to himself the nature of his police work, "the close-woven stuff of relations between conspirator and police" (*TSA*, 85), by suppressing the truth of what links him to the contingent plot hatched at Brett Street. His view of "what is normal in the constitution of society" offers, as a sort of incidental insight, a disturbing enough picture of everyday police work, more chilling than Winnie's matter-of-fact explanation of the benevolent protection the local constable supposedly offers the population at large. What Heat's view of "normal" class society fails to grasp is his relation to the Special Crimes Department, where "special" implies a political element whose significance Heat neither can nor wishes to imagine. In this respect, the Assistant Commissioner is that much better equipped to deal with the task of solving the crime. His course of action, too, is determined by the need to protect his own interests. Just as Heat wants to suppress the identity of his secret agent, Verloc, the Assistant Commissioner wants to prevent the incrimination of Michaelis, which would disrupt both his marital relations and his standing in high society.

But the Assistant Commissioner brings something else to this bureaucratic machinery, which has its heroic side, making him seem "like the vision of a cool, reflective Don Quixote" (*TSA*, 147). Linked to an imperial ethos evoked by the ironic image of Westminster as "the centre of the Empire on which the sun never sets" (*TSA*, 214), his "crusading instinct" is hardly more benevolent than Chief Inspector Heat's conception of police work. His place is as administrator of Empire: "He knew that a department is at the mercy of its subordinate officers, who have their own conceptions of loyalty. His career had begun in a tropical colony. He had liked his work there. It was police work. He had been very successful in tracking and breaking up certain nefarious secret societies amongst the natives" (*TSA*, 99). His suspicion of Heat's loyalties, resting as much on his resentment of Heat's success as on his need to be accepted into British society and his desire to protect Michaelis, yields an extraordinary analogy when he finds a resemblance between Heat and one of his former native intermediaries:

> A mistrust of established reputations was strictly in character with the Assistant Commissioner's ability as detector. His memory evoked a certain old fat and wealthy native chief in the distant

colony who it was a tradition for the successive Colonial Governors to trust and make much of as a firm friend and supporter of the order and legality established by white men; whereas, when examined sceptically, he was found out to be principally his own good friend, and nobody else's. Not precisely a traitor, but still a man of many dangerous reservations, caused by a due regard for his advantage, comfort, and safety. A fellow of some innocence in his naïve duplicity, but none the less dangerous. He took some finding out. (*TSA*, 118)

There is, indeed, a connection between the Assistant Commissioner's use of such subordinates in the colonial context and his role at suppressing secret societies. That discovery is overstated, however, by an excess of description: "He was physically a big man, too, and (allowing for the difference of colour, of course) Chief Inspector Heat's appearance recalled him to the memory of his superior. It was not the eyes nor yet the lips exactly. It was bizarre" (*TSA*, 118). The Assistant Commissioner's inability to put his finger on the exact resemblance serves to underscore his alienation from the basis of the comparison: that each is simply a subordinate to be used for his own administrative ends. What the Assistant Commissioner misrepresents to himself, in the conduct of his police work, is the obscure connection between his former task of "tracking down and breaking up certain nefarious secret societies among the natives" and his current work of exposing the "political" nature of Vladimir's plot as a "sham."

But the difficulty of resemblance is much more complicated than an inability to discern the common *human* element. As if to dismiss the irritating phenomenon of alienation, the narrative asks a curious rhetorical question: "But does not Alfred Wallace relate in his famous book on the Malay Archipelago how, amongst the Aru Islanders, he discovered in an old and naked savage with a sooty skin a peculiar resemblance to a dear friend at home?" (*TSA*, 102). This "peculiar resemblance," like the "resemblance" of Winnie's face to her brother's, is one that draws attention to those bonds of humanity that escape detection by systems of classification. Wallace's *The Malay Archipelago* is a classic product of evolutionary theory, notable, as I have already mentioned in relation to *Lord Jim*, for its ambitious classification of the variation of species and cultures throughout the Malay Archipelago. His discussion of the Aru Islanders, however, is striking for the attention he himself draws to the overarching conclusions of his study, the discovery of a dividing line—now named "the Wallace line"—splitting the Malay Archipelago into two regions, separating "the Malayan and all the Asiatic races, from the Papuan and all that inhabit the Pacific" with a "corresponding zoological division of the Archipelago into an Indo-Malayan and Austro-Malayan region."[26] The Aru Islanders, living "along the line of junction" where "intermigration and commixture have taken place," present a problem to which Wallace is obsessively drawn: "the complicated mixture of races in Aru" he writes, "utterly confound an ethnologist. "[27] The Assistant Commissioner—or the narrator of *The Secret* Agent—happens to recall Wallace's self-dramatization of ethnologist confounded, which is not only premised on the now paradigmatic problem of ethnographer observed, but turns, too, on a question of the proper name of one's country of origin:

> Two or three of them got round me and begged me for the twentieth time to tell them the name of my country. Then, as they could not pronounce it satisfactorily, they insisted that I was deceiving them, and that it was a name of my own invention. One funny old man, who bore a ludicrous resemblance to a friend of mine at home, was almost indignant. "Unglung!" said he, "who ever heard of such a name?—anglang—anger-lang—that can't be the name of your country; you are playing with us. . . . Do tell us the real name of your country and then when you are gone we shall know how to talk about you."[28]

Conrad's novel may not directly invite a rereading of this battle over how to pronounce the name of England, but the quality of the narrator's rhetorical question ("does not Alfred Wallace relate in his famous book?"), ambiguously addressed either inward, in the Assistant Commissioner's interior monologue, or outward toward the reader, captures something of the extraordinary instability of the reader's implied or actual relation to the proliferating marks of psychological or ethnographic otherness.[29]

One of a series of effects of alienation by which the novel decenters and diffuses attempts to fix the origins of human agency and political loyalty, the satirical point of this allusion to Wallace is revealingly magnified by reference to the original text. That satirical point turns on an ironic reversal of the Assistant Commissioner's sense of "home" by comparison to Wallace's. The Assistant Commissioner, it becomes clear, is more at home abroad. It is just this that unhinges the formalism of plotting a foreign subversion of domestic order and determines the importance of his riddle of territorial double-crossing as the solution of the novel's "special" crime. Thus the standoff between Vladimir and the Assistant Commissioner looks, from Vladimir's perspective, toward the stage of European politics eclipsed in *Under Western Eyes*, and, from the Assistant Commissioner's perspective to the colonial scene of political struggle, the view of a world ordered around London as imperial center of an East–West mapping of the world. This standoff enables classification of *The Secret Agent* as reflecting a shift in Conrad's underlying imaginative investments, from an ironic grasp of the deluded East–West mapping of a world governed by British imperial hegemony to the redefinition of European politics in terms of the struggle to define a new "good European" order—of governments and of men.[30] This gives perspective to that double-mapping of Europe and Empire with which the Russian idea of the West fixes European legacies in a singular "Western" history, imposed retrospectively on a social evolution that might alternatively be regarded as evolving further (as by Toynbee), or declining (as by Spengler).

Winnie Verloc's Place: Outside the Maps of Europe and Empire

Led by the piece of triangular broadcloth, the Assistant Commissioner's colonial sense of adventure prompts him to confront the geometry of Verloc's unique place, marked, from the start, by the cryptic triangle that is his code:

> Brett Street was not very far away. It branched off, narrow, from the side of an open triangular space surrounded by dark and mysterious houses, temples of petty commerce emptied of traders for the night. Only a fruiterer's stall at the corner made a violent blaze of light and colour. Beyond all was black, and the few people passing that direction vanished at one stride beyond the glowing heaps of oranges and lemons. No footsteps echoed. They would never be heard of again. The adventurous head of the Special Crimes Department watched these disappearances from a distance with an interested eye. He felt light-hearted, as though he had been ambushed all alone in a jungle many thousands of miles away from departmental desks and official inkstands. (*TSA*, 150)

The romance of the Commissioner's adventure creates an imagistic impression that prepares for an aftereffect even once he has himself disappeared from the narrative and Winnie faces the consequences of the simulated anarchist activity, simulating a plot of romance with Ossipon:

> The fruiterer at the corner had put out the blazing glory of his oranges and lemons, and Brett Place was all darkness, interspersed with the misty halos of the few lamps defining its triangular shape, with a cluster of three lights on one stand in the middle. The dark forms of the man and woman glided slowly arm in arm along the walls with a loverlike and homeless aspect in the miserable night. (*TSA*, 173)

The aesthetic impression seems to mark an overlap between various impossible romantic versions of topography: the Assistant Commissioner's, Winnie's and Ossipon's. The "violence" of the first colorful blaze, set against the snuffed-out "glory" of the last, allows for a kind of interpretive multiple reading, with the whole cast of characters assigned to various positions within the two moments of the fruiterer's mundane evening occupation. Indeed, it would be impossible to exclude from these metaphors a displaced symbolism of the explosion that fragments Stevie's body.

The relevance of the imported commodity of the citrus fruit itself, though ultimately outside the economic equations of the novel, leaves an irreducible aesthetic trace in the repetition of "oranges and lemons" (though in the different contexts of "violence" and "glory"). It is a representation on which the narrative insists, though it cannot ultimately be accommodated by the geometry of the triangular space to which it points. As the last form of "petty commerce" that the Commissioner encounters, it testifies to the requirement to signify a continuation of foreign-grown products for domestic consumption. Appropriated for the different and incompatible perspectives that light it up as an aesthetic moment—carrying the very possibility of narrative sequence when movement has long since been reduced to perspectival distortion of place—the commerce in citrus fruits incorporates a desire (perhaps some "Sehnsucht nach dem Suden") into a geometry of the lack of desire. Such a desire could only be fully satisfied—or worked out, perhaps even produced—elsewhere.

That elsewhere, excluded in the "topographical mysteries" of Conrad's London, becomes for Winnie Verloc the impossible geographic place of escape: "And perceiving the utter impossibility of walking as far as the nearest bridge, Mrs. Verloc thought of a flight abroad. It came to her suddenly. Murderers escaped. They escaped abroad. Spain or California. Mere names. The vast world created for the glory of man was only a vast blank to Mrs. Verloc" (*TSA*, 270). For Winnie the oppression of "mere names" on the map is overdetermined by the psychological trauma of her inability to escape a whole set of naming systems—including the name of Greenwich—and most obviously the patriarchal naming system of bourgeois marriage, which has displaced her family name. The complete absence from the novel of her original family name is not so much a sign of lost family inheritance as it is a constitutive displacement from political affiliations. Her predicament, indeed, subverts the logic of the Assistant Commissioner's assumptions: "'A genuine wife and a genuinely respectable, marital relation.'" The Assistant Commissioner's assumptions only exaggerate the contradictions of his own sense of "home," evident in his remarking that "'[Verloc] felt certain that his wife would not even hear of going abroad. Nothing could be more characteristic of the respectable bond than that'" (*TSA*, 221).

The "vast blank" to which Winnie's predicament reduces the "vast world created for the glory of man" recalls the series of "blank spaces" in Conrad's works, including the autobiographical rewriting of Marlow's passion for maps into the, so to speak, neutral predicament of imagining political community in *A Personal Record* with the mere claim, "I shall go *there*." Here, of course, the "blank space" becomes a "vast blank" in a perspectival shift which deflates the masculine heroism of geographical exploration. The references to Spain and California, however, are not entirely emptied. In recalling these names to Winnie's mind, *The Secret Agent* pinpoints the fault line between recent fictions of a "good European" Western order and older fictions of the West with which *Nostromo*, in its still more far-reaching genealogy of revolutionary discourses, unearths the colonial origins of European political representations.

Political Genealogies in Nietzsche and Conrad

To speak of Conrad's political novels in terms of genealogies is to invite analogy to the critical leverage Friedrich Nietzsche gave the term genealogy in his critique of European humanism, most notably in *On the Genealogy of Morals*. There is more to the analogy than a mere coincidence of political reaction against revolutionary ideals. For Nietzsche, the guiding term "genealogy" does not imply an antiquarian respect for the ancestral family tree. Legitimacy of ancestry is linked, rather, to "the lordly right of giving names";[31] and its critical leverage comes from an attention to the mistakes and accidents of birth always likely to show up on the genealogical table.[32] What Nietzsche and Conrad share is not belief in aristocratic traditions but skepticism about modern forms of representing continuities of social, political, or cultural history.

Nietzsche's characteristic manner of ironizing the "historical sense, to which we Europeans lay claim as our specialty,"[33] has a number of important points of connection to Conrad's very different grasp of the mistaken identity of European historical origins. One that is particularly relevant to *The Secret Agent* is Nietzsche's coinage of the "good European" perspective. More important than the brief allusion to that formulation in the text of *The Secret Agent*, however, is the manner in which it signals the absence in Nietzsche's work of that later formulation of "the West" with which it has since been conflated.[34] One touchstone for Nietzsche's ironic sense of the "good European" perspective is precisely its perspectival relation to the satirized "historical sense" of the nineteenth-century European, as seen through the lens of evolutionary theories: "the hybrid European—a tolerably ugly plebeian, all in all," who "definitely requires a costume" to represent that historical sense which "has come to us in the wake of the mad and fascinating *semi-barbarism* into which Europe has been plunged through the democratic mingling of classes and races."[35] Nietzsche's emphasis on Europe's "hybrid" origins is a characteristic deflation of the noble claims of European humanism. Nietzsche does not write of a "Western" cultural tradition. The "good European" perspective that might appear to approximate that idea is quite explicitly linked to Europe's "ignoble" racial and class origins.

Where Nietzsche's philosophical work perhaps most strikingly intersects with Conrad's political genealogies, however, is over an autobiographical fiction Nietzsche developed at various stages in his writing career, the fiction of a noble Polish ancestry. As he writes in the opening to *Ecce Homo*:

> Even by virtue of my descent, I am granted an eye beyond all merely local, merely nationally conditioned perspectives; it is not difficult for me to be a "good European." On the other hand, I am perhaps more German than present-day Germans, mere citizens of the German *Reich*, could possibly be—I, the last *anti-political* German. And yet my ancestors were Polish noblemen: I have many racial instincts in my body from that source—who knows? In the end perhaps even the *liberum veto*.[36]

The ironic claim to a privileged perspective on world events, reinforced by the characteristic Nietzschean quotation marks around "good European," helps define both the similarities and the differences between Nietzsche and Conrad. Each participated in an entirely problematic late-nineteenth-century critique of European enlightenment ideals.

Moreover, Nietzsche's claims depend upon a particular emphasis on Polish ancestry that is by no means simply an accidental coincidence of personal genealogy. The telling difference in the manner in which a Polish lineage determines Nietzsche's genealogical fiction compared with Conrad's lies in Nietzsche's selective choice of two antithetical distinctive Polish traits for genealogical self-fashioning. One is the "liberum veto," or unrestricted veto, a traditional privilege for members of the Polish Diet and a mark of the historical importance of Poland as a political example for European forms of constitutional democracy. The other is the insinuation of "the many racial instincts from that source" (insinuating not only Slavic, but also Jewish racial stereotypes). Poland, for Nietzsche, embodies a juxtaposition of extreme European perspectives: an extreme of enlightened political ideas, and an extreme of racial confusion and mixture. The claim to Polish ancestry, indeed, uniquely embodies the rhetorical force of his coinage "we good Europeans" which cuts both against claims to racial superiority so characteristic of the emerging "official nationalism" of the German *Reich* and against the "noble posterity" of European democratic revolutionaries. A sign of the uniqueness of Nietzsche's coinage "we good Europeans," however, is the eclipse of its rhetorical force with the consolidation of the rhetorical invention of the West, which works precisely to disconnect European political traditions from the confusing entanglement of racial and national differences.

Clearly Conrad's relation to Poland is very different from Nietzsche's fabrication of Polish ancestry. One way to clarify the difference is to point out how much more seriously Conrad must have grasped what for Nietzsche is a joke at the expense of inflated European ideals—that Europe's first constitutional democracy collapsed the moment it was born. This implicit joke is more explicit in those versions of Nietzsche's Polish genealogy which preceded the publication of *Ecce Homo*; indeed, Conrad himself might have read one version quoted in an article on Nietzsche published in *Blackwood's Magazine* in October 1897:

> "The Poles were for me the most gifted and chivalrous among the Slavonic peoples, and the endowment of the Slavs seemed to me superior to that of the Germans. Indeed, I thought that it was only in consequence of a strong infusion of Slavonic blood that the Germans had become a gifted nationality. I thought with pleasure on the right of a Polish nobleman by his simple veto to overturn the resolution of an assembly. The political unruliness and weakness of the Poles," he adds characteristically, "were for me rather proofs of their capacity than the reverse."[37]

Where Nietzsche can refer to a political idea like the "liberum veto" to consolidate the ironic perspectives of a "good European," Conrad's investment in imagining political community makes his genealogy substantially different from Nietzsche's. One might say that Conrad takes seriously what Nietzsche applies to the genealogy of morals: a genealogy of political discourses in general and of revolutionary discourses in particular.

For Conrad, there is always a political difference between the psychological experience of extreme cultural disorientation and the ethnographic designation of a "people." The Conradian political dilemma is a predicament of being caught between cultures, the bewilderment of exile from community, and isolation through a betrayal that implicates a crossed set of cultures. It is this dilemma, crossed with the compelling need to imagine an authentic political community, that gives Conrad's fiction more leverage as a political genealogy than the Nietzschean play on the "good European" perspective.

It leads Conrad, most notably in *Nostromo*, to which I turn last, to carry the politics of Nietzsche's Polish joke a step further. If Poland embodies Europe's "noble" legacy of democratic revolution, its failure to achieve the form of a modern nation-state is exemplary not only as a comment on the formal limits of democracy, but also because its historic failure as the first European nation to follow the American model points to the extra-European origins of modern nation-building.

Notes

1. Howe, *Politics and the Novel*, 76.

2. A review in *The Manchester Guardian* complained, "We associate Mr. Conrad with memorable experiences of thrilling adventure, of heroical tension, of the glowing East; we seem to be losing something very precious when he compels us to the grim comedy of anarchism" (Sherry, *Conrad*, 182); a review in the *Glasgow News* opened, "It is not an irrelevant reflection upon *The Secret Agent* that its author, Joseph Conrad, is of Polish birth" (ibid., 195).

3. Cited in Iszak, "*Under Western Eyes*," 436.

4. This confusion is not plotted simply as the *narrator's* confusion. Nathalie herself implies here, as elsewhere, that social contests in Europe *can* be explained in terms of class conflict, while in Russia "it is something different." But what has been elided in the inauguration of this dialogue is not simply the significance of the "Russian way" for European debates, but also the manner in which Nathalie's argument is in dialogue with Russian "Westerners" who argued that only European-style reform provided a credible alternative for Russians. Nathalie's mother, the unobtrusive third party to their exchange, might figure as participant in this hidden or oblique dialogue, particularly given the importance of the generation gap in articulating the nihilism or iconoclastic thinking of the 1860's that so dramatically altered and intensified the Slavophile–Westerner debates.

5. By contrast, Eugène Melchior, writing about Turgenev in 1883, goes to great lengths to explain why "it is necessary to be up-to-date in Russian polemical debates and their terminology, in order to understand what storms can be unleashed by the appellation 'Occidental'" (*Revue des deux mondes* [Oct. 15, 1883]: 793; my translation).

6. Kropotkin, *Memoirs of a Revolutionist*, 194.

7. Dostoyevsky, *Crime and Punishment*, 4.

8a. Bakhtin, *Problems of Dostoevsky's Poetics*, 74, 251.

8b. Characteristically, the repetitions are premised on an original displacement of origins. A "quarter-life-size" representation, the statue is itself possibly a copy ("quarter-life-size" perhaps in relation to the original sculpture). Since there is no such sculptor, Spontini, the reference appears as a deliberately mistaken allusion to the famous Italian composer Gasparo Spontini (1774–1851), a displacement of sight and sound reproduced in the synaesthetic effects of oblique reading described above. This invented work of art provides a condensed model for how the novel's underlying antipathy toward Russia's mimicry of European culture also subverts the idea of a supposedly original European culture. Viewed through the lens of its imitation and displacement, the aura of the work of art produces a cultural effect synonymous with the novel's production of "the West" as cliché.

9. Compare Frank Kermode's rather different stress on the "narrative secrets" of *Under Western Eyes* in "Secrets and Narrative Sequence."

10. Ian Watt, in *Conrad in the Nineteenth Century*, offers a persuasive reading of the symbolist power of the title *Heart of Darkness*, but one might note that Marlow is the first to destroy the poetic integrity of the title: "The reaches opened before us and closed behind, as if the forest had stepped leisurely across the water to bar the way for our return. We penetrated deeper and deeper into the heart of darkness. It was very quiet there" (*Y*, 35).

11. Emily Iszak, charting the late appearance of the title (in January 1911), notes that Methuen, the publisher, read the title as cliché, objecting that it promised "a book of descriptive impressions" ("*Under Western Eyes* and the Problems of Serial Publication," 436).

11. Williams, *The English Novel*, 121.

13. The importance of the image of the face in *Under Western Eyes* is alluded to in Fried, "Almayer's Face." Although his suggestive reading of upturned faces in a much more general field of textual production seems particularly suggestive for *Under Western Eyes*, we await his disclosure of the full dimensions of the upturned face in *Under Western Eyes*.

14. See *Zionism and the Western Jew: A Symposium*, London Zionist League, Dec. 14, 1908.

15. Aschheim, *Brothers and Strangers*, 79.

16. Jean-Aubry, *Conrad Letters*, 1:336; emphasis mine.

17. Conrad, *Collected Letters*, 2:229–30.

18. Ibid., 3:434

19. See Howse, *Greenwich Time*.

20. For critical accounts of Conrad's sources for *The Secret Agent*, see Fleishman, *Conrad's Politics*; Hay, *Joseph Conrad*; Sherry, *Conrad's Western World*; and Watt, ed., *Conrad: The Secret Agent*.

21. For details of Conrad's expansion of *The Secret Agent* from the serialized version and from the précis of the ending, see the Introduction to the Cambridge edition of *The Secret Agent*, ed. Bruce Harkness and S. W. Reid, especially xxxvii.

22. See Foucault, *The Order of Things*, 373–86.

23. The quotation is from *Beyond Good and Evil*, pt. 2, sec. 22: "You must pardon me as an old philologist who cannot refrain from the maliciousness of putting his finger on bad arts of interpretation: but 'nature's conformity to law' of which you physicists speak so proudly, as though—it exists only thanks to your interpretation and bad 'philology'—it is not a fact, not a 'text,' but rather only a naïve humanitarian adjustment and distortion of meaning with which you go more than half-way to meet the democratic instincts of the modern soul!" (52).

24. In February of 1905 Conrad wrote to Cunninghame Graham: "The stodgy sun of the future—our early Victorian future—lingers on the horizon, but all the same it will rise—it will indeed—to throw its sanitary light upon a dull world of perfected municipalities and WC's sans peur et sans reproche. The grave of individual temperaments is being dug by GBS [George Bernard Shaw] and HGW [H. G. Wells] with hopeful industry" (*Collected Letters*, 3:217–18).

25. Fleishman, *Conrad's Politics*. See esp. 187–214.

26. Wallace, *The Malay Archipelago*, 2:452–53.

27. Ibid., 232.

28. Ibid., 246.

29. This battle over how to pronounce the name of England, together with all the various battles over names that I discuss in Conrad's work, might productively be compared to Jacques Derrida's famous reading of Claude Lévi-Strauss's *Tristes Tropiques* in "The Battle of Proper Names," in *Of Grammatology*, 107–118.

30. The term "good European" has, as discussed below, a specifically Nietzschean nuance; but Nietzsche's term had, by 1907, been translated—along with the rest of Nietzsche's work—into the intensified and racialized vortex of artistic and political discourses of the first decade of the twentieth century—in England in such new journals as *The New Age* and *The English Review*. The formation, in Scotland, of a "Good European Society," which flourished between 1903 and 1915 around some of the key promoters of Nietzsche in the British Isles, provides an index not only of the resonance of the term, but also of the problematic terms of its translation. Each issue of the society's "notes for Good Europeans" was headed by a quotation from Nietzsche: "In a word—and it shall be an honourable word—we are Good Europeans . . . the heirs of thousands of years of the European spirit." This is a slightly doctored version of paragraph 377 of *The Gay Science*, in which Nietzsche's ironic grasp of the term "good European" is silently edited out: "the *too deeply pledged heirs* of millenniums of European thought."

31. Nietzsche, *On the Genealogy of Morals*, 26.

32. It is worth calling attention to the number of radically different evaluations of Nietzsche's work that have a direct bearing on the force of any such analogy between Conrad and Nietzsche. In singling out Nietzsche's idea of "genealogy," I have in mind primarily the recent critical appropriation of Nietzsche's term by Gilles Deleuze and Michel Foucault. Deleuze offers a concise summary of the concept of genealogy at the beginning of his study *Nietzsche and Philosophy* (1–3), as well as a more extensive elaboration of its implications throughout the entire work. It is this concept that Michel Foucault develops in his influential outlines for historical practice. See, in particular, "Nietzsche, Genealogy, History," in *Language, Counter-memory, Practice*. Conrad's political fictions may be read as genealogies of political discourse almost in the Foucauldian sense, with the important additional point that they call into question one of the leading motifs of Foucault's work, its concentration on the formation of discourses "in the West."

The intersection between Conrad and Nietzsche is also, however, to be viewed through the lens of English translations and discussions of Nietzsche. We have already discussed the links between Nietzsche's influence and Dostoyevsky's, beginning around 1907. As early as 1899, however, Conrad was exposed to an important example of the English reception of Nietzsche, in the form of Edward Garnett's article. What is significant, most of all, about this English Nietzsche is the fact that he was enlisted in the cause of socialism—most notably by A. R. Orage, whose newspaper *The New Age* led the way in establishing Nietzsche as the philosopher à la mode from 1909 to 1913 (see Thatcher, *Nietzsche in England*, 42).

33. Nietzsche, *Beyond Good and Evil*, 152.

34. See the discussion of Heidegger on Nietzsche in the Epilogue.

35. Nietzsche, *Beyond Good and Evil*, 152.

36. Nietzsche, *Ecce Homo*, 225.

37. *Blackwood's Magazine* (Oct. 1897): 476–93, esp. 480.

ROBERT HAMPSON

Absence and Presence in Victory

Said, discussing the interplay between writing, speaking and seeing in Conrad's fiction, has suggested that, characteristically, Conrad's narratives 'originate in the hearing and telling presence of people' (95).[1] But these narratives also often assume (as Chapter 6 has demonstrated) the currency of rival versions and, indeed, are often positioned among competing narratives. Although these spoken narratives evoke a community, their existence as writing implicitly sets that evoked community against the actual isolation of the scene of writing and the scene of reading. Where gossip anticipates a community, writing produces the reader as solitary individual. Conrad's narratives circulate gossip within a community, but also, as in 'Karain' or *Lord Jim*, repeatedly return to the solitary scenes of writing and of reading.

Said argues further that writing sets the illusion of presence against the fact of 'the absence of everything but words' (WTC, 95). Conrad's narrative is grounded epistemologically in utterance 'as speech reported or spoken' (WTC, 101). Thus, in *Lord Jim*, Marlow listens to Jim and then remembers Jim 'at length, in detail and audibly' (LJ, 33) in front of other audiences. However, as Said notes, 'Jim does not speak to Marlow, but rather in front of him, just as Marlow cannot by definition speak to the reader but only in front of him' (WTC, 103). In the same way, in *Victory*, Lena has the consciousness that Heyst, when addressing her, 'was really talking to himself' (V, 196). Ironically,

From *Cross-Cultural Encounters in Joseph Conrad's Malay Fiction*, pp. 146–60, 223–25. © 2000 by Robert Hampson.

Lena's final words, though addressed to Heyst, are also performed in front of him rather than engaging with him in a moment of mutual understanding:

> 'Who else could have done this for you?' she whispered gloriously.
> 'No one in the world,' he answered her in a murmur of unconcealed despair. (V, 406)

What should be their moment of union, in the romantic script according to which Lena sacrifices herself, is actually marked by division and divergence. In other words, intradiegetically in both *Lord Jim* and *Victory*, speech conveys 'the presence to each other of speaker and hearer' but not necessarily 'a mutual comprehension' (WTC, 103–4). Something similar happens extradiegetically. Lena and Heyst talk in front of each other and in front of the reader. They are presented dramatically through dialogue, and the reader is left to gauge the degrees of understanding and misunderstanding, reading and misreading, involved in their interaction through her own (mis)understandings and (mis)readings. The scene of narration—with its speaker and hearer—creates the illusion of presence, if not the actuality of mutual comprehension, but the scene of writing and the scene of reading are both involved in a problematics of absence that foregrounds interpretation.[2]

Island Gossip

In *Victory*, Conrad returned to many of the issues he had raised in *Lord Jim*. The most obvious of these is gossip. From the start *Victory* establishes the oral community within which Heyst has taken refuge, and returns to an exploration of gossip. Part I is presented by an unnamed narrator, who invokes the group ('We "out there"') to which he belongs (V, 3). He reports on Heyst's observable characteristics and recycles various attempts to interpret Heyst's behaviour made by this community. He notes that 'from the first there was some difficulty in making him out' (V, 6). This difficulty is demonstrated by the succession of labels that are attached to him ('Enchanted Heyst', 'Hard facts', 'Heyst the Spider', 'Heyst the Enemy'), each of which memorialises some incident or utterance. In the first part of *Victory*, as in the first part of *Nostromo*, various labels and public identities circulate around an absence.

The most important of the early incidents is Heyst's rescue of Morrison and the events that follow from that. The narrator introduces the incident by reference to competing narratives current in the community of gossip: 'Some said he was a partner, others said he was a sort of paying guest' (V, 10). The dominant narrative, however, is that circulated by Schomberg: 'that Heyst, having obtained some mysterious hold on Morrison, had fastened himself on him and was sucking him dry' (V, 20). Hence the label: 'Heyst the Spider'.[3] Subsequently, the Tropical Belt Coal Co. provides the stimulus for further gossip: 'Everybody in the islands was talking of the Tropical Belt Coal' (V, 24). This time, however, the gossip is prompted by the threat the Tropical Belt Coal Co. represents to the livelihood of the gossipers: 'the end of the individual trader, smothered under a great invasion of steamers' (V, 24). The beginning of the 'era of steam' (V, 21) for the islands marks the end of the era of sail.[4] Steamers keeping regular timetables render redundant the traders with their sailing-ships, dependent on wind and weather, who have consti- tuted an important part of the oral community of Conrad's Malay novels. This gossip, in other words, is professional talk, prompted by self-interest. If the narrative is grounded epistemologically in utterance, that utterance, in turn, is grounded in the material conditions of the archipelago, though these are only seen darkly through the text's circulation of gossip and rumour.

The Tropical Belt Coal Company also generates its own form of gossip. There is, for example, Heyst's promotional talk of the 'great stride forward for these regions', which is heard by 'more than a hundred persons in the islands' (V, 6). There is the related talk of 'offices in London and Amster- dam'—though this, in practice, might amount to no more than 'one room in each' (V, 21). There is also the prospectus with its map:

> On it Samburan was represented as the central spot of the Eastern
> Hemisphere. . . . Heavy lines radiated from it in all directions
> through the tropics . . . (V, 23)

This map is very obviously not a neutral and objective representation but an expression of value.[5] More important, as GoGwilt observes, the 'ironic failure of this map to represent a corresponding power' graphically registers the gap between 'representation and reality' (IW, 67).[6] The promotional literature that accompanies the map also produces a new label for Heyst: 'A. Heyst, manager in the East' (V, 29). The designation 'manager in the East' suggests a large concern with various managers, and again there is an obvi- ous gap between the representation and the reality of Samburan.

Schomberg, too, is involved in this form of textual production—and to the same effect. The narrator refers to his 'famed table d'hôte dinners' and the accompanying advertising slogan 'catering "white man for white men"' (V, 97). But Schomberg's financial affairs do not match up to his rhetoric: indeed, they 'had never been so unpromising since he came out East directly after the Franco-Prussian War' (V, 96). In 'Falk', Schomberg made a promotional speech to the narrator: 'I only charge a dollar for the tiffin, and one dollar and fifty cents for the dinner. Show me anything cheaper. Why am I doing it? . . . I do it for the sake of a lot of young white fellows here that hadn't a place where they could get a decent meal and eat it decently in good company' (Ty, 174). The narrator had undermined this speech by observing that the 'convinced way he surveyed the empty chairs made me feel as if I had intruded upon a tiffin of ghostly Presences' (Ty, 174). Again, the effect is to emphasise the gap between representation and reality.

It is Schomberg who keeps Heyst's name current in island gossip. He is Conrad's anatomy of gossip: 'asking everybody about everything, and arranging the information into the most scandalous shape his imagination could invent' (V, 30).[7] Part I ends with Schomberg's narrative of Heyst, in which Heyst's actions are interpreted in line with this rule (V, 61). Heyst's rescue of Lena gives Schomberg an even stronger motive to make Heyst the object of his gossip. Part II describes how it became 'a recognised entertainment to go and hear his abuse of Heyst' (V, 95). If Schomberg has a 'genius' for catering, he also has granted to himself a licence for 'the inventing, elaborating and retailing of scandalous gossip' (V, 97). Schomberg's gossip has become commodified. For his audience, it is no longer primarily a communicative act but rather a performance. Like Jim, Schomberg speaks 'in front of' rather than 'to' his audience. Nevertheless, it is Schomberg's version of Heyst—'a Heyst fattened by years of private and public rapines, the murderer of Morrison, the swindler of many shareholders' (V, 156)—which circulates and will direct Ricardo and Jones to Heyst's island in Part III.[8]

Victory effectively equates gossip with exile. At least, it is the condition of exile that underlies the construction of this particular European community through gossip. Schomberg's successive hotels are the emblem of this rootless society, and it is no accident that they are a centre for the production and distribution of gossip. However, Schomberg's production of gossip does not protect him from becoming himself the subject of gossip. With Lena's escape, for example, he briefly becomes a character in others' gossip. Davidson is told about Schomberg's fight with Zangiacomo when he arrives at Schomberg's hotel, and that story opens onto other story-telling:

> The captains of vessels, coming on shore later in the day, brought tales of a strange invasion, and wanted to know who were the two offensive lunatics in a steam-launch, apparently after a man and a girl, and telling a story of which one could make neither head nor tail. (V, 49)[9]

These stories are subsequently re-circulated by Davidson to Heyst ('the story of the violent proceedings following on the discovery of his flight' [V, 56]). It is also gossip about Schomberg that has brought Ricardo and Jones to his hotel. When Schomberg discovers from Jones that he has been the subject of talk rather than the source of talk, he is 'astounded' (V, 101)—a response that prefigures Heyst's, when Lena reveals to him that she had heard talk about his partner: 'The idea of being talked about was always novel to Heyst's simplified conception of himself' (V, 206). Discovering that you are the subject of talk risks encountering others' objectification of you. Thus Heyst is forced to realise that he is not 'above the level of island gossip' (V, 206), as he had imagined. But that objectification of himself through gossip also intrudes into his relationship with Lena. It reinforces Lena's sense of insecurity; it also affects how Heyst regards himself. Lena repeats the story she has heard—how Morrison's partner 'first got all there was to get out of him' and then 'sent him out to die somewhere' (V, 208). She tells Heyst how she heard that 'everybody in these parts knew the story' (V, 208), and Heyst considers, for the first time, 'how the business looked from outside' (V, 208). In the privacy and isolation of Samburan the oral community catches up with Heyst: first, through Lena; subsequently, through Jones and Ricardo.

When they arrive on the island, Jones tells Heyst that he is 'a much talked-about man' (V, 377). For Ricardo, the 'Schombergian theory of Heyst' becomes 'a profound conviction' (V, 264). It is a conviction that has prompted their voyage to Samburan and will end in the death of all the Europeans on the island. The awareness of these 'ugly lies' (V, 381) also has an impact on Heyst's ability to defend himself against Ricardo and Jones. Thus he writes his own possible responses to their presence into the Schombergian script: 'after luring my friend and partner to his death from mere greed of money', he would now be said to have 'murdered these unoffending shipwrecked strangers from mere funk' (V, 361). However, despite the influence of Schomberg's gossip in the narrative, gossip is actually a sign of powerlessness rather than of power. As Spacks suggests, 'gossip gets its power by the illusion of mastery gained through taking imaginative possession of another's experience' (*Gossip*, 22). Schomberg's gossip thus becomes the measure of his powerlessness: if 'verbal acts' are designed to 'extend our control over a world that is not naturally disposed to serve our interests', then gossip both epitomises that desire for control and, by the same measure, declares the lack from which that desire springs.[10]

The Privileged Reader

In *Lord Jim*, for much of the novel the written text aspires to the condition of orality—with the recovery of the immediacy, community and presence of oral storytelling. The last part of the novel, however, complicates this picture. Although, as Chapter 6 demonstrated, the narrative is still presented as oral testimony from a variety of sources, that oral testimony has not been reproduced orally by Marlow, but has been sent as writing to the 'privileged man' (LJ, 337). The introduction of the 'privileged man' emphasises distance, isolation, and absence as components of the scene of reading—just as immediacy, community, and presence, were the characteristics of oral narration. One of the problems, however, is why this particular individual was chosen as the privileged reader.[11] As Marlow emphasises, this man is, on the surface, the least likely to be receptive to Jim's narrative. He is, after all, the member of the audience for Marlow's oral story-telling who believed that 'giving your life up to them . . . was like selling your soul to a brute'; he insisted, instead, that 'we must fight in the ranks' (LJ, 339).

When Marlow's narration ends, the temporary community constituted by the act of narration disperses, and each returns to the condition of being separate individuals ('Each of them seemed to carry away his own impression' [LJ, 337]). Unlike the end of 'Karain', where the narrator's encounter with Jackson on the Strand reconvenes a version of the European group that had featured in the tale, the end of *Lord Jim* emphasises separateness. It does this by turning from oral narration to written texts, from the collectivity of an audience to the isolation of the scenes of writing and reading. The privileged man, whom Marlow contacts some two years later, is presented with a packet containing four texts: a letter to Jim from his father; 'a good many pages closely blackened and pinned together'; 'a loose square sheet of greyish paper'; and 'an explanatory letter from Marlow' (LJ, 338). The novel insists not just on the written sources of the final stage of the narrative but also on the materiality of that writing. At the same time, each of these texts asserts a sense of isolation, exclusion, and absence. The 'loose square sheet of greyish paper', for example, contains Jim's attempt to write after the catastrophe, but the attempt is unsuccessful—and it is not clear even who is addressed.[12] The letter from Jim's father is the last letter Jim received from home—received just before he joined the *Patna* (LJ, 341). This letter, full of 'mild gossip' about his family (LJ, 342), four pages of 'family news' offering him the possibility of 'converse' (LJ, 342), represents that family circle from which his actions on the *Patna* have excluded him. The final document, the many closely-written pages of text, is the narrative assembled by Marlow—a substitute for the unavailable narrative which Marlow invokes: 'the story in [Jim's] own words, in his careless yet feeling voice' (LJ, 343). Marlow's invocation of Jim's voice emphasises Jim's absence. Jim's voice is displaced by writing, and these documents are all that is left to gesture towards the life that has passed. However, while Jim's voice is unavailable, the written nature of Marlow's final narrative is de-emphasised: there is no marked stylistic difference between Marlow's oral narration that occupies most of the novel and the written text with which it ends. If Jim's voice is unavailable, Marlow's voice apparently 'cannot be silenced' (Y, 97). Marlow's written text resurrects Marlow's speaking voice and produces the illusion of Marlow's presence. However, the condition for that 'speaking' remains the irremediable absence of Jim and the temporary absence of Marlow.

Magic Books

In *Victory*, Heyst is the 'privileged man' insofar as he is the privileged reader of his father's texts. In Part 3, as he contemplates his own uprootedness, he consults his father's book, *Storm and Dust*. The text is supplemented by the icon of his father's scene of writing, the portrait of his father 'with the quill pen in his hand' (V, 195), the primal textual scene. It is also supplemented by Heyst's memories of his father's voice. As he said earlier, 'They read his books, but I have heard his living word' (V, 196). Now, as he reads, 'it seemed to him that he was hearing his father's voice' (V, 219): 'He abandoned himself to the half-belief that something of his father dwelt yet on earth—a ghostly voice, audible to the ear of his own flesh and blood' (V, 219). Despite the emphasis on writing, the bond between Heyst and his father is founded on presence—or the illusion of presence—and presence as signified by speech. The absent father is present in the text through Heyst's memory; he is, above all, present in his shaping influence on Heyst's life. This is the marvellous irony of the scene in which Ricardo enters Heyst's house in search of 'clues', sees the room full of books and the portrait, but can't see the clue that stares him in the face. He has the key to Heyst in front of him, but does not realise it: 'what guess could one make out of a multitude of books' (V, 286). Heyst's father is the determining absence for the scheme of drifting that has been Heyst's life. Heyst invokes his father's voice as prior to his father's writing; but his father's writing, in the broader sense, has determined Heyst's own speaking. Where Heyst hears his father's voice authorising his texts, Heyst's own existence has been programmed by his father.

Heyst has taken refuge in the oral community of the archipelago from the metropolitan print community associated with his father. After leaving school at eighteen, he had spent three years living in London with his father, who was then 'writing his last book' (V, 91). Heyst's mourning for his father has a similar textual aspect: his tears are prompted by the reading of 'a few obituary notices generally insignificant and some grossly abusive' (V, 175). This textual reference is maintained in the relics of his father Heyst brings to Samburan: his father's books and the portrait of his father in the act of writing 'pen in hand above a white sheet of paper' (V, 189). For Heyst, the portrait of his father is 'a wonderful presence in its heavy frame on the flimsy wall' (V, 218). This icon of writing has, however, an ambiguous status.[13] The portrait is described as 'looking exiled and at home, out of place and masterful' (V, 219). The figure in the portrait is represented as 'looking at home' and 'masterful', but the portrait shares with Heyst the sense of being displaced, 'transplanted', with the consequent problematising of its 'mastery'. Furthermore, insofar as the portrait is a copy of the father, the father is also displaced. From Heyst's perspective, the portrait represents two versions of origin: the father and the father's writing. However, the 'wonderful presence' of the father is in fact the mark of his absence. In addition, as Barthes has argued, 'writing is the destruction of every voice, of every point of origin'.[14] With writing, 'the voice loses its origin, the author enters into his own death' (IMT, 141). Or, as Derrida puts it, against the self-presence of the father in speech, writing is the 'miserable son' orphaned and wandering the world.[15] The condition of being 'exiled and at home, out of place and masterful' thus corresponds to the ambiguities of presence and absence, apartness and power that the novel explores in relation to spoken and written language.

Intertextuality plays a part in that exploration. The Heyst who 'had plunged himself into an abyss of meditation over books' (V, 180) in Samburan is also a re-enactment of Prospero. His existence on Samburan is a version of Shakespeare's *The Tempest*—with Lena as Miranda; Wang as Ariel; Mr Jones as Duke Ferdinand; Pedro as Caliban.[16] As Jerry Brotton has observed, the power of books and the power of possession of books is an important feature of *The Tempest*.[17] Prospero's 'immersion in "the liberal arts" (I.ii.73)' allows him 'unprecedented access to the arcane mysteries of the elements most feared and respected by early modern cosmographers and travellers— the sea and the stars' (TT, 29). Brotton notes how Prospero's involvement in books is constantly emphasised. He was banished from Milan for neglecting 'worldly ends' (I.ii.89) by treating his library as 'dukedom enough' (I.ii, 109–10). In the conspiracy to overthrow Prospero, Caliban admonishes Stephano and Trinculo: 'Remember / First to possess his books' (III.ii.89–90) (TT, 29). In *Almayer's Folly*, Almayer's office was imaged as a 'temple' and his ledgers were perceived as 'magic books'. *Victory*, too, is concerned with books, but the power of books is much more problematic. In Part III, Heyst comes to appreciate the power of words, but this appreciation comes as a result of the calumnies of Schomberg. He then reads one of his father's books, but his father's written words are experienced by him through the evocation of his father's voice. The text is used by him to produce the illusion of presence, but that illusion is based on the assumed priority of speech to writing. However, speech and presence also cause him problems. Indeed, where he converts text into the illusion of presence, when confronted with Otherness he converts presence into text. Thus, when he turns to Lena, she becomes reduced to a script, but, unlike his father's text, Lena is 'a script in an unknown language' or 'like any writing to the illiterate' (V, 222).[18] The magic does not work: this text does not give a comforting illusion of presence, but insists instead on its opacity—its Otherness. Heyst's scheme of drifting has been a way of avoiding contact with Otherness. It has also been a way of avoiding the strangeness of exile. In Kristeva's words, 'as he chooses a program he allows himself a respite or a residence' (SO, 6). Lena's presence on the island forces Heyst to engage in an interrogation of Otherness. He is 'intensely aware of her personality' (V, 192), but; if he tries to go beyond primary sense data, he runs into difficulties. Thus, 'in the intimacy of their life her grey, unabashed gaze forced upon him the sensation of something inexplicable reposing within her' (V, 192). If he tries to explore this Otherness, presence immediately turns into its opposite: 'something inexplicable' under the pressure of his interrogation becomes 'simply an abysmal emptiness' (V, 192).

Metropolitan Problems

Paul Brown has pointed out that *The Tempest* 'bears traces of the contemporary British investment in colonial expansion'.[19] More recently, Peter Hulme has written on the dual location of *The Tempest*: how it fuses the Mediterranean and the West Indies.[20] Conrad transplants that hybrid to a third location: the East Indies. Here the South American, Pedro, is a Caliban out of his element, and none of the characters (with the possible exception of the almost invisible Alfuros) are native to the island.[21] Hulme notes how class-conflict was an aspect of the Bermuda narrative and how Shakespeare re-figures that class-conflict in the Stephano/Trinculo sub-plot, the conspiracy of the lower orders against the nobles. In *Victory*, this re-surfaces as a component of the sexual relationship between Ricardo and Lena: their similar class background is emphasised, and Ricardo indeed sees their relationship as a conspiracy against the two 'gentlemen'. This concern for the metropolitan experience is signalled by Ricardo's nostalgia for the West India Docks (V, 127) and the life of 'walking the pavement and cracking jokes and standing drinks to chums' (V, 129).[22] It is signalled also by Lena's memories of 'poor lodging-houses' (V, 78) in North London (V, 191). It is confirmed by the account of Heyst's years in London with his father and by Jones's world of gentlemen's clubs and 1890s sexual scandal. In the colonial setting of *Victory*, it is not the colonial encounter that is foregrounded but rather metropolitan problems.[23]

However, if metropolitan problems are foregrounded, the colonial encounter is not ignored. The introduction of the 'privileged man' at the end of *Lord Jim* raised questions about English views of colonised peoples that were not resolved. *Victory* addresses some of those questions. Although the colonial encounter is kept in the background—and the cross-cultural encounter that is foregrounded in *Victory* is between different English cultures rather than European and non-European cultures—this is another case where the background gradually comes to the fore. English attitudes towards colonised peoples are thematised from early on along with the intrusion of metropolitan concerns into Heyst's Samburan retreat. From the start, there is Heyst's general tendency to disregard Wang: Heyst is represented (and represents himself) as living alone on Samburan. Lena shares this attitude: 'There is no one here to think any thing of us good or bad' (V, 188). Wang is like the invisible servants in Austen novels, or like the slave-girl, Taminah, in *Almayer's Folly*.[24] In Chapter 8 of *Almayer's Folly*, Reshid tries to make use of Taminah, 'an apparition of daily recurrence and of no importance whatever' (AF, 110), to spy on Almayer's household. Ironically, the powerless and disregarded Taminah is already in possession of the important information that Reshid seeks. In *Victory*, however, this is not just an issue of class. Chapter 20 of *Lord Jim* provides an instructive comparison. Here Marlow is guided to Stein's study by a Javanese servant who, after throwing open the study door, 'vanished in a mysterious way as though he had been a ghost only momentarily embodied for that particular service' (LJ, 204). This figure of the ghostly, disembodied servant that appears briefly as an embellishment in *Lord Jim* is built into *Victory* as one of its constituent parts. Conrad's translation of *The Tempest* to the archipelago casts Wang in the role of Ariel, and, if Conrad does not make much space for their voices, he at least makes visible the invisibility of servants and subject peoples.[25] When Schomberg and Ricardo are considering obstacles in the way of a visit to Samburan, both agree that 'native craft' can be ignored:

> Both these white men looked on native life as a mere play of shadows. A play of shadows the dominant race could walk through unaffected and disregarded in the pursuit of its incomprehensible aims and needs. (V, 167)

Later, discussing Wang, Ricardo and Jones agree that he can safely be disregarded, 'a Chink was neither here nor there' (V, 268). In addition to the manifestation of these racist attitudes, the idea of 'race' itself is explicitly articulated in the narrative. There is, for example, the casual working-class racism of Lena: she and Heyst, discussing Wang, seem to agree that 'One Chinaman looks very much like another' (V, 182). Later still, when Lena realises that Heyst had planned to send her to the Alfuros' village for safety, she protests: 'That was a strange notion of yours, to send me away. . . . To these savages, too! . . . You can do what you like with me—but not that, not that!' (V, 349). For Mr Jones, racism is not casual but a conscious ideology.

He asks Heyst 'Do you believe in racial superiority, Mr Heyst?' and, without waiting for a reply, adds 'I do, firmly' (V, 382).

Wang, for obvious reasons, becomes the focus of English attitudes towards non-Europeans. Wang, first of all, represents the Chinese community of the archipelago, making visible this group which is glimpsed at the edges of Conrad's Malay world. They are most prominent in the form of the Chinese coolies on board the *Nan-Shan* in 'Typhoon'. They are pervasive in the Macassar of *An Outcast* as servants in the Sunda Hotel, billiard markers; tellers in Hudig's office; shipowners; serangs and pirates. They are also present as the shopkeepers in Patusan; as Davidson's shipowners in *Victory*; as the silent servants in Schomberg's hotels in *Lord Jim* and *Victory*. Wang's own career also produces a catalogue of Chinese roles in the archipelago through his transition from miner to cultivator, from coolie labour to entrepreneur, as he cultivates his patch of ground and markets his produce to Heyst. Where Ariel's magic powers perhaps explain Wang's mysterious ability to appear and disappear, Ariel's invisibility becomes the 'invisibility' of servants and the colonised. Wang as a version of Ariel foregrounds the notion of invisible agency, of work which is done 'magically'—in other words, the mystification and occlusion of labour by class and imperial ideologies. At the same time, through the narrative, Wang also asserts his agency. Wang, in a noticeable reversal of colonial positions, 'annexes' both Heyst's keys and his gun (V, 180, 314). Wang similarly annexes the ground next to his hut and turns it over to cultivation (V, 181). More significantly, Wang is disregarded by Jones and Ricardo, but is instrumental in their defeat: he shoots Pedro and shoves off their boat. Finally, when all the Europeans are dead, it is Wang and his Alfuro wife who remain in possession of the Diamond Bay settlement.

In the final act of *The Tempest*, Prospero shows Alonzo his 'cell' and 'discovers' Ferdinand and Miranda playing at chess. In the equivalent moment in *Victory*, Mr Jones makes Heyst return to his bungalow and discovers Ricardo and Lena engaged in a much less innocent game: 'Behold the simple Acis kissing the sandals of the nymph' (V, 393). In the following chapter, Ricardo's rhetoric ('What you want is a man, a master that will let you put the heel of your shoe on his neck' [397]) and his actions ('She advanced her foot forward a little from under the hem of her skirt; and he threw himself on it greedily' [V, 400]) continue this notion of foot fetishism. Fetishism—like 'racial superiority'—is thematised in the novel.[26] Early on, Morrison's 'famous notebook' is described as 'the fetish of his hopes' (V, 18). Later on, when Ricardo is reflecting on Jones's fear of women, the narrator suggests that 'there is no real religion without a little fetishism' (V, 161). If the logic of fetishism involves the over-valuation of objects, then fetishism recurs throughout the novel. Heyst has made a fetish of his father's books and portrait. Lena makes a fetish out of Ricardo's knife. Indeed, as this last example suggests, various objects are fetishised by the narrative: Heyst's keys; Heyst's revolver; Ricardo's knife. The revolver that Wang takes from Heyst leaves him 'a man disarmed'. In the same way, Lena's acquisition of Ricardo's knife similarly disarms him, even while her purpose is to empower Heyst.[27] The narrative focus on the capturing of Ricardo's knife might itself be seen as a kind of narrative fetishising of it. These instances call out for a psychoanalytic decoding. More important, however, fetishism can also be related to the invisibility (or concealment) of labour. As McClintock notes, Marx's account of commodity fetishism hinges on the over-valuation of commodity exchange and the undervaluation of labour. The reverse side of fetishism, in other words, is the disregarded labour of the colonial subject, the making invisible of the colonised people. *Victory* shows how colonised peoples can be made invisible, and, in foregrounding that 'making invisible', points towards the realm that it cannot represent.

Exchange

If the narrative method of *Victory* engages with the problem of representation by foregrounding the circulation of discourses among the European community of the archipelago, the narrative itself, like that of Conrad's earliest Malay fiction, is firmly grounded in the material conditions of the archipelago: commodities, trade, technological developments. Thus Willems, in *An Outcast*, recalls a successful period of trade as Hudig's agent, when he was involved in 'ponies' from Lombok; opium; 'the illegal traffic in gunpowder'; 'the great affair of smuggled firearms' (OI, 8). Lingard, too, with his monopoly of trade in Sambir has access to an 'inexhaustible' supply of 'guttah and rattans' (OI, 43), and, when Willems arrives in Sambir, he watches 'the up-country canoes discharging guttah or rattans, and loading rice or European goods' (OI, 52) on the wharf of Lingard and Company. In *Victory*, however, as part of the novel's sense of belatedness, 'exchange' also seems to have broken down. In Part I, Chapter 2, the narrator describes Morrison's 'trade':

> He was the dearly beloved friend of a quantity of God-forsaken villages up dark creeks and obscure bays, where he traded for 'produce'. He would often sail through awfully dangerous channels up to some miserable settlement, only to find a very hungry population clamorous for rice, and without so much 'produce' between them as would have filled Morrison's suitcase. (V, 10)

Morrison is equally unlucky in his dealings with the local colonial powers. When Heyst rescues him, he has fallen foul of 'the Portuguese authorities' in Dilli, who, 'on some pretence of irregularity in his papers, had inflicted a fine upon him and had arrested his brig' (V, 12). Heyst's attempt at imperial capitalism, the Tropical Belt Coal Company, is no more successful, producing little more than a lot of 'island gossip' and the prospectus with its proleptic trap of the triumph of commodities. Schomberg seems little more successful as a hotel-keeper. He has been a hotel-keeper 'first in Bangkok, then somewhere else, and ultimately in Sourabaya' (V, 20). Whatever his reasons for moving, his hotel in Sourabaya (to judge by his actions in the novel) is hardly a major success: through Zangiacomo, he is effectively involved in prostitution; while through Jones and Ricardo, he becomes involved in gambling. Wang alone sets up a successful (though small-scale) commercial venture—selling vegetables to Heyst. The oral community of island traders is just waiting to be put out of business by steam.

Lena's attempt to exploit her transplantation to a new environment is equally unsuccessful. In Part III, Chapter 9, she appears in 'a hand-woven cotton sarong' (V, 252). She is described as 'exotic yet familiar' with her 'white woman's face and shoulders above the Malay sarong' (V, 253). Lena's change of dress registers her new life in Samburan. It suggests her attempt to find a new identity for herself outside of European models.[28] As she tells Heyst, she is 'not what they call a good girl' (V, 198). But here, on Samburan, 'There's no-one . . . to think anything of us, good or bad' (V, 188). Heyst's rescue of Lena from Schomberg can thus be seen also as an escape from European terms of reference. The arrival of Jones and Ricardo, however, checks that exploration of other possibilities. Henricksen observes:

> Narrative knowledge ... is a powerful constituent in the lives of individuals, where it creates a sense of selfhood and identity while at the same time creating subject positions that people can and often must occupy in the narrative of a community's values and actions. (NV, 13)

Ricardo, in particular, brings back to Lena the working-class culture of her London childhood. To deal with Ricardo, Lena draws on the 'narrative knowledge' of that childhood—specifically, Sunday School narratives of guilt and redemption and cultural constructions of self-sacrificing womanhood. She writes a script for herself rooted in the metropolitan culture of her childhood, and the sarong is finally exchanged for a black dress (V, 371) that she had brought with her from her former life.

In *The Rescue*, Conrad returns to the exploration of metropolitan conflicts in the colonial context. The cross-cultural encounter is again both that of Europeans and non-Europeans and also that of different kinds of European.

Again, he uses performance and theatricality as a focus. However, where the main theatrical elements in *Victory* are the dramatic handling of dialogue and the use of a Shakespearean intertext, in *The Rescue* the scenic method is supplemented by a proliferation of theatrical imagery and a closer attention to cultural cross-dressing.

NOTES

1. Edward Said, 'Conrad: the Presentation of Narrative', in *The World, The Text and The Critic (1984*; London: Vintage, 1991), 90–110; 95; hereafter cited as WTC.

2. As Robert Eaglestone puts it, 'the text's very existence is based on absence': 'representation comes into existence in order to represent what is absent' (*Ethical Criticism: Reading After Levinas* [Edinburgh: Edinburgh University Press, 1997], 46).

3. The incident hinges on the treatment of country traders by the colonial powers. In this case, the Portuguese authorities in Dilli had 'inflicted a fine' (V, 12) and arrested Morrison's brig with the intention of taking the ship from him. 'Freya of the Seven Isles' similarly shows a Dutch gunboat captain using his powers to arrest (and wreck) the ship of his rival in love, an English country-trader.

4. The Suez Canal, the replacement of sailing ships by steam, and the laying of telegraph cables are the late-nineteenth-century technological developments that radically re-shape the archipelago. In 'Falk', the narrator, the young captain of a sailing ship, who is waiting for Falk to tow his ship down-river to the sea, observes: 'I never realised so well before that this is an age of steam. The exclusive possession of a marine boiler had given Falk the whip hand of us all' (Ty, 181).

5. See J. B. Hartley, 'Maps, knowledge, and power', in D. Cosgrove and S. Daniels (eds), *The Iconography of Landscape: Essays on the symbolic representation, design and use of past environments* (Cambridge: Cambridge University Press, 1988), 277–312.

6. The image of radiating lines centred on Samburan also resonates with the earlier name given to Heyst by the island gossip: 'the Spider'.

7. As Spacks puts it, 'At one extreme, gossip manifests itself as distilled malice. It plays with reputations, circulating truths and half-truths and falsehoods' (*Gossip*, 6).

8. Earlier gossip by Schomberg has brought Jones and Ricardo down on him. They tell him of someone they met in Manila who gave them his name: 'He said you set a lot of scandal going about him once' (V, 101). As Spacks observes: 'rarely can one locate with precision the damage gossip causes, yet the chance of damage always remains' (*Gossip*, 51). In this case, the damage Schomberg caused by circulating gossip about another has been repaid by the circulation of gossip about him to Jones and Ricardo.

9. Earlier in the day, Davidson had been told by one of Schomberg's customers that Zangiacomo 'ran amuck' (V, 48), a formula that turns Zangiacomo into a Malay.

10. Barbara Herrnstein Smith, *On the margins of discourse: the Relation of Literature to Language* (Chicago: University of Chicago Press, 1978), 85.

11. GoGwilt, for example, reads Marlow's written report to the 'privileged man' in terms of 'a contest for readership between the "Little Englanders" ... and

the promoters of a "Greater Britain"' (IW, 89). Henricksen's approach through prag-matics proposes a reading of the Gentleman Brown episode as 'a dialogic response to this particular narratee', whose belief in his own ethnic group 'is darkly mirrored in Brown's "blind belief" in the rightness of his will against all mankind' (NV, 101).

12. The obvious addressee is Marlow. Bongie suggest that Jim's letter is, in effect, an answer to the 'gossipy letters' Marlow wrote in Chapter 15, while Jim came to terms with the collapse of his old world: 'Perhaps remembering that distant night, Jim himself, when his new world has been folded back into the old, tries to write' (EM, 178).

13. Consider also, on a more trivial level, the ambiguity of whether the 'won-derful presence' refers to the portrait of the father or to the 'heavy frame'.

14. Roland Barthes, *Image Music Text* (London: Fontana, 1977), 141–8, here-after cited as IMT.

15. J. Derrida, *Dissemination* (Chicago: Chicago University Press, 1981), 146.

16. See Hampson, Introduction to the Penguin edition of *Victory* (1989), 17–19.

17. Jerry Brotton, '"This Tunis, sir, was Carthage": Contesting colonialism in *The Tempest*' in Ania Loomba and Martin Orkin (eds), *Postcolonial Shakespeares* (Routledge, 1998), 23–42; hereafter cited in the text as TT.

18. See Leslie Heywood, 'The Unreadable Text: Conrad and "The Enigma of Woman" in *Victory*', *Conradiana*, 26.1 (Spring 1994), 3–19, for an interpretation of this motif that contests the idea of absolute difference.

19. Paul Brown, '"This thing of darkness I acknowledge mine": *The Tempest* and the discourse of colonialism', in Jonathan Dollimore and Alan Sinfield (eds), *Political Shakespeare: New essays in cultural materialism* (Manchester: Manchester University Press, 1985), 48–71.

20. Peter Hulme, *Colonial Encounters: Europe and the Native Caribbean 1492–1797* (1986; Routledge, 1992), 88–134. Brotton notes how *The Tempest* 'car-ries resonances of different geographical trajectories' (TT 31). Where (post)colonial criticism of the play has emphasised the 'New World' encounter, Brotton attends to the Mediterranean and 'Old World' aspects of the play, the neglected 'eastern fron-tier' of maritime expansion, to situate the play precisely at the 'geopolitical bifurca-tion between the Old World and the New'.

21. The Alfuros were originally from the northern provinces of Celebes.

22. Indeed, Peter Bagnall has convincingly connected Ricardo with the Rip-per murders. See Peter Bagnall, 'Joseph Conrad and Jack the Ripper', Unpublished D.Phil. Thesis, University of Oxford, 1998.

23. This is the shift that takes place between Conrad's early and late Malay novels. See Chapter 8 on *The Rescue*.

24. Consider, for example, Mrs Norris (in *Mansfield Park*) who also 'lives alone'.

25. Women also fall into this category. Note Davidson's surprise when he engages Mrs Schomberg in conversation: 'one was inclined to think of her as an It—an automaton, a very plain dummy, with an arrangement for bowing the head at times and smiling stupidly now and then' (V, 40). Silenced by her husband, she nevertheless shows that she has a voice. She also acts: she helps Lena to escape (and perhaps also tries to kill Jones and company by giving them salt water for their voyage).

26. I am following McClintock's use of 'fetishism' to denote practices in which mundane objects become invested with power. McClintock records how Binet

brought 'fetish' into the discourse of sexuality in 1880 to signify 'the sexual adoration of inanimate objects' (IL, 189). His major work in this area, 'Le Fetichisme dans l'amour', published in *La Revue Philosophique* in 1887, suggested that all people are fetishists to some extent.

27. Betty Vanderweilen, 'Gender Performance in *Victory*', *Conradiana* 26.2/3 (Autumn 1994), 201–10, interestingly reads this incident in terms of Lena attempting to invest Heyst 'with what she conceives as his proper patriarchal attitudes' (207).

28. It also registers the material culture of the region. Thus, in Part IV, Chapter 2, she appears in 'the brown and yellow figured Celebes sarong' (V, 293), traditional Bugis cloth.

TERRY COLLITS

Anti-Heroics and Epic Failures: *The Case of* Nostromo

Conrad made several voyages to the French Antilles when scarcely out of his teens, claiming to have glimpsed South America and to have been briefly in Venezuela.[1] Only in the year before he died did he set foot in the United States. Although his relationships with the Old World were somewhat tangential, as a true European he maintained a wary distance from the New. Not remaining exclusively Polish, or French, or British, he used his writings to create a pan-European perspective towards the interconnections of Europe's empires. Arguably the first internationalist novelist, Conrad saw the old European colonialism as dying. But far from feeling his present to be the dawn of a new world order, his diagnosis of the *Zeitgeist*—before, during, and after the Great War—corresponded roughly with the description of the crowd gathered at Schomberg's in Surabaya, as "the age in which we are camped like bewildered travellers in a garish, unrestful hotel" (*Victory*, 3).

Conrad made one early literary journey to "the Americas" in the form of his masterpiece *Nostromo*. The epic scope and detached narrative perspective of this least personal of his novels (to that date) involved considerable self-distancing. According to Conrad's "Author's Note" of 1917, *Nostromo*, set in an imaginary Latin American republic, was assembled out of a few personal memories from his earlier Marseilles period (1874–78) and much reading.[2] The novel marginalizes British imperial power at the same time that Conrad

From *Conradian* 29, no. 2 (Autumn 2004): 1–13. © 2004 by the Joseph Conrad Society.

himself was taking up permanent residence in the heartland of middle-class England. Set in what was, strictly speaking, a *post*-colonial Latin America, *Nostromo* describes new forms of imperialism based on multinational capitalist interests and projects a vision of empire beyond the demise of European colonialism. Well before Old World colonialism had run its course, it descries on its furthest horizon the dim outlines of a future global economic system dominated by American capital.

The social and political realities of Costaguana are approached in terms that go beyond the dualism of the colonizer/colonized nexus. In 1823, President James Monroe had told Congress of the need to remain aloof from European colonial wars but also insisted that Europe stay out of the Americas. This had the long-term effect of leaving Latin America to the United States to "manage." *Nostromo* catches that history on the very cusp of change: the moment of American intervention in Panama/Columbia, which coincided with the construction of the Panama Canal. That event opened the way to further "new worlds." At the time of *Nostromo*'s Costaguana, with the canal not yet built and a United States controlled Canal Zone yet to be established (both were just around the corner), Conrad situates his backwater province on the Pacific side of South America, thus doubly removed for a moment longer from the "mainstream."[3]

Early in the novel Charles Gould comments: "There's a good deal of eloquence of one sort or another produced in both the Americas" (83). The critical edge of this remark can be felt if one recalls Conrad's endemic mistrust of "eloquence," whether that found in Mr Kurtz's infamous humanitarian report or the rhetoric of the billionaire businessman Holroyd:

> Now, what is Costaguana? It is the bottomless pit of 10 per cent. loans and other fool investments. European capital had been flung into it with both hands for years. Not ours, though. We in this country know just about enough to keep indoors when it rains. We can sit and watch. Of course, some day we shall step in. We are bound to. But there's no hurry. Time itself has got to wait on the greatest country in the whole of God's Universe. We shall be giving the word for everything: industry, trade, law, journalism, art, politics, and religion, from Cape Horn clear over to Smith's Sound, and beyond, too, if anything worth taking hold of turns up at the North Pole. And then we shall have the leisure to take in hand the outlying islands and continents of the earth We shall run the world's business whether the world likes it or not. The world can't help it—and neither can we, I guess. (76–77)

Several generations after the "Monroe Doctrine" had laid down a blue-print for future American imperialism, Holroyd's discourse appears like a cross between Graham Greene's evangelical "quiet American" and Hegel gone mad. From the vantage point of the present, the mild fanaticism of this genially quixotic, polite Christian businessman sounds a more foreboding note. The satirical distancing of this new type is accompanied by the precise insight that the development Holroyd envisions lies beyond the control even of "the greatest country in the whole of God's Universe." The wider horizon that comes into view includes a self-regulating global system beyond indi-vidual or even national agency. Its more alarming intimation is of a powerful America unable to take moral responsibility for its interventions. The novel's impersonal vision also contains the seeds of mid-twentieth-century world-systems analysis and later globalization theory.[4] Conrad's scepticism towards America, on the other hand, persisted, coming up years later, for instance, in a letter of October 1922 to Bertrand Russell on the publication of his *The Problem of China:* "[Your deductions] strike a chill into one's soul especially when you deal with the American element. That would indeed be a dreadful fate for China or any other country" (cited in Russell 1967: 1:160).[5]

Political discussions of *Nostromo* often repeat the familiar criticism of "Heart of Darkness": that it is unclear where Conrad "stands" in terms of his sympathetic allegiances and on the broad question of imperialism. A minor but revealing example comes from one of his admirers, the late Edward Said, who in an assessment of *Nostromo* commented that the novel "embodies the same paternalistic arrogance of imperialism that it mocks in characters like Gould and Holroyd" (1994: xx). Said identifies this surely disabling prejudice, that native Latin Americans are incapable of having their own culture, let alone governing themselves or even of responding to *any* form of governance, by attributing to the author the unquestioning recollection of a *bon mot* of the legendary liberationist, Simón Bolívar: "governing them, he [Conrad] says, quoting Bolívar, is like ploughing the sea" (1994: xviii). Taking this reference to characterize Conrad's general attitude towards non-European peoples, Said mis-remembers the passage he had more carefully cited in his major essay on *Nostromo* in *Beginnings.* "The heritage of South America is, as the great libera-tor Bolívar had said in the bitterness of his spirit, 'America is ungovernable. Those who worked for her independence have ploughed the sea'" (1975: 111; *Nostromo* 186). Said is not alone in attributing Bolívar's utterance to Conrad. Not the narrator but the sceptic Martin Decoud quotes the "Liberator," his reflection following an intense argument with his beloved Antonia Avellanos, Costaguana's quintessential "patriot." That is, it is rendered purely dramatically so that its exact political meaning is to be found in that total dramatic context.

The question of what "Conrad himself" might have thought is a perfectly reasonable one, but before it can be put, the nature of each textual location needs to be determined, as the above example shows. The text here reveals a critical distance between the disparaging and racist sentiment that emanates from Bolívar and is enclosed within Decoud's meditation, and what might be taken to be Conrad's position. The distancing is both a function of *Nostromo*'s acknowledged breadth of vision and fundamental for understanding the complexity of Conrad's politics. But rather than looking for Conrad's politics directly (as it were), the discussion here will begin by comparing the novel's panoramic political vision with that of traditional epic. By common consent, this is the one Conrad novel and one of the few English-language novels that on the grounds of its epic scope can plausibly be compared with Homer, Virgil, or Tolstoy.[6] The question of literary genre will be extended by asking what kind of *political* knowledge becomes possible from the perspective of the epic.

Conrad: "The artist of the whole matter"
Not long after *Nostromo*'s publication Henry James wrote a letter to Conrad that contained an extraordinary (and much-quoted) tribute: "No-one has known—for intellectual use—the things you know . . . you have, as the artist of the whole matter, an authority that no-one has approached" (Edel, ed. 1987: 368).[7] The relationship between Conrad and James is hard to pin down. James's own masterpiece *The Golden Bowl* was published in the same year as *Nostromo*. It, too, has a certain transnational scope: a different kind of visionary from Conrad's Holroyd, James's Adam Verver sets himself the task of buying up the great art works of Europe to display in America. In his idealism and untold wealth, he envisions a kind of grand, high-cultural Disneyland of the future. Perhaps James felt, however, that his own internationalist perspective was narrow in comparison with the younger novelist's life-experience. His letter to Conrad, which includes the Sibylline utterance quoted above, stresses the latter's totality of vision ("the artist of the whole matter") as the key to Conrad's *authority*, "that no-one has approached." It is hard to believe that this does not refer, at least partly, to the novel Conrad had most recently published. James's carefully chosen terms go to that novel's scope, its epic fullness, and depiction of a world at a significant turning-point in human history. Novels on an epic scale were a long way from James's own stated aesthetic preferences, which makes his assessment even more intriguing. He once called novels such as *War and Peace* "large loose baggy monsters," (James 1962, 84) and of George Eliot's monumental *Middlemarch* asked: "If we write novels so, how are we to write History" (Haight, ed. 1965: 87).

Fredric Jameson's high evaluation of *Nostromo* also links the grandeur of the novel's narrative design with its author's authoritative knowledge. His reading of Conrad might even provide an answer to James's question: *Nostromo* both works on an epic scale *and* presents a model for writing history. Jameson sees the novel's refusal of closure as the key to its method. This enables it to go beyond the cognitive limitations of *Lord Jim*. The earlier novel's "deep" insights into the politics and ideology of imperialism can only be recovered from the text's unconscious: "it is well, in conclusion, having shown all the things which Conrad chose not to see, to show what he *could see* in a demanding and ambitious effort of the social and historical imagination" (Jameson 1981: 269; emphasis added).

Nostromo's non-linear and de-centred narrative structure enables its greater access to history. Its first signification of the success of the Monterist rebellion—the donkey flight of the sad Ribiera—is often taken simply as an instance of the author's scepticism towards all forms of political hope. It announces that the ultimate futility of political idealism, combining with Conrad's supposed counter-revolutionary tendencies, represent the novel's final "message." But the Ribierist failure is never dramatized. Like Jim's jump from the *Patna*, it is anticipated and later recorded as having happened, a central event that is therefore "present/absent in the most classic Derridean fashion" (Jameson 1981: 272). The absence of *the* momentous event in *Nostromo*, only glimpsed through the cracks between the opening section's bold temporal and spatial narrative shifts, brings into being a consciousness of history inaccessible to classical realism, which belonged to a different historical moment. In recompense for that partial loss, however, Jameson argues that it is an enabling factor for producing a different kind of "grand narrative" altogether: "this hole at the centre of the narrative is itself but an external emblem of the greater one around which the gigantic system of events of the novel pivots as on some invisible axis" (1981: 272).

Nostromo thus answers the question of how, in the inherited forms of prose fiction, that collective and de-centred process that may be interpreted retrospectively as the coming of capitalism to Latin America can be represented. Individual lives are now shown as relative to greater collective processes, ideals, and life choices that all become absorbed into an impersonal History. Narrative traces of the earlier realism, such as character and action, persist like the *bourgeoisie*'s collective memory of its heroic past in Karl Marx's *Eighteenth Brumaire*. They are there partly to parody the pretensions of Costaguana's chief citizens to become important figures in history and founders of a new political order. *Nostromo*'s "absent-centredness" does not produce a hollow into which the conflictual terms of political struggle fall but creates a perspective with its own specific insights into contemporary (and even future) reality.[8] The problem of writing (and reading) that reality becomes the centrepiece of Jameson's reading. "The resonance of his book springs from a kind of unplanned harmony between this textual dynamic and its specific historical content" (1981: 280). Jameson claims that *Nostromo* was the furthest point Conrad reached in terms of political insight. In doing so, he tacitly acknowledges a place of agreement he found with a writer whom he quite clearly regarded elsewhere as "counter-revolutionary"

"For life to be large and full": Conrad and Homer

The title-phrase for this section is borrowed from Emilia Gould's melancholy meditation some years after the novel's central action. That was staged at a time when, as Captain Mitchell might have said, everything hung in the balance. It comes at the end of the chapter that follows the unnoticed suicide of Martin Decoud, the novel's most intellectually trenchant character, and immediately before the high melodrama of Nostromo's death, the stuff of grand opera. She reflects: "It had come into her mind that for life to be large and full, it must contain the care of the past and of the future in every passing moment of the present" (520–21). Mrs Gould's interior monologue closes a long exchange, Chekovian in mood, between herself and Dr Monygham. The disappointment of her life's hopes leads to her final bleak judgement on the "material interests" that formed the basis for her husband's finer ambitions. Her private tragedy is almost routinely seen as Conrad's final judgement on the politics of modernity, the capitalist world order, and all forms of human idealism and striving. That interpretation privileges both Mrs Gould as a character and the world of private and family relationships to a degree that the novel's greater perspective distinctly challenges. They are certainly twin focus points of the mainstream nineteenth-century novel, at the expense of other ones: the broad unfolding of historical process, and the public world of politics and nation-building. This is not to say, however, that the narrative assumes a posture of uncritical detachment. Its most intimate scenes are shot through with passions and investments, but privileging even the most poignant personal tragedies distorts the full picture to which they belong.

Conrad's world-view is no more deterministic in any simple sense than Marx's. In the wake of other defeated revolutionary hopes, those of 1848, Marx posed the problem of the interplay of free-will and determining structure as a paradox: "Men make their own history, but not of their own free-will; not under circumstances they themselves have chosen but under the given and inherited circumstances with which they are directly confronted." He added: "The tradition of the dead generations weighs like a nightmare on the minds of the living" (Fernbach, ed. 1973: 146). This could well serve as an epigraph for *Nostromo*, echoing as it does so many of its themes. Surprisingly, however, the problem is that its attitude is *too* pessimistic for that purpose. its usefulness is that it insists on the dynamic interplay between broad social forces and the energies and desires of individuals that drive historical process. For that reason, *Nostromo*'s full meaning does not coincide with the experience of Mrs Gould or any single character.

The literary genre that matches Emilia Gould's desire for "life to be large and full" is the epic. Further, *Nostromo* is the only English candidate from the great age of European imperialism to match (say) Virgil's official state paean to Augustus' Rome, *The Aeneid*. The late twentieth century saw one majestic comic epic on the imperial theme: Salman Rushdie's *Midnight's Children* (1980), but its grand narrative is the story of Indian independence, where Britain's imperial greatness is relegated. Rushdie's privileged position of knowledge is derived from his origins among the colonized. That enabled him and not a "real" Englishman to write a comic counter-epic that could match the tale of the Empire itself. E. M. Forster's *A Passage to India* (1924), a plausible contender, opens with a truly impressive sweep across the divided terrain of British India but finally becomes locked into its characters' needs and dramas. It cannot sustain the necessary distancing (even of its humanistic faith) to understand the supra-personal action that provides the structure for individual destinies. Paul Scott's later *Raj Quartet* (1966) adopts some of the trappings of epic. The story of the last days of the British Raj has the "high seriousness" for an epic narrative to match Homer's Trojan War or Virgil's story of Rome's origins, but its achievement is rather the opposite of epic fullness. It opens a place in the story of empire for the feminine, the world of *memsahibs* and other unsung heroines who occupied the other side of the imperial stage.

There are other reasons, too, for this apparent lacuna in the literature of England during her imperial heyday. There was always enough nationalist sentiment and imperialist exultation to fuel such a project, and the earlier, heroic period of British ascendancy on the subcontinent held the ingredients for the narrative. Robert Clive's military and administrative achievements alone would have been sufficient for an epic, especially if spectacular and horrific events such as the Black Hole of Calcutta or the extension to India of Britain's struggles against French power were thrown into the mix.[9] England, however, never seemed fully to "own" her colonial achievements. A succession of impressive individuals created her most glorious possession. They include Warren Hastings and Clive, both of whom ended their days back "home" in semi-disgrace. Partly, their mixed achievements were judged through popular middle-class contempt from as far back as the early nineteenth century for the nabob. Their acquisition of wealth in the colonies and supposed vulgarity sullied their acquired social and economic status. Consequently, British India did not quite cut the mustard for epic treatment by a talented laureate.

Although once dubbed such, Conrad was not even to be an unofficial "prose laureate" (Sherry, ed. 1973: 61). If his imperialist novels recall any laureate at all, it might be Virgil, who, having a dark side, was chosen by Dante as a guide through the underworld. Conrad's imaginative journey into his own "heart of darkness" contains Virgilian as well as Dantesque echoes. *The Aeneid* is more touched by the "tears of things" than impressed by Augustan triumphalism, and his most memorable passages record the human costs of pursuing the imperial ideal. Like Conrad's novels, the poem more often appeals as a critique of imperialism's crimes and moral contradictions than as an act of homage. Nevertheless, Homer rather than Virgil provides the closer comparison with the epic perspective of *Nostromo*.

To explain this comparison's validity, it may be useful to revisit an old distinction between so-called primitive epics, such as Homer's, and literary epic, such as Virgil's, Dante's, or Milton's. The former were thought to be somehow closer to the "real thing." The assumption behind this categorization was that they appear to have arisen spontaneously out of the folk culture of the worlds they depict, in contrast with the latter group's more obviously literary and fictitious works. The "real thing" Homer represents is a past heroic world of the Aegean Bronze Age kingdoms and their warlords, whose power and exploits pre-dated any social organization resembling the modern state. In Hegel's phrase, they were "sufficient unto themselves" and bequeathed to literature the type of the larger-than-life hero upon whom the whole community depended (Paolucci, ed. 1962: 98–112). *The Iliad* records the most famous of their wars, and the deaths of the greatest among them. *The Odyssey*, on the other hand, represents the aftermath of that heroic struggle and tells of a precarious attempt to restore the old world order and recreate something of the fullness and largeness of a life that passed away on the plains of Troy.

It is not, however, to the heroic self-sufficiency of the Homeric hero that one must look to discover Homeric affiliations in *Nostromo*. It is true that Giorgio Viola, the old Garibaldino, looks back on moments of heroic struggle under his legendary leader, just as Conrad sometimes meditated on the Napoleonic era as a time when heroism, adventure, and the making of history appeared to come together. Likewise, Costaguana's Blancos remember their "liberator," the legendary Simón Bolívar. But Nostromo, whose character, physical appearance, and exploits virtually mimic the traditionally heroic, is situated in a novel whose every page describes the coming into being of an un-heroic world.

The practice of self-conscious artistic distancing is also strongly present in *The Odyssey*. Like *Nostromo*, the poem announces its legendary theme only immediately to baffle the reader/listener with puzzling deferrals of the story and complications of plot and chronology. It does not begin with the heroic itself but with the hero's absent presence. Homer, like his imagined listeners, inhabits a world remote from the events described, but so does the poem's eponymous hero. At a turning-point in Odysseus' epic journey, he is received hospitably by King Alkinous of the Phaeacians. At the feast in his honour, the anonymous Odysseus listens to his own deeds rendered in song by the minstrel Demodokos. The "real" Odysseus weeps as he hears the moving account of himself and his companions now become the subject for poetry only a few years after the events recited. *The Odyssey* is deeply post-Iliadic and belongs to a world cut off from the "thing itself."

Nostromo is equally self-conscious about its status as writing, which, in turn, determines its representation of history. It affects the tone of its recollections of past greatness through the allusions to Garibaldi and also colours the different memorializing and monumentalizing habits of Captain Mitchell and Don José Avellanos, respectively—the tone-deaf myth-making of the one, the pious chronicling of *Fifty Years of Misrule* of the other. Its narrative strategy fixes events simultaneously as past, present, and future. That is how its "unplanned harmony" of form and narrative content links it to the Homeric perspective of *The Odyssey*. That perspective establishes no hierarchy of values between public and private, family and nation, Blanco politicians, mine-owners, and ordinary Costaguaneros. This does not mean that there are not differences of value throughout—judgements made, stimulated, or simply allowed—either in specific cases or in the narrative's overall trajectory. In *Nostromo* above all, Conrad has succeeded in creating a narrative method and perspective that subsumes his personal preferences, supposing these to be capable of articulation in the first place, into a vision of the impersonal processes of history in one world historical instance.

Notes

1. Van Marle (1991) on the basis of extensive archival research establishes only a small window of opportunity for a voyage to South America and returns an open verdict on whether or not Conrad went there.

2. For a powerful and imaginative attempt to penetrate the mysteries that lie behind the scant record of Conrad's turbulent Marseilles years prior to his English rebirth, see Lesage (2003).

3. Giovanni Arrighi well catches the ambiguities of the United States in the history of imperialism, comparing the American position towards European imperialism at the end of the nineteenth century with that towards China: "An analogous role was played by the United States in Latin America, where the application of the Monroe Doctrine had effectively contained European expansionist tendencies. It is true that American policy in this area already prefigured, by its intimidating acts of intervention, the limits of its support for national sovereignty. But that did

not stop the USA from presenting itself as an anti-colonialist power faithful to its image of the 'first ex-colony,' or from being perceived as such on the world arena" (1978: 93).

4. See, for example, Wallerstein (1979) and Frank (1984); both writers are prominent world-systems theorists.

5. If Conrad was averse to Americanism, North American scholarship, by contrast, has served him well, with steady and rigorous attention to his work from the period immediately following the Second World War. Notably, and unlike England, American Conrad studies have been attentive to Conradian politics. At the start of the Cold War, Howe's brilliant discussion of the politics of *Nostromo* appeared in *Kenyon Review* in 1953–54 (1957); Hay (1963) remains one of the finest studies of the subject (or, indeed, of Conrad in general); Fleishman (1967) established a framework and set of givens for future analyses of Conrad and politics. A full analysis of Conrad's attitude to the United States is developed in several of Hay's chapters.

6. Tillyard (1958) offers a not very trenchant early address to the question of Conrad and epic. More recently, Adams (2003) has essayed a searching discussion that includes Conrad more than any other English novelist within his category. The focus on *The Odyssey* as a journey poem, however, makes his discussion of *Nostromo* diverge from my sense of what makes the novel "Homeric."

7. For detailed discussions of this letter, see Hay 1963: 12, and Harpham 1996: 150–51.

8. Jameson's reading of *Nostromo* follows the lines of an (undeclared) argument with his English Marxist counterpart Terry Eagleton about a question of form. For Eagleton, *Nostromo*, like all Conrad's novels, is marked by a "central absence": "It is precisely in these absent centres, which 'hollow' rather than scatter and fragment the organic forms of Conrad's fiction, that the relation of that fiction to its ideological context is laid bare" (1975: 138–39). His unusually perfunctory analysis of the novel incorporates its non-linear, decentred narrative into a general account of Conrad, whom he sees as helplessly determined to "speak" but not to "know" the ideological contradictions within which it is trapped. The text's refusal of "coherent historical intelligibility" involves a form that foregrounds action and the concrete, but that must forever produce the "corrosive negation" of all certitude. The ideological upshot of such textual processes of exclusion and self-cancellation is to leave things precisely as they were.

9. For an attempt to retrieve something of the grandeur of Clive's Indian career (with a certain historical irony), see Chaudhuri, who quite deliberately sets out to redress a balance by contesting the field directly with British historians and biographers: "Clive has not had a better deal at the hands of his biographers than the Empire has had from its historians. The fact is that, so long as it lasted, it never moved into the light of history, but remained subject to polemics, for or against. The polemical approach has not been given up, though the Empire has disappeared" (1975: iv).

Works Cited

Adams, David. *Colonial Odysseys: Empire and Epic in the Modernist Novel.* Ithaca, NY: Cornell University Press, 2003.

Arrighi, Giovanni. *The Geometry of Imperialism.* London: New Left Books, 1978.

Chaudhuri, Nirad C. *Robert Clive of India.* Bombay: Jaico Publishing House, 1975.

Conrad, Joseph. *The Collated Edition of the Works of Joseph Conrad*. 22 vols. London: J. M. Dent & Sons, 1946–55.

Eagleton, Terry. *Criticism and Ideology*. London: New Left Books, 1975.

Fleishman, Avrom. *Conrad's Politics: Community and Anarchy in the Fiction of Joseph Conrad*. Baltimore: Johns Hopkins Press, 1967.

Frank, André Gunder. *Critique and Anti-Critique: Essays on Dependence and Reformism*. London: Macmillan, 1984.

Harpham, Geoffrey Galt. *One of Us: The Mastery of Joseph Conrad*. Chicago: University of Chicago Press, 1996.

Hay, Eloise Knapp. *The Political Novels of Joseph Conrad*. Chicago: University of Chicago Press, 1963.

Hegel, G. W. P. *Hegel on Tragedy*. Edited and introduced by Anne and Henry Paolucci. Garden City, NY: Anchor Books, 1962.

Howe, Irving. *Politics and the Novel*. New York: Horizon Press, 1957.

James, Henry. *The Art of the Novel: Critical Prefaces*. New York: Scribner's, 1934.

———. "George Eliot's *Middlemarch*" (1873). In *A Century of George Eliot Criticism*, edited by Gordon S. Haight. London: Methuen, 1965.

———. *Henry James: Selected Letters*. Edited by Leon Edel. Cambridge, MA: Harvard University Press, 1987.

Jameson, Fredric. *The Political Unconscious: Narrative as a Socially Symbolic Act*. Ithaca, NY: Cornell University Press, 1981.

Lesage, Claudine. *Joseph Conrad et le Continent*. Montreuil-sur-Mer: Michel Houdiard Éditeur, 2003.

Marle, Hans van. "Lawful and Lawless: Young Korzeniowski's Adventures in the Caribbean." *L'Époque Conradienne* 17 (1991): 91–113.

Marx, Karl. *Surveys from Exile*. Edited and translated by David Fernbach. London: Allen Lane, 1973.

Russell, Bertrand. *The Autobiography of Bertrand Russell. 3 vols*. London: Allen & Unwin, 1967–69.

Said, Edward. *Beginnings: Intention and Method*. New York: Columbia University Press, 1975.

———. *Culture and Imperialism*. London: Chatto & Windus, 1993.

Sherry, Norman, ed. *Conrad: The Critical Heritage*. London: Routledge & Kegan Paul, 1973.

Tillyard, E. M. W. *The Epic Strain in the English Novel*. London: Chatto & Windus, 1958.

Wallerstein, Immanuel. *The Capitalist World-Economy*. Cambridge: Cambridge University Press, 1979.

J. HILLIS MILLER

"Material Interests": Conrad's Nostromo *as a Critique of Global Capitalism*

Joseph Conrad's *Nostromo* is extremely complicated in its narrative organization. It offers narratologists great opportunities to demonstrate in detail the various kinds of narrative complexity employed by modernist authors such as Faulkner, Woolf, James, or Conrad himself. Just about every narrative device specialists in narrative form have identified is employed in one way or another: time shifts; analepsis; prolepsis; breaks in the narration; shifts in "focalization" from one character's mind to another by way of the "omniscient" (or, as I should prefer to say, following Nicholas Royle, "telepathic")[1] narrator's use of free indirect discourse, or by way of interpolated first person narration or spoken discourse; shifts by the narrator from distant, panoramic vision to extreme close-ups; retellings of the same event from different subjective perspectives; citations of documents, and so on.[2] The chronological trajectory of Sulaco history can be pieced together from these indirections. The story begins in the middle and then shifts backward and forward in a way that the reader may find bewildering, as he or she wonders just where on a time scale a given episode is in relation to some other episode. It is as though all these episodes were going on happening over and over, continually, in the capacious and atemporal mind of the narrator, like the endless succession of similar days and nights over the Golfo Placido in the setting of *Nostromo*. The story is presented in an almost cubist rendering,

From *Joseph Conrad: Voice, Sequence, History, Genre*, edited by Jakob Lothe, Jeremy Hawthorn, and James Phelan, pp. 160–77. © 2008 by Ohio State University.

rather than by way of the impressionist technique Conrad is often said to have employed. I suggest that if the goal of *Nostromo* is to reconstruct the history of an imaginary Central American country, the formal complexity of the novel does more than implicitly claim that form is meaning, that is, that the complexity was necessary if Conrad was to tell at all the story he wanted to tell. *Nostromo*'s narrative complications also oppose what it suggests is false linear historical narration to another much more complex way to recover through narration "things as they really were." I shall return at the end of this essay to the question of the social, political, and ethical "usefulness" of modernist narration of this sort.

Fredric Jameson's slogan, "Always Historicize," means that we should read modernist English literature, or any other literary work of any time, in its immediate historical context. He is no doubt right about that. Nevertheless, certain works of English literature from the beginning of the twentieth century have an uncanny resonance with the global situation today. Examples would be the exploitation of Africa by the Wilcox family in E. M. Forster's *Howards End*, or the presentation of the effects of combat on Septimus Smith in Virginia Woolf's *Mrs. Dalloway*. Charles Gould and the American financier Holroyd, in Joseph Conrad's *Nostromo*, are even better examples. Their collaboration is remarkably prophetic of the current course of American global economic aspirations as well as of the effects of these on local cultures and peoples around the world. I shall indicate some of those disquieting consonances later.

If *Nostromo* is a novel not so much about history as about alternative ways to narrate history, this means its goal is not to recover a single life story (as, say, *Lord Jim* does), but to recover the story of the ways a whole group of individuals were related, each in a different way, to their surrounding community as it evolved through time. *Nostromo* is a novel about an imagined community, a fictitious one based on Conrad's reading about South American history.

A spectrum or continuum of different ways the individual may be related to others can be identified, going from smaller groups to larger. At the small end is my face-to-face encounter with my neighbor, with my beloved, or with a stranger, in love, friendship, hospitality, or hostility. A family, especially an extended family or a clan, is a larger group, in this case bound by ties of blood or marriage. A community is somewhat larger. A community is a group of people living in the same place who all know one another and who share the same cultural assumptions. They are not, however, necessarily related by blood or marriage. A nation is larger still. Most commonly a nation is made of a large number of overlapping but to some degree dissonant communities. Largest of all is the worldwide conglomeration of all human beings living on the same planet and all more and more subject to the same global economic and cultural hegemony. At each of these levels the individual has a relation to others, different in each case and subject to different constraints and conventions. It is of course often, in a given case, difficult, if not impossible, to maintain a sharp boundary between the different-sized groups.

Each form of living together, or of what Heidegger called "Mitsein," has been the object of vigorous theoretical investigation in recent years, for example, Lévinas's focus on the face-to-face encounter of two persons, or Jacques Derrida's similar focus in *The Politics of Friendship*, or work by Bataille, Blanchot, Nancy, Lingis, and others on the concept of community. In what I shall say about Conrad's *Nostromo* I shall interrogate primarily the relation of the individual to the community, or lack of it, in this novel, in the context of an intervention by one stage of global capitalism.

It can certainly be said that the citizens of Sulaco, the province of Conrad's imaginary Central American country of Costaguana, the setting for *Nostromo* (1904), form a community, at least in one sense of the word "community." The inhabitants all live together in the same place. All share, more or less, the same moral and religious assumptions. Whether rich or poor, white, black, or native American, they have been subjected to the same ideological interpellations, the same propaganda, the same political speeches, proclamations, and arbitrary laws. Most of all, they share the same history, what Don José Avellanos calls, in the title of his never-to-be-published manuscript, "Fifty Years of Misrule" (though the narrator, magically and quite improbably, has read it and can cite from it [Conrad 1951, 157; henceforth identified by page number alone]). Though Sulaco is a community of suffering, as one revolution after another brings only more injustice and senseless bloodshed; nevertheless, it can be argued, it is a true community. It is small enough so that most people know one another. Don Pépé, who runs the mine, knows all of the workers by name. Almost all belong to a single religious faith, Catholic Christianity.

If the reader reconstructs the story from a distance, putting the broken pieces of narration back in chronological order, *Nostromo* appears as a tale of nation-building, the creation of one of those "imagined communities" Benedict Anderson describes in his book of that name. After fifty years of misrule by the central government of Costaguana in Santa Marta, Sulaco, through a series of seriocomic events and accidents, becomes a prosperous, modern, peaceful, independent state, the Occidental Republic of Sulaco. An example of the fortuitous "causes" of this historical change is the cynical plan for secession devised by the skeptic Decoud shortly before his death. His plan is motivated not by political zeal or belief, but by his love for Antonia Avellanos. Nevertheless, Captain Mitchell, in his fatuous incomprehension, recounts the creation of the Republic of Sulaco as a connected story whose destined endpoint is the present-day prosperous nation. He recounts the sequence, in tedious detail, "in the more or less stereotyped relation of the 'historical events' which for the next few years was at the service of distinguished strangers visiting Sulaco" (529).

The pages following the citation just made give an example of Captain Mitchell's version of Sulaco history. Captain Mitchell is the spokesperson for an exemplary "official history," with its naïve conception of "historical events" as following one another in a comprehensible linear and causal succession. Conrad quite evidently disdains such history-writing. That false kind of history is represented, in one degree or another, by those source books on South American history, by Masterman, Eastlake, Cunninghame Graham, and others that Conrad had read.[3] Though *Nostromo* is about the nation-building of an imaginary South American republic, not a real one, nevertheless it is, among other things, a paradigmatic example of an alternative mode of history-writing, much more difficult to bring off. Conrad implicitly claims that this counterhistory is much nearer to the truth of human history and much more able to convey to readers the way history "really happens."

If the reader looks a little more closely at what the narrator says about Sulaco society, however, it begins to look less and less like a community of the traditional kind, that is, less and less like a community of those who have a lot in common, like those egalitarian rural English villages on the Welsh border Raymond Williams, in *The Country and the City*, so much admires, even though he resists idealizing them. For one thing, Sulaco "society" is made up of an extraordinary racial and ethnic mixture, product of its sanguinary history, as the narrator emphasizes from the beginning. The Spanish conquistadors enslaved the indigenes, the Native Americans. Wars of liberation from Spain led to wave after wave of military revolutions, one tyranny after another, with incredible bloodshed, cruelty, and injustice. Nevertheless, a large class of aristocratic hacienda-owning, cattle-ranching, pure-blooded Spanish people, "creoles," remain. They are the core of the "Blanco" party. Black slaves were imported. Then a series of migrations from Europe, people coming either as workmen, political exiles, or as imperialist exploiters, brought English, French, Italians, even a few Germans and Jews. Sailors, like Nostromo, deserted from merchant ships to add to the mix. Much intermarriage of course has occurred. Bits of three languages other than English exist in the novel: Spanish, French, and Italian. The narrator often uses Spanish names for occupations and ethnic identifications, as well as for place names like Cordillera, the name of the overshadowing mountain range. A good bit of the conversation in the novel must be imagined to be carried on not in the English the narrator gives, but in Spanish. Decoud and Antonia are native-born Costaguanans, but they have been educated in France. They talk to one another in French. Giorgio Viola, the old Garibaldino, and his family are Italian, as is Nostromo. They speak Italian to one another. This is signaled even in this English-language book by the way Nostromo addresses Viola as "Vecchio," Italian for "old man." Conrad does not specify what language the descendants of black slaves and the indigenes speak, but presumably some original languages persist beneath their Spanish. Charles Gould and all his family are English, though Gould was born in Costaguana and educated in England, as is the custom in that family. His wife is English, though her aunt has married an Italian aristocrat, and Charles Gould meets his future wife in Italy. The railroad workers are partly locals, "Indios," but engineers from England run the operation, and some workmen are European.

Sulaco, I conclude, is a complex mixture of races, languages, and ethnic allegiances. Sulaco is not all that different in this from the United States, by the way, though we have had, so far, only one, successful, "democratic revolution," ushering in government of the people, by the people, and for the people, with liberty and justice for all. I say those words with only a mild trace of irony, though the liberty, justice, and equality did not of course in 1776 extend to black slaves, or to Native Americans, or to women. My houses in Maine are on land taken from the Native Americans who had lived in the Penobscot Bay region for at least seven thousand years before the white man came and destroyed their culture in a few generations. "Liberty and justice for all" still has a hollow ring for many Americans, for example, the African American men and women who populate our prisons in such disproportionate numbers, or who swell the ranks of the unemployed.

The Sulaco noncommunity exists, moreover, like the United States one, as a complex layering of differing degrees of power, privilege, wealth, with the African Americans and Indios at the bottom, extending up through European working-class people, to the Creoles and the dominating quasi-foreigners like Charles Gould. Though the Gould family has been in Sulaco for generations, they are still considered Anglos, Inglesi. They are English in appearance, sensibility, mores, and language. The chief form of social mobility in Sulaco is through bribery, chicanery, or outright thievery, such as Nostromo's theft of the silver, or by way of becoming the leader of a military coup and ruling the country through force, as the indigene Montero momentarily does in *Nostromo*. It isn't much of a community.

Martin Decoud at one point sums up succinctly the nature of the Sulaco noncommunity in a bitter speech to his idealistic patriotic beloved, Antonia Avellanos. He quotes the great "liberator" of South America, Simón Bolívar, something for which the "Author's Note," oddly enough, apologizes. I suppose that is because the citation is a parabasis suspending momentarily the dramatization of a purely imaginary Central American state with an intrusion from actual history. In the "Note" Conrad has been defending, ironically, the "accuracy" of his report of Sulaco history, based as it is on his reading of Avellanos's "History of Fifty Years of Misrule." The joke (almost a "postmodern" rather than "modernist" joke) is that Avellanos's "History" is fictitious, along with the whole country of which it tells the story. No way exists to check the accuracy of Conrad's account against any external referent, nor any way to check what the narrator says against what Avellanos says. This reminds Conrad that some actual historical references do exist in the novel, and that these are a discordance:

> I have mastered them [the pages of Avellanos's "History"] in not a few hours of earnest meditation, and I hope that my accuracy will be trusted. In justice to myself, and to allay the fears of prospective readers, I beg to point out that the few historical allusions are never dragged in for the sake of parading my unique erudition, but that each of them is closely related to actuality—either throwing a light on the nature of current events or affecting directly the fortunes of the people of whom I speak. (5)

"Actuality"? "Current events"? The words must refer here to the pseudo-actuality of Costaguana history. One such parabasis-like intrusion is Decoud's citation of Bolívar: "After one Montero there would be another," the narrator reports, in free indirect discourse, Decoud as having said,

> the lawlessness of a populace of all colors and races, barbarism, irremediable tyranny. As the great liberator Bolívar had said in the bitterness of his spirit, "America is ungovernable. Those who worked for her independence have ploughed the sea." He did not care, he declared boldly; he seized every opportunity to tell her [Antonia] that though she had managed to make a Blanco journalist of him, he was no patriot. First of all, the word had no sense for cultured minds, to whom the narrowness of every belief is odious; and secondly, in connection with the everlasting troubles of this unhappy country it was hopelessly besmirched; it had been the cry of dark barbarism, the cloak of lawlessness, of crimes, of rapacity, of simple thieving. (206)

It should be remembered that though what the narrative voice reports Decoud as having said agrees more or less with what the narrative voice itself says, speaking on its own, nevertheless Decoud is explicitly presented as an "idle boulevardier" who only thinks he is truly Frenchified. His corrosive skepticism leads ultimately to suicide. One might say that Decoud is a side of Conrad that he wants to condemn and separate off from himself, leaving someone who is at least earnestly committed to the endless hard work of the professional writer who earns his daily bread by putting words on paper. Conrad's letters to Cunninghame Graham often express, it must be said, a skeptical pessimism that is close to Decoud's, as in one famous passage about the universe as a self-generated, self-generating machine: "It knits us in and it knits us out. It has knitted time, space, pain, death, corruption, despair, and all the illusions—and nothing matters" (Conrad 1969, 57). In any case, what Decoud says matches closely what the narrator says about Sulaco's deplorable history.

How did Sulaco come to be such a noncommunity, or, to give Jean-Luc Nancy's term a somewhat different meaning from his own, how did Sulaco come to be an inoperative or "unworked" community, a *communauté désoeuvree*? Nancy's book begins with the unqualified statement that "The gravest and most painful testimony of the modern world, the one that possibly involves all other testimonies to which this epoch must answer (by virtue of some unknown decree or necessity, for we bear witness also to the exhaustion of thinking through History), is the testimony of the dissolution, the dislocation, or the conflagration of community" (Nancy 1991, 1). *Nostromo*, it might be said, is a parabolic fable or allegory, a paradigmatic fiction, of the dissolution, dislocation, or conflagration of community. Just how does this disaster come about, according to Conrad? Who are the villains in this sad event? It is an event that can no longer even be understood historically. Nancy's view of "thinking through History," the reader will note, is quite different from Jameson's. The dislocation of community must be borne witness to as something that we, or rather I, have experienced even if we (I) cannot explain it: "I have witnessed the conflagration of community. I testify that this is what has happened. I give you my personal word for it." The magically telepathic narrative voice in *Nostromo* is such a witness.

No doubt, Conrad, quite plausibly, ascribes a lot of stupidity, knavery, limitless greed, thievery, and wanton cruelty to his Costaguanans. Someone had to obey orders and torture Dr. Monygham or Don José Avellanos. Someone had to do as they were told and string Señor Hirsch up to a rafter by his hands tied behind his back, just as someone has had to commit all the recent violence in Iraq, Rwanda, Kosovo, and elsewhere. We have seen a lot of examples of this human propensity for murder, rape, and sadistic cruelty all over the world in recent years. *Nostromo* provides a parabolic representation of this aspect of human history. These traits of human nature, organized in civil wars and revolutions, have certainly stood in the way of Sulaco, in Conrad's fictitious history, becoming a community, to put it mildly.

Nevertheless, one needs to ask just what has made these deplorable aspects of "human nature," aspects that always stand in the way of law, order, democracy, and civil society, especially active in Sulaco. The answer is two-fold. First there was the murderous invasion of South America by the Spanish that killed many of the indigenous population and enslaved the rest, driving them to forced labor and destroying their culture. Mrs. Gould has a sharp eye for the present condition of the indigenous population. She sees them during her travels all over the country with her husband to get support for the new opening of the mine and to persuade the Indios to come as workmen for the mine:

> Having acquired in southern Europe a knowledge of true peasantry, she was able to appreciate the great worth of the people. She saw the man under the silent, sad-eyed beast of burden. She saw them on the road carrying loads, lonely figures upon the plain, toiling under great straw hats, with their white clothing flapping about their limbs in the wind; she remembered the villages by some group of Indian women at the fountain impressed upon her memory, by the face of some young Indian girl with a melancholy and sensual profile, raising an earthenware vessel of cool water at the door of a dark hut with a wooden porch cumbered with great brown jars. (98)

This passage is a good example of that shift from a panoramic view to the specificities of an extreme close-up, in this case in a report of Mrs. Gould's memory, as it diminishes from her general knowledge of "the great worth of the people" to that "earthenware vessel of cool water at the door of a dark hut with a wooden porch cumbered with great brown jars." Conrad's narrator observes that many bridges and roads still remain in Sulaco as evidence of what slave labor by the Indios accomplished (99). Whole tribes, the narrator says, died in the effort to establish and work the silver mine. At several places the narrator describes the Native American remnant in their sullen reserve.

"For whatsoever a man soweth, that shall he also reap" (Gal. 6:7). The consequences of the Spanish conquest still remain as the inaugural events in that whole region. The effect of these events cannot be healed or atoned for even after hundreds of years. They still stand in the way of the formation of any genuine community, Christian or secular, in the usual sense of the word community. This "origin" was not a unified and unifying originating event, like the big bang that initiated our cosmos, from which Costaguanan history followed in a linear and teleological fashion toward some "far off divine event" of peace and justice for all. It was rather a moment of what Jean-Luc Nancy calls, in a play on the word, "dis-position." The indigenous community, what-ever it was like (and it will not do to idealize it too much; pre-Columbian his-tory in South America was extremely bloody too), was disposed of by being displaced, posed or placed beside itself, unseated, dis-posed. This happened through the violent occupying presence of an alien culture bent on converting the savage heathens to Christianity and on enslaving them as workers in the Europeanizing of Sulaco.

This divisive violence at the origin, or origin as *polemos*, division, dis-position, also helps account for the way South American history, in what Con-rad in *A Personal Record* calls this "imaginary (but true)" version of it (Conrad 1923, 98), is a long story of civil wars, tyrannies, and revolutions. Nor has this history come to an end. Twentieth-century events in Brazil, Argentina, Panama, Uruguay, Chile, or in Haiti bear witness to this. (A bloody rebellion against the Haitian government of Jean-Bertrande Aristide, led by armed paramilitary forces and parts of the army, was taking place at the moment I first drafted this essay, on 10 February 2004. The Bush government, in typical United States interventionist fashion, put its support behind Aristide's ouster. Never mind that he was the democratically elected president. The issue is the privatization of Haitian state-owned companies. The parallel with the central political event in *Nostromo* is striking.) These sad "true" histories are the back-ground, or the assumed subsoil, of the "imaginary" story Conrad tells.

The next phase of Sulacan society the narrator records is the subsequent invasion of Europeans, in a second wave, after South American republics achieved independence. This was the invasion of global capitalism. It was already in full swing in Conrad's day. Of course that invasion is still going on today. It is more often now transnational corporations, often, but not always, centered in the United States, rather than in Europe, that are doing the exploiting. *Nostromo*'s main action is a fable-like exemplum of the effects of Western imperialist economic exploitation. The novel can be read with benefit even today as an analysis of capitalist globalization. The novel circles around one signal event in such a history, the moment when foreign capital, what Conrad calls "material interests," makes it possible to resist a threatened new local tyranny. This happens by way of a successful counterrevolution, and the establishment of a new regime. The Occidental Republic of Sulaco will allow foreign exploitation, in this case the working of the San Tomé silver mine, to continue operating peacefully in a stable situation, a nation with law and order. The silver will flow steadily north to San Francisco to make rich investors constantly richer. This prosperity leaves the men who work the mine still earning peasants' wages, though they now have a hospital, schools, better housing, relative security, and all the benefits that the Catholic Church can confer. Nevertheless, references to labor unrest, strikes, and the like are made

toward the end of the novel. Conrad's narrator gives a haunting picture of the
mine workers at a moment of the changing of shifts:

> The heads of gangs, distinguished by brass medals hanging on their
> bare breasts, marshaled their squads; and at last the mountain would
> swallow one-half of the silent crowd, while the other half would
> move off in long files down the zigzag paths leading to the bottom of
> the gorge. It was deep; and, far below a thread of vegetation winding
> between the blazing rock faces, resembled a slender green cord, in
> which three lumpy knots of banana patches, palm-leaf roofs,[4] and
> shady trees marked the Village One, Village Two, Village Three,
> housing the miners of the Gould Concession. (111)

What is most terrifying about this process of exploitation is Conrad's
suggestion of its inevitability, at least in the eyes of the capitalist exploiters.
It does not matter what are the motives of the agents of global capitalism,
how idealistic, honest, or high-minded they are. They are co-opted in spite of
themselves by a force larger than themselves. Charles Gould has inherited the
Gould Concession from his father, who was destroyed by it, since, though he
was not working the mine, constant levies were made on him by the central
government in Santa Marta, until he was ruined financially and spiritually.
"It has killed him," says Charles Gould, when the news of his father's death
reaches him in England. He resolves to atone for that death by returning to
Sulaco, raising capital on the way, and working the mine, just as, it might be
argued, one of George W. Bush's motives for the invasion of Iraq was a desire
to make up for his father's failure to "take out Saddam Hussein" and secure
Iraqi oil for Western use.

Charles Gould was, as I have said, born in Sulaco. His sentimental and
idealistic belief is that what he calls "material interests" will eventually bring
law and order to his unhappy homeland, since these will be necessary to the
working of the mine. "What is wanted here," he tells his wife,

> is law, good faith, order, security. Anyone may declaim about
> these things, but I pin my faith on material interests. Only let the
> material interests once get a firm footing, and they are bound to
> impose the conditions on which alone they can continue to exist.
> That's how your money-making is justified here in the face of
> lawlessness and disorder. It is justified because the security which it
> demands must be shared with an oppressed people. A better justice
> will come afterwards. That's your ray of hope. (92–93)

That noble but naïve confidence finds its echoes in today's neoconservative arguments for bringing democracy to Iraq by way of securing the smooth working of the oil industry there, our present-day form of "material interests." The latter (oil exploitation) is bound to bring the former (Western-style capitalist democracy)—in good time—since oil exploitation requires law and order.

Actually Gould is, in spite of his English sentimental idealism and practical efficiency, no more than a tool of global capitalism. The latter is represented, as every reader of the novel will remember, by the sinister American businessman and entrepreneur from San Francisco, Holroyd. Holroyd funds the reopening of the San Tomé mine as a kind of personal hobby. It is one small feature of his global enterprise. That enterprise includes, as a significant detail, a commitment to building Protestant churches everywhere the influence of his company reaches. Or, rather, Holroyd funds not the mine, but Charles Gould. It is Gould he has bought, not the mine, out of his confidence in Gould's integrity, courage, practicality, mine engineering know-how, and fanatical devotion to making the mine successful at all costs. Holroyd's recompense is the steady flow of large amounts of silver north by steamer to San Francisco from the port of Sulaco.

Holroyd has a canny sense of the precariousness of the San Tomé enterprise. He is ready at a moment's notice to withdraw funding if things go badly, for example, through a new revolution installing another tyrannical dictator who will take over the mine for his own enrichment. Nevertheless, Holroyd sees global capitalism as destined to conquer the world. He states this certainty in a chilling speech to Charles Gould. Gould does not care what Holroyd believes as long as he gets the money necessary to get the mine working. Holroyd's speech is chilling because it is so prescient. A CEO of ADM, "Supermarket to the World," or Bechtel, or Fluor, or Monsanto, or Texaco, or Halliburton, or Dick Cheney, for example, might make such a speech today, at least in private, to confidantes or confederates. It is not insignificant that Holroyd's big office building of steel and glass is located in San Francisco, since so many transnational corporations even today are located in California, if not in Texas. Conrad foresaw the movement of global capitalism's center westward from Paris and London first to New York and then to Texas and California. What Conrad did not foresee is that it would be oil and gas rather than silver or other metals that would be the center of global capitalism. Nor did he foresee that the development and use of oil and gas would cause environmental destruction and global warming that would sooner or later bring the whole process of economic imperialism to a halt, if nuclear war does not finish us all off before that.

Western-style industrialized and now digitized civilization, as it spreads all over the world, requires oil and gas not just for automobiles and heating, but for military might and explosives; for the airplanes that span the globe; for plastics, metal, and paper manufacture; for producing fertilizers and pesticides that grow the corn and soybeans that feed the cattle that make the beef that feeds people, and now for the production of personal computers, television sets, satellites, fiber optic cables, and all the rest of the paraphernalia of global telecommunications and the mass media. Surprisingly, it takes two-thirds as much energy to produce a PC as to produce an automobile, a large amount in both cases. When the oil and gas are gone, in fifty years or less, we are going to be in big trouble.

Holroyd, by the way, is a perfect United Statesian, that is, a mixture of many races. He is also a splendid exemplar of religion's connection to the rise of capitalism, this "millionaire endower of churches on a scale befitting the greatness of his native land" (84). "His hair was iron gray," says the narrator, "his eyebrows were still black, and his massive profile was the profile of a Caesar's head on an old Roman coin. But his parentage was German and Scotch and English, with remote strains of Danish and French blood, giving him the temperament of a Puritan and an insatiable imagination of conquest" (84). Here is this insatiable capitalist's prophetic account of the way United States–based global capitalism is bound to take over the world:

> Now what is Costaguana? It is the bottomless pit of ten per cent loans and other fool investments. [The reader will remember the huge losses the Bank of America and other banks incurred not long ago from bad South American loans.] European capital has been flung into it with both hands for years. Not ours, though. We in this country know just about enough to keep in-doors when it rains. We can sit and watch. Of course, some day we shall step in. We are bound to. But there's no hurry. Time itself has got to wait on the greatest country in the whole of God's universe. We shall be giving the word for everything—industry, trade, law, journalism, art, politics, and religion, from Cape Horn dear over to Smith's Sound, and beyond too, if anything worth taking hold of turns up at the North Pole. And then we shall have the leisure to take in hand the outlying islands and continents of the earth. We shall run the world's business whether the world likes it or not. The world can't help it—and neither can we, I guess. (85)

Holroyd makes this remarkable statement to Charles Gould, during the latter's visit to Holroyd's office in San Francisco to raise venture capital for the mine. The "great Holroyd building" is described as "an enormous pile of iron, glass, and blocks of stone at the corner of two streets, cobwebbed aloft by the radiation of telegraph wires" (89). That sounds pretty familiar, except that today such a building would have more glass and less visible iron and stone. The cobweb of telegraph wires would be replaced by invisible underground optic cables or by discrete satellite dishes. Nevertheless, Conrad's circumstantial account of the determining role of the telegraph and of transoceanic cables in Sulaco's affairs anticipates the role of global telecommunications today.

Gould's reaction to Holroyd's speech about the way the United States will take over the world is a slight disagreeable uneasiness caused by a sudden insight into the smallness, in a global perspective, of the silver mine that fills his whole life. Holroyd's "intelligence was nourished on fact," says the narrator, and, oddly, says his words were "meant to express his faith in destiny in words suitable to his intelligence, which was unskilled in the presentation of general ideas" (85). This commentary is odd, because Holroyd's speech, it seems to me, expresses with great eloquence the "general idea" or ideological presuppositions of United States' "exceptionalism," its presumption that it is our destiny to achieve imperialist economic conquest of the world, with military help when necessary. Holroyd's grandiose conceptions are not all that solidly nourished on fact. Charles Gould, on the other hand, "whose imagination had been permanently affected by the one great fact of the silver-mine, had no objection to this theory [Holroyd's] of the world's future. If it had seemed distasteful for a moment it was because the sudden statement of such vast eventualities dwarfed almost to nothingness the actual matter in hand. He and his plans and all the mineral wealth of the Occidental province appeared suddenly robbed of every vestige of magnitude" (85).

My own reaction to Holroyd's speech is that chill or frisson I mentioned as a reaction to Conrad's prescience. It is also the reflection that United States global economic imperialism may already be coming to an end, like all imperialisms, as China is about to become the world's largest economy, as Indian software displaces Silicon Valley, as United States jobs flee by the hundreds of thousands to worldwide "outsourcing" and manufacturing (a million jobs lost to China alone in the last few years), and as non-Americans like the Australian Rupert Murdoch are coming to dominate the worldwide cable and satellite media. The triumph of global capitalism means the eventual end of nation state imperialist hegemony. That includes the United States. We should make no mistake about that.

Somewhat paradoxically, one of the best ways to understand what is happening now in our time of globalization is to read this old novel by Conrad, written just a hundred years ago. That is one answer to the question of literature's "usefulness" I posed at the beginning of this essay. The way military intervention by the United States is necessary to secure and support its world-wide economic imperialism is indicated in one small detail in *Nostromo*. The narrator notes that at the climax of the successful secession and establishment of the new Occidental Republic of Sulaco, a United States warship, the *Powhatan* (ironically named by Conrad for a Native American nation located in the eastern United States), stands by in the offing to make sure that the founding of the new Republic does not go amiss (544). This parallels the historical fact that when Panama, through United States conniving, split off from Colombia after Colombia refused to approve the Panama Canal, an American naval vessel, the *Nashville*, stood by to make sure the split really happened and the Columbians did not try to take Panama back.

It would be too long a tale here to tell the whole story of United States military and economic intervention, not to speak of covert action, in South America. Conrad's *Nostromo* gives an admirable emblematic fictional example of it. Whether or not Conrad himself agreed unequivocally with Holroyd's economic determinism is another question, just as it is questionable whether Conrad expresses without qualification his own radical skepticism in the Parisian dandy Decoud, "the man with no faith in anything except the truth of his own sensations," as though he were a perfect "impressionist." I think the answer is no in both cases.

The biographical evidence, for example, that provided succinctly by Cedric Watts, indicates that though Conrad learned a lot about South American history and topography from Eastlake, Masterman, and others, it was especially through his friendship and conversations with the Scottish socialist aristocrat R. B. Cunninghame Graham, descendent of Robert the Bruce, and through reading Graham's writings, that Conrad achieved his understanding of, and attitude toward, the bad things Western imperialism over the centuries had done in South America.

I conclude that, as many distinguished previous critics, for example, Edward Said and Fredric Jameson, have noted, *Nostromo* is, among other things, an eloquent and persuasive indictment of the evils of military and economic imperialism exercised by first-world countries, especially the United States, against so-called third-world countries everywhere. The reader needs, however, to be on guard against confusing analogy with identity. I have used words like "allegory" or "parable" or "fable" or "consonance" or "uncanny resonance" to indicate that *Nostromo* is a commodious emblem of historical events, economic imperialism in this case. Such historical events have recurred from time to time in post-Renaissance world history. They always happen, however, in significantly different ways at different moments in history, as, for example, oil and gas have replaced silver as the preferred loot from third-world countries, or as new telecommunications, e-mail, cellphones, and the Internet have replaced the telegraph lines and undersea cables of Conrad's day. The differences, we must always remember, are as important as the similarities. A parable is not a work of history. It is a realistic story that stands for something else in an indirect mode of reference. One might call each such literary work a reading of history. Literature, to express this in Conrad's own terms, is a way of using language in a mode that is "imaginary (but true)."

The claim I am making is complex and problematic. I am sticking my neck out in making this claim. It is impossible to do justice to the complexity in question in a short paper. A parable is not the same mode of discourse as an allegory, nor is either the same as an emblem, or as a paradigm, or as a reading. Careful discriminations would need to be made to decide which is the best term for Conrad's procedure of making an imaginary story "stand for" history in *Nostromo*. That little word "for" in "stand for" is crucial here, as is the word "of" in the phrases "parable of," or "emblem of," or "allegory of," or "paradigmatic expression of," or "reading of." What displacement is involved in that "for"? What is the force of "of" in these different locutions? What different ligature or separation is affirmed in each case? The differences among these "ofs" might generate a virtually endless analysis of *Nostromo* in their light.

I have used a series of traditional words for Conrad's displacement of "realist" narration to say something else. The multiplicity is meant to indicate the inadequacy of all of them. *Nostromo* is neither a parable, nor an emblem, nor an allegory, nor a paradigm, nor a reading. Each of these words is in one way or another inadequate or inappropriate. A parable, for example, is a short realistic story of everyday life that stands for some otherwise inexpressible spiritual truths. An example is Jesus' parable of the sower, in Matthew 13:3–9. *Nostromo* is hardly like that. All the other words I have used can be disqualified in similar ways. Nevertheless, it is of the utmost importance not to read *Nostromo* as a straightforward piece of "historical fiction." Historical realities as Conrad knew them, primarily from reading, but also through conversations with Cunninghame Graham, not from direct experience, are used as the "raw material" for the creation of a fictive "world" that is "imaginary (but true)." Conrad's own phrase is perhaps, after all, the best way to express the use of realist narrative techniques to create a place swarming with people and events that never existed anywhere on land or sea except within the covers of copies of *Nostromo*, and in Conrad's imagination, of course. The magnificent opening description of the sequestered province of Sulaco, cut off from the outside world by the Golfo Placido and by the surrounding mountains, is one way this isolation of Sulaco's imagined (non)community is expressed in *Nostromo*. The second part of Conrad's phrase, "but true," argues that the fictive events that take place in *Nostromo* correspond to the way things really happened in Central America at that stage of its history, that is, the moment of

United States imperialist and global capitalist interventions. The words "but true" suggest a claim by Conrad that this transformation of historical fact into a complex modernist narrative form is better than any history book at indicating the way history actually happens. History happens, that is, in ways that are distressingly contingent. History is "caused" by peripheral factors such as Decoud's love for Antonia Avellanos or Nostromo's vanity. Conrad's phrase, "imaginary (but true)," is, after all, echoing, with his own modernist twist, what Aristotle said in the *Poetics* about the way poetry is more philosophical than history because "[history] relates what has happened, [poetry] what may happen" (*Poetics*, 1451b; Aristotle 1951, 35). The "modernist twist" is the implicit claim that the narrative complexities and indirections I have been identifying get closer to "what has happened" than "official" histories. Aristotle would probably not have approved of those complexities, any more than Plato, in *The Republic*, approved of Homer's "double diegesis" in pretending to narrate as Odysseus.

In spite of these complexities, the bottom line of what I am saying is that *Nostromo's* indirect way of "standing for" the real South American history he knew from books and hearsay also means that, *mutatis mutandis*, it is also an indirect way of helping to understand what is going on in the United States and in the world today, in 2007.[5] That understanding would then make possible, it might be, responsible action (for example by voting) as a way of responding to what is going on. This, I am aware, is an extravagant claim for the social, ethical, and political usefulness of literature.

I conclude also, finally, that *Nostromo* demonstrates, to my satisfaction at least, that all its notorious narrative complexities of fractured sequence, reversed temporality, and multiple viewpoints are not goods in themselves. Not telling a story by way of a single point of view and in straightforward chronological order can be justified only if, as is the case with *Nostromo*, such extravagant displacements or "dis-positions" are necessary to get the meaning across more successfully to the reader's comprehensive understanding.

NOTES

1. See Royle 2003, 256–76.

2. The best interpretation of Conrad's work from a narratological perspective is Lothe 1989.

3. See Cedric T. Watts's succinct account of Conrad's sources in "A Note on the Background to 'Nostromo,'" in Conrad 1969, 37–42. A fuller account is given in Watts 1990.

4. The text has "roots," as does the Dent edition, but surely that is a misprint for "roofs." "Palm-leaf roots" doesn't make sense.

5. F. R. Leavis, in *The Great Tradition*, first published in 1946, makes a strikingly similar claim for the relevance of *Nostromo* to understanding the history of Leavis's own time. Speaking of "Charles Gould's quiet unyieldingness in the face of

Pedrito's threats and blandishments," Leavis says this episode "reinforce[s] dramatically that pattern of political significance which has a major part in *Nostromo*—a book that was written, we remind ourselves in some wonder, noting the topicality of its themes, analysis, and illustrations, in the reign of Edward VII [1901–1910]" (Leavis 1962, 218). I owe this reference to Jeremy Hawthorn. I am no Leavisite, but am, nevertheless, always happy to find myself in agreement with Leavis. Leavis would no doubt have had little sympathy with my insistence on the way *Nostromo* is "parabolic," that is, "imaginary (but true)."

Works Cited

Acts of Narrative. Edited by Carol Jacobs and Henry Sussman. Stanford, CA: Stanford University Press, 2003. 93–109.

Aristotle. *Poetics*. In Aristotle's *Theory of Poetry and Fine Arts*, critical text, translation, and commentary by S. H. Butcher. N.p.: Dover, 1951.

Conrad, Joseph. *A Personal Record*. London: Dent, 1923.

———. *Nostromo*. New York: Modern Library, 1951. All references to *Nostromo* are to this edition. I have used it because it reprints the first book version and has some passages Conrad later cut.

———. *Letters to Cunninghame Graham*. Edited by Cedric T. Watts. Cambridge: Cambridge University Press, 1969.

Leavis, F. R. *The Great Tradition*. Peregrine Books edition. Harmondsworth: Penguin, 1962.

Lothe, Jakob. *Conrad's Narrative Method*. Oxford: Clarendon Press, 1989.

Nancy, Jean-Luc. *The Inoperative Community*. Edited by Peter Connor, translated by Peter Connor, Lisa Garbus, Michael Holland, and Simona Sawhney. Minneapolis: University of Minnesota Press, 1991.

Royle, Nicholas. "The 'Telepathy Effect': Notes toward a Reconsideration of Narrative Fiction." In *The Uncanny*. Manchester: Manchester University Press, 2003. 256–76; also available in *Acts of Narrative*, edited by Carol Jacobs and Henry Sussman. Stanford, CA: Stanford University Press, 2003, 93–109.

Watts, Cedric T. "A Note on the Background to 'Nostromo,'" in Conrad 1969, 37–42.

———. *Conrad's "Nostromo."* London: Penguin, 1990.

TOM HENTHORNE

"There Will Be Fighting":
Insurgency & Postcoloniality in
Almayer's Folly & An Outcast of the Islands

Almayer's Folly

In the novelty of its local color, in the daring originality of its dramatic force, in the fresh disclosure of new scenes and characters, in the noble and imaginative handling of life's greatness and littleness, *Almayer's Folly* has no place in the prevalent fiction of the hour, which, like a flooded stream, sweeps past us into oblivion. It leaps at once to a place of its own—a place which ought to rank its author high among novelists worthy of the name in its best sense

—UNSIGNED REVIEW of *Almayer's Folly*
in *Literary News*, September 1895

[*Almayer's Folly*] departs altogether from the conventional happy ending, as well as from many other conventions of the novelist's art. But it is distinctly powerful, and not less distinctly original.

—UNSIGNED REVIEW of *Almayer's Folly*, *Speaker*, June 1895

As these two reviews suggest, many of Conrad's earliest critics recognized that his first novel, *Almayer's Folly*, was "remarkable" and even "unique," even though it was marketed by T. Fisher Unwin and Company as popular exotic fiction (Sherry 1973, 48; Watt 1994, xli–xlv). Unlike the works of writers such as Pierre Loti and Carlton Dawes, however—books

From *Conrad's Trojan Horses: Imperialism, Hybridity, and the Postcolonial Aesthetic*, pp. 32–63, 181–85. © 2008 by Tom Henthorne.

169

that sold well but were largely ignored by literary critics—Conrad's first novel was, as H. G. Wells puts it, "praised . . . rather more than it was read" (Sherry 1973, 73). Writing many years later, Edward Garnett, Conrad's first editor and lifelong friend, seems to confirm Wells's observation, noting that the first printing of the novel "rested for years on the booksellers' shelves" and the "title *Almayer's Folly* long remained a jest in 'the trade'" because they were unable to sell it (Garnett 1956, 16). That *Almayer's Folly* did not sell well despite positive reviews can be explained in part by the fact that the book violated genre conventions.[1] In a sense, *Almayer's Folly* is an adventure book without an adventure. Although the title character contemplates a gold expedition into the interior of Borneo that will result in "wealth and power" for himself and his daughter, no such expedition takes place (5). Indeed, by the end of the first chapter, it becomes clear that Kaspar Almayer is a dreamer and a fool and therefore no adventurer at all: he is a man of mediocre abilities whose only outstanding characteristic is his white skin.

Almayer's Folly is not without a hero, however, for as the novel proceeds, Nina Almayer, Kaspar's "half-caste" daughter, emerges as the protagonist, albeit an unconventional one, of a romance (15). Through her, Conrad depicts not only an alternative perspective on imperialism but also the formation of national consciousness as she comes to reject her European heritage and declare herself Malay. By presenting her as heroic, Conrad suggests that Nina is correct in preferring Malay culture to European culture, thereby radically challenging European presumptions of superiority. Conrad also challenges imperialist ideology by representing alternative points of view and histories through his Sulu, Balinese, and Malay characters and by employing a seemingly omniscient narrator whose sympathies appear to shift from the colonizers to the colonized as the novel proceeds. Such features distinguish Conrad's first novel from others published in Great Britain in the 1890s: rather than monologically affirming Britain's civilizing mission as most British fiction of the period does, *Almayer's Folly* contests imperialist ideology and ongoing forms of oppression from colonized perspectives, perspectives Conrad was better able to represent after his own postcoloniality began to emerge in the early 1890s.[2]

Almayer's Folly and Conrad's Emerging Postcoloniality

In terms of sensibilities at least, the man who completed *Almayer's Folly* in 1894 was not the same person who carried drafts of the early chapters with him to Africa in 1890. Conrad himself told his friend Garnett that until he went up the Congo, he had "not a thought in his head," that he "was a perfect animal" (Garnett 1956, 8). Recalling the conversation, Garnett comments, "The sinister voice of the Congo with its murmuring undertone of human fatuity, baseness and greed had swept away the generous illusions of his youth, and had left him gazing into the heart of an immense darkness" (8). As Garnett suggests, the horrors Conrad witnessed in Africa forced him to rethink not only his attitudes toward imperialism and imperialist ideology but also his own complicity in what he describes in "Geography and Some Explorers" as "the vilest scramble for loot that ever disfigured the history of human conscience" (25).[3] One could argue, of course, that Conrad's change in consciousness is similar to the political one George Orwell underwent as a result of his experiences in colonial Burma: both Conrad and Orwell were European-educated white men who reacted against British imperialism only after participating in it.[4] Orwell was neither a colonial subject nor an ethnic "other" to the British, however, and therefore could only imagine, in texts such as *Burmese Days*, what it was like to be a subject person. Conrad, in contrast, knew from his childhood in Russian-occupied Ukraine what it was to be "othered," even though during his long career as a merchant sailor, he had occupied many other positions in the colonial social hierarchy. As a result of his own particular subjectivity, Conrad's change in consciousness was more than just a political one: he became "postcolonial" in the sense that his experiences as a colonial subject coupled with his experiences in Africa led him to develop the sort of "contestatory/oppositional consciousness" that de Alva and others identify with postcoloniality (245). In this regard, at least, Conrad's change in consciousness resembles Gandhi's, whose postcoloniality emerged only after he had lived in both Great Britain and South Africa and developed a broader perspective on imperialism.[5]

Such an account of Conrad's changing sensibilities is necessarily specu-lative, at least from a biographical point of view, since little of Conrad's cor-respondence from the period survives, and his autobiographical writings are notoriously unreliable.[6] Indeed, the best record we have of Conrad's emerging postcoloniality is the manuscript of *Almayer's Folly*, since Conrad's changing sensibilities are reflected in it. That fact that he carried the manuscript with him as he traveled back and forth between Europe, Africa, and Australia dur-ing this critical period of his life explains at least in part why Conrad treats the manuscript itself "as if it were a sort of hero in an adventure story" in *A Personal Record* (GoGwilt 1995, 112): it becomes a metonym for his own developing consciousness. As we shall see, Conrad's "puzzled wonder as to the meaning of all [he] saw" in Africa in 1890 led him not only to revise the chapters he had written the previous fall but to reconceptualize the entire novel, beginning with its title character (*Letters* 1:294).

The Man Who Would Be White:
Kaspar Almayer and the Folly of Racism

Kaspar Almayer certainly lacks the outstanding qualities generally associated with adventure heroes (White 5; Dryden 52, 106–7): he is not brave, smart, or intrepid. He does, however, share one important characteristic with the typical adventure hero: his white skin. Although most critics focus little attention on his racial identity, Kaspar seems to regard his whiteness as his greatest asset, and, like Daniel Dravot in Kipling's "The Man Who Would Be King," he tries to use it to his advantage. Kaspar lacks the initiative, charisma, and drive of Dravot, however, and therefore is unable to exploit his "quality" as a "white man" (31): he is a pathetic figure rather than a vainglorious one, a man who considers himself European even though he has never been there, holding himself above the "savages" around him.

Raised in Java by a father who "grumbled all day" about the "stupidity" of the natives and a mother who "bewailed the lost glories of Amsterdam" from her easy chair, Kaspar demonstrates no propensity for greatness (6). He does, however, learn English and arithmetic well and so manages to find work as a clerk with a successful trader in Macassar and then with Tom Lingard, an English adventurer who has acquired a lucrative trade monopoly in Sambir, a river settlement in Eastern Borneo (6). Kaspar, who left "the poisonous shores of Java" in order "to conquer the world" soon finds what he believes is an opportunity to make his fortune (6): Lingard, it seems, has informally adopted a Sulu girl he had captured in a battle with "pirates," and he has "sworn a mighty oath to marry her to a white marl' (8). Kaspar agrees to be that white man, thinking that once Lingard is gone, it would be "easy enough to dispose of a Malay woman, a slave after all, to his eastern mind" (10).[7]

Almayer's decision to advance his material interests by exploiting his racial identity rather than his abilities quickly proves to be a mistake. Immediately following the wedding, Lingard builds the couple "a pretty little house" in Sambir, where Kaspar becomes Lingard's exclusive agent (20). Kaspar thus begins his life as the only white settler on the east coast of Borneo, "eager and full of hope," thinking that "the world was his" (20). The Almayers' marriage quickly fails, however, and his trading success is limited, in part because Mrs. Almayer provides Lakamba—her lover and one of Kaspar's business rivals—with "secret" information about his financial affairs (20). Eventually, with the help of Mrs. Almayer and Syed Abdullah, an Arab trader who has established a post in Sambir, Lakamba rises to power and shuts Kaspar out of the local trade entirely. Kaspar's troubles are compounded when Lingard loses his fortune, for it soon becomes apparent even to Kaspar that the "great piles of shining guilders" that he expected in exchange for marrying Lingard's adopted daughter will never materialize and that his decision to marry a Sulu woman was a tremendous folly: it becomes the "greatest regret" of his life (32).

As Kaspar's hopes for an easy fortune fade, his relations with his wife and the Malay community deteriorate further. Although Mrs. Almayer's intimate relationship with Lakamba ends once he becomes the local Rajah, she treats her husband with "savage contempt expressed by sulky silence, only occasionally varied by a flood of savage invective," and Kaspar, in turn, contemplates murdering her (21). With Lingard appearing in Sambir only infrequently, Kaspar lives in what he regards as isolation, since to him, Malays are not fit "company for a white man" (92). His only companionship comes from his daughter, Nina, who seems to prefer him to her mother (21). He does not want her to grow up in a "savage" environment, however, so he sends her to Singapore to live with a white family so she can receive "Christian teaching, social education, and a good glimpse of civilized life" (34). Despite his efforts to ensure that Nina is "taught properly" (22), Kaspar cannot "make her white," as his friend, Captain Ford, reminds him (25). In fact, he cannot even make her wish to be white. On the contrary, after returning to her parents' home following "an outburst of contempt from white people for her mixed blood" (34), Nina becomes "gradually more indifferent, more contemptuous of the white side of her descent represented by a feeble and tradition-less father" (35).

Not surprisingly, perhaps, given his racial arrogance, Kaspar is oblivious to his daughter's change in attitude: it is unthinkable to him that she would want anything but to live as a white woman. Until the very end, he believes that Nina shares his dreams of leaving Borneo for Europe, where no one "would think of her mixed blood in the presence of her great beauty and of his immense wealth" (5).[8] Accordingly, when he learns of the establishment of the British Borneo Company, he builds a large "new house for the use of the future engineers, agents or settlers of the new Company" in the hopes of making his fortune (26). Once again Kaspar tries to profit from his white skin, fully expecting that business from the European company will come to him rather than to his Malay and Arab rivals. His plans come to nothing, however, when the British give up their claim to Sambir, leaving it "under the nominal power of Holland" (28). Soon afterward, visiting Dutch naval officers dub the unfinished house "Almayer's Folly" sine Kaspar wasted "every available guilder" on it (30).

Kaspar makes one last effort to exploit his "quality" as a "white man" after finding Lingard's notes on gold expeditions he made in the Bornean interior (48): in particular, Kaspar hopes that his racial prestige will allow him to succeed "with the up-river tribes" that control "Gunong Mas—the mountain of gold" (31, 63). To make such an expedition, however, he needs laborers, and he is unwilling to trust either Lakamba or Abdullah, the only men who can provide them. When Dain Maroola appears in Sambir hoping to procure gunpowder to use in his fight against the Dutch, Kaspar's labor problem appears to be solved. He agrees to help the desperate insurgent acquire gunpowder if Maroola and half his men will accompany him on a gold expedition upriver once Maroola's brig and the other half of his men get underway with their cargo.

Kaspar Almayer's illicit dealings with Dain Maroola eventually lead to disaster, not only financially but personally, since Nina, whom he hoped to "make" white, elopes with Maroola to become a Rani. It is at this point in the novel that Kaspar's race consciousness surfaces a final time. Although he briefly considers setting aside his prejudices and leaving Sambir with Nina, ultimately, Kaspar does what he considers "his duty to himself—to his race—to his respectable connections" and disowns his daughter. "I will never forgive you, Nina," he tells her: "And tomorrow I shall forget you" (144). He spends what remains of his life trying to forget, an effort that the narrator calls "the undying folly of his heart" (151). Indeed, he goes so far as to erase "carefully with his hand all traces of Nina's footsteps" from the beach after she leaves, making himself ridiculous before his servant, Ali, who looks on with "great dismay" (147).

As the scene on the beach suggests, Kaspar becomes increasingly ridiculous as the novel proceeds, a process that culminates with him being led around by his pet monkey, who "seemed to have taken complete charge of his master" (152). That Kaspar, who consistently held himself above those who are not European, ultimately subordinates himself to an animal is significant: he undergoes a reversal so extreme that he becomes a subject of comic irony. Equally important is the fact that he becomes a comic figure under the gaze of subject peoples: by the end of the novel, Almayer is a caricature of sorts, an object of fun. In effect, Conrad reverses the colonialist gaze so prominent in novels such as Kipling's *Kim* and Joyce Cary's *Mr. Johnson*, subjecting white colonists to a form of irony that has become a part of the postcolonial aesthetic as evidenced by characters ranging from "Big Jim" Walton in A. R. F. Webber's *Those That Be in Bondage*, a drunken white colonist named after his mule, to Mr. Winterbottom in Chinua Achebe's *Arrow of God*, a man who tries to impress fellow Europeans with his knowledge of a language he does not even speak. In this sense, at least, Conrad's representation of Almayer seems to become increasingly postcolonial as the novel proceeds.

Nina Almayer: The Half-Caste Hero of an Unconventional Romance

Conrad's negative depiction of Kaspar Almayer has led a number of critics, including Ian Watt, to conclude that Kaspar is an antihero and that, therefore, Conrad can be considered a modernist since, as Malcolm Bradbury and

James McFarlane put it, in Conrad's "nihilistic," fictional worlds, the "central figures are men on the point of test, threatened by a secret or alternative self, or a void at the center of their values" (616). Such a description could only be applied accurately to *Almayer's Folly* if Kaspar were the novel's only protagonist.[9] As Ruth Nadelhaft suggests, however, Kaspar is one of several central figures in the novel. Indeed, she argues that Nina Almayer and her mother "carry the weight of the novel in a number of ways, not least by their presence in so many scenes that the first quarter of the novel must be said to be about them" (1991, 20). If Nadelhaft is correct, then *Almayer's Folly* cannot be categorized as nihilistic unless all of the central characters are devoid of values, something that is certainly not true of Nina. As we shall see, far from being an antihero, by the end of the novel, Nina emerges as a powerful, independent character whose decision to be Malay rather than European is represented as being correct.

Nina's emergence as a protagonist is significant not only because she provides Conrad with a means of representing postcolonial consciousness but because, like the narrative's increasingly ironic treatment of Almayer, it illuminates Conrad's own developing postcoloniality. In the initial draft of chapter 1, Nina does not appear at all: she is introduced in what was originally chapter 2 as a seemingly minor character. When Conrad revised his early draft following his return from the Congo, however, he not only restructured the opening chapters so that Nina is introduced in the first chapter but also mentions her on the very first page. He also provides more detail about Nina's experiences in Singapore in what is now the third chapter and adds Captain Ford's comment cited earlier about Kaspar's efforts to "make her white." Taken as a whole, the changes Conrad made to his initial drafts of the opening chapters suggest that he did not conceive of Nina as a protagonist until after his experiences in Africa: what began as a study of a failed adventurer becomes an unconventional romance about a colonial subject who develops a postcolonial consciousness. In this reconceived version of the novel, Nina becomes so important that Conrad considered titling the Polish translation "Almayer's Daughter" (McLauchlan 81).[10]

Predictably, perhaps, most nineteenth-century reviews of the novel did not recognize Nina's significance as a character.[11] The *World*, for example, reports that *Almayer's Folly* is simply the "dreary record of the still more dreary existence of a solitary Dutchman doomed to vegetate in a small village in Borneo" (Sherry 1973, 51), and *Athenaeum* identifies Kaspar Almayer as the "central figure," listing Nina and Mrs. Almayer with "an old servant, Ali, and sundry other retainers" as supporting characters (Sherry 1973, 52). As Nadelhaft suggests, the failure of such readers to recognize Nina's significance can be explained in part by gender prejudice: "Although from his earliest novels

Conrad created and developed powerful and credible images of women, male friends, colleagues, and critics disregarded those images and focused instead on images of men" (Nadelhaft 1991, 2). To many of Conrad's readers, a female protagonist was simply unthinkable. Nina's status as a "half-caste" also seems to have contributed to the inability of many of Conrad's original reviewers and critics to recognize Nina's role as hero. This, too, perhaps, should not be surprising, since the heroes of nineteenth-century European novels were almost exclusively white. Indeed, *Almayer's Folly* may be the first novel published in Great Britain to feature a "half-caste" as a protagonist.[12] What is surprising is the fact that a number of reviewers failed to assign Nina any significance at all. The reviewer for *Academy*, for example, apparently groups Nina with "the wily, half-savage Malays" that surround Almayer (Sherry 1973, 54), and *Nation* places her in "a mob of raging heathen" (Sherry 1973, 60). The latter review adds, "Borneo is a fine field for the study of monkeys, not men." Apparently, non-European heroes were as unimaginable to Conrad's original readers as female ones.

Although most of the novel's reviewers seem to have missed it, Nina's role as a hero is signaled in the opening chapter in her encounter with her father after he has learned that Dain Maroola has returned to Sambir, presumably to accompany him on his gold expedition. To Nina, whose "dreamy eyes" signal her "impatient expectancy," Maroola's reappearance has a different significance—her lover has returned. The narrator's description of Nina makes it clear from the very beginning that the novel is a hybrid of sorts and can be read in at least two different ways: as an adventure story and as an exotic romance.[13] As if to underscore this, in the very next passage Conrad represents her in terms characteristic of the latter genre—she is at once what Linda Dryden identifies as the "oriental *femme fatale*" and a vulnerable European woman in need of rescue (94):[14]

> She was tall for a half-caste with the correct profile of the father modified and strengthened by the squareness of the lower part of the face inherited from her maternal ancestors—the Sulu pirates. Her firm mouth with the lips slightly parted and disclosing a gleam of white teeth put a vague suggestion of ferocity into the impatient expression of her features. And yet her dark and perfect eyes had all the tender softness of expression common to Malay women, but with a gleam of superior intelligence. (15)

If on one level Conrad suggests that *Almayer's Folly* can be read as an exotic romance by including an "oriental *femme fatale*" and a vulnerable European woman, on another level he indicates that the novel is anything but conventional by conflating the two in Nina: her hybrid identity makes it clear that the novel is more than just formulaic entertainment and that Nina is more than just a stock character. Indeed, the description just quoted helps establish Nina as a potential hero since it suggests that she has the best features of both her father and her mother. It also highlights Kaspar's deficiencies, particularly his weak chin: Almayer may be a central character, but as a hero he shows little promise. Nina, in contrast, has all the attributes one might expect of the lead female character in a romance, which suggests that her story is the dominant one.

The conversation that ensues between father and daughter seems to confirm that her story is at least as important as his. Kaspar, who seems oblivious to the fact that his daughter is now grown, repeatedly calling her "little girl," expresses his hope that the success of the gold expedition will allow him to take his daughter to Europe where they can live a "glorious life" (15, 16). Nina, however, is "unmoved" by her father's fantasies of wealth (16). As her father prattles on about his coming triumphs, she gazes into the night, thinking about Maroola. The chapter ends by contrasting Nina directly to her father: "Undisturbed by the nightly event of the rainy monsoon, the father slept quietly, oblivious alike of his hopes, his misfortunes, his friend and his enemies;—and the daughter stood motionless, at each flash of lightning, eagerly scanning the broad river with a steady and anxious gaze" (17). That the first chapter ends by juxtaposing Nina's alertness with her father's lethargy is important since it suggests that the two are essentially different: Nina is an active, independent woman, while her father is a foolish, self-indulgent dreamer. Nina's evident anxiety is also significant: the reader knows why Kaspar is ebullient upon Maroola's return, but the reason for Nina's nervousness is not explained immediately, generating a tension that makes Nina's mysterious response one of the main focuses of the first part of the novel.

Nina's importance in the narrative remains evident in the chapters that immediately follow as the narrator begins to tell Nina's story, beginning with her childhood. We learn that she was born two years into the Almayers' failing marriage, that as a child she had an "evident preference" for her father (21), and that her father sent her to Singapore to "be brought up decently" (22). When she returns unexpectedly to Sambir ten years later, she has become "a woman, black haired, olive skinned, tall and beautiful, with great sad eyes, where the startled expression common to Malay womankind was modified by a thoughtful tinge inherited from her European ancestry" (24). Nina, we are told, "was never happy over there," in part because she was "slighted" by the European women (25). Eventually, her hosts force her to leave their household, because, as Captain Ford explains to Kaspar, having a beautiful young "half-caste girl in the house" is "deucedly awkward" (25). Although Captain

Ford offers her a place in his own household, Nina decides to return to Sambir unannounced, apparently tired of being treated with contempt by whites.

In the chapter that follows, the narrator describes how Nina's relationships with her mother and father change after her return to Sambir. Although
she still has great affection for her father, her experiences in Singapore taught
her to despise not only colonial society but whites in general, something that
becomes most clear in chapter 9 when she tells a Dutch naval officer, "I hate
the sight of your white faces," and then, "touching lightly her father's cheek,"
adds, "I hoped to live here without seeing any other white face but this" (106).
It is her relationship with her mother that changes the most, however. At first,
Nina approaches her mother "curiously, guarding her skirts from the betel
juice" her mother had spit on the floor (33). Eventually, her mother's descriptions of her own childhood, "the glories of the Sultan of Sulu," and the "fear
which benumbed the hearts of white men at the sight of his swift piratical
praus" make a strong impression upon Nina:

> And listening to the recital of those savage glories, those barbarous
> fights and savage feasting, to the story of deeds valorous, albeit
> somewhat bloodthirsty, where men of her mother's race shone far
> above the Orang Blanda, she felt herself irresistibly fascinated, and
> saw with vague surprise the narrow mantle of civilized morality, in
> which good-meaning people had wrapped her young soul, fall away
> and leave her shivering and helpless as if on the edge of some deep
> and unknown abyss. Strangest of all, this abyss did not frighten her
> when she was under the influence of the witch-like being she called
> her mother. (33)

The more Nina reflects on her experiences in Singapore, particularly the
final "outburst of contempt from white people for her mixed blood" that led
to her departure, the more she falls "under the influence of her mother" (34,
35). Eventually, she decides that "the savage and uncompromising sincerity
of purpose of her Malay kinsmen" is preferable to the "sleek hypocrisy, . . .
the polite disguises, [and] to the virtuous pretenses of such white people as
she had the misfortune to come into contact with" (43).

Because of the influence of her mother's stories, Nina is predisposed to
admire Dain Maroola when he first appears in Sambir, an event the narrator
describes in chapter 4. When Maroola first looks at her with "an uncontrolled
expression of admiration and desire," Nina feels "a hitherto unknown feeling of shyness mixed with alarm and some delight, enter and penetrate her
being" (43). Their mutual attraction soon leads to romance, one that they and
Mrs. Almayer are careful to hide from Kaspar and everyone else in Sambir.

To Nina, Dain Maroola is "the ideal Malay chief of her Mother's tradition," and her relationship with him allows her to escape her humiliating life as a "half-caste":

> She recognized with a thrill of delicious fear the mysterious consciousness of her identity with that being.—Listening to his words it seemed to her she was born only then to a knowledge of a new existence, that her life was complete only when near him, and she abandoned herself with a feeling of dreamy happiness, while with half veiled face and in silence—as became a Malay girl—she listened to Dain's words giving up to her the whole treasure of love and passion his nature was capable of with all the unrestrained enthusiasm of a man totally untrammeled by any influence of civilized self-discipline. (50)

As the passage suggests, Nina is attracted to Maroola in part because he makes her feel as if she were "a Malay." Her relationship with him helps her to forget her earlier existence as a "half-caste" among whites. It is for this reason that, toward the end of the novel, circumstances force her to decide whether to continue life with her parents in Sambir or leave with Maroola for Bali, she chooses the latter, telling her father, "I am not of your race. Between your people and mine there is . . . a barrier nothing can remove" (134). As John McClure notes, Conrad casts Nina "in the role of judge," and she "chooses Malay culture over European" (105).[15]

Nina Almayer and the Malay Insurgency

Many critics, including Thomas Moser and D. C. R. A. Goonetilleke, dismiss Nina's decision to join Dain Maroola as "romantic."[16] To do so is to ignore the political context of her decision. Dain Maroola is not a trader or a pirate but a prince who has come to procure gunpowder to fight encroaching Dutch imperialists. That he does so "at a time when the hostilities between Dutch and Malay threaten to spread from Sumatra over the whole archipelago" is even more significant (62): as we shall see, he is part of a larger revolutionary struggle to drive Europeans from the archipelago. Nina, it seems, wants to be part of the insurgency as well. When she learns from a naval officer that Dain Maroola has killed two white men by exploding his boat when Dutch sailors are near, she exclaims, "Two only!" as if disappointed that more had not died as Maroola had hoped (105). Leaving Sambir with Dain Maroola affords Nina the opportunity to participate in the insurgency. Although she feels that, as a woman, she cannot "slay the white men" herself, she can "give him [Maroola] his kriss" and "bid him go" as her mother suggests (115). That she intends to do just that becomes clear in her final conversation with her father when she says of Maroola, "He is brave; he will be powerful, and I hold his bravery and strength in my hand, and I shall make him great" (134).

Not surprisingly, given the pro-imperialist sentiment of the 1890s, Nina's rejection of her European heritage and her decision to join the insurgents bothered many of Conrad's late nineteenth-century British readers, implying as it did that Malay culture was, in some ways at least, superior to European culture and that resistance to European imperialism was legitimate. One early critic asserts that "Conrad, beyond all others has identified himself with the standpoint of the natives," and another complains that the "moral" of *Almayer's Folly* "seems to be that white Christians can be much worse than black pagans, and generally are, along the Straits of Macassar" (Sherry 1973, 119, 81). Despite their limitations and obvious prejudices, these early critics see what many contemporary critics miss: by contrasting Nina's undoubted happiness and success as a Malay to her father's continuing failure, Conrad affirms that Nina has made the right choice. Whereas Kaspar Almayer dies miserable and alone as an opium addict, Nina renounces her European identity, helps the fugitive, Dain Maroola, escape to Bali, and becomes Rani of a powerful, independent state.[17] Through Nina, then, Conrad provides his readers with an alternative perspective on imperialism. More important, perhaps, as Christopher GoGwilt argues, "Nina's rejection of the 'white side of her descent' shows Conrad imagining an alternative political and historical consciousness," one that will eventually provide a basis for a new national identity (GoGwilt 1995, 82). This becomes most clear when Nina tells her father, "I have been rejected with scorn by the white people, and now I am a Malay!" (134). Nina's formal assertion of Malay identity is significant since it anticipates the formation of a national identity for the many peoples of the Malay Archipelago.[18] She is not Dutch, Sulu, or a "half-caste" but Malay—part of an emerging nationality that will eventually challenge European hegemony in the archipelago.[19]

Other Ways of Seeing:
Indigenous Perspectives and the Provincializing of Europe

Conrad's "half-caste" hero, Nina Almayer, is only one of the novel's radical features, for in addition to developing a critique of imperialism through Nina, Conrad develops alternative frames of reference through indigenous characters. By including such perspectives, Conrad not only recognizes that the peoples of the Malay Archipelago have distinct interests and points of view but also suggests that resistance to imperialism takes many forms and operates on many levels. Moreover, as we shall see, Conrad's dialogization of various perspectives on imperialism challenges the "master narrative" offered by European histories of the colonization of the archipelago, effectively provincializing them (Chakrabarty 43).

Set in the 1870s, *Almayer's Folly* offers an alternative to imperialist accounts of the pacification of the Sulu—accounts that deny the legitimacy of Sulu beliefs, values, and practices—through the thoughts, words, and actions of Sulu characters such as Mrs. Almayer.[20] Despite enduring years of indoctrination in colonial institutions following her capture by Lingard, Mrs. Almayer retains her sense of Sulu identity and continues to regard the world much as she did before she became a colonial subject, "concealing her hate and contempt" for her "new life" (19). Years later, after her daughter is grown, Mrs. Almayer still "glories" in her Sulu past, communicating the history of her people to Nina in a "monotonous recitative" (33). Ultimately, Mrs. Almayer makes the intent of her recitations clear, telling Nina, "When I hear of white men driven from the islands then I shall know that you are alive and that you remember my words" (115). As this passage suggests, Mrs. Almayer recognizes that maintaining a sense of cultural identity is essential to resisting domination on both a personal and a communal level.

Babalatchi, Lakamba's "prime minister, harbour master, financial advisor, and general factotum," another character "of Sulu origin," shares many of Mrs. Almayer's attitudes toward Europeans and their culture (31). Like her, he believes that whites are "stronger" but not "better" (113), and he hopes that the peoples of the archipelago will eventually rebel, telling Captain Ford "with energy" toward the end of the novel, "There will be fighting. There is a breath of war in the islands" (154). He realizes, however, that the peoples of the archipelago cannot resist European domination militarily and so "circumvent[s]" white colonists rather than fights them, commenting, "White men were strong but very foolish. It was undesirable to fight them, but deception was easy. They were like silly women; they did not know the use of reason and he [Babalatchi] was a match for any of them" (66, 64). Although the narrator indicates that Babalatchi's "confidence" in his ability to deceive Europeans is based on "deficient experience," Babalatchi successfully manipulates Europeans, not only engineering Dain Maroola's escape to Bali after he kills two Dutch sailors but also shielding the Rajah from the consequences (64). More important, perhaps, with Kaspar's demise, which Babalatchi is at least partially responsible for, Europeans no longer have a permanent resident in Sambir, thus diminishing their power there. Although Sambir is still nominally controlled by the Dutch, indigenous peoples can live there without fear of European interference in their day-to-day lives.

Conrad offers yet another perspective on European imperialism through Nina's lover, Dain Maroola, a Balinese prince who fights the Dutch because they threaten Balinese autonomy. As the subject of an independent state, Maroola's attitude toward imperialism is very different from that of subjects such as Mrs. Almayer and Babalatchi: he believes that the colonization effort can be effectively resisted through direct action. To Maroola, the struggle against the Dutch is not merely local, a point the novel reinforces by having Maroola's appearance in Sambir coincide with what it terms the "Acheen war"—a lengthy conflict in which the Aceh effectively resisted Dutch efforts to occupy parts of northern Sumatra for more than forty years (38).[21] The inability of the Dutch to defeat the Aceh outright diminished their military reputation, which, in turn, made their control of the archipelago all the more tenuous. This problem became particularly acute for the Dutch when the Aceh defeated the first expedition against them in 1873, and, as the narrator of *Almayer's Folly* notes, "the hostilities between the Dutch and Malays threatened to spread from Sumatra over the whole archipelago" (62). By introducing Maroola in such a context, the novel suggests that although Maroola acts primarily to preserve Balinese autonomy, he is also part of a larger struggle in which peoples throughout the archipelago resist the Dutch colonization effort. Maroola demonstrates his commitment to this broader insurgency when, pursued by a Dutch frigate far from Bali, he tries to kill the Dutch sailors rather than simply escape them (167).[22] Like Mrs. Almayer and Babalatchi, he wants to "see white men driven from the islands" (200). Rather than simply hope for such a struggle, however, he participates in it.

Until recently, Maroola has been generally dismissed by critics as a mere love interest.[23] He is more than just a convention of a popular romance, however, for it is through him that Conrad represents what it is to be an anticolonial insurgent. Certainly, the Indonesian novelist Pramoedya Ananta Toer recognizes this, recalling *Almayer's Folly* as a "story about a Balinese prince who is smuggling guns to organize resistance against Dutch colonial rule" (GoGwilt 1996, 156). To Toer, Maroola is the novel's central character. Toer goes on to comment that in the novel, "Conrad was writing about the history of armed struggle against colonialism not recorded in Dutch historiography" (156).

Toer is not the only one to credit Conrad with recording events ignored by European histories, of course: the Indonesian historian G. J. Resink also recognizes that Conrad's fictions provide useful supplements to official European historical accounts (GoGwilt 1995, 83). In effect, Conrad "provincializes" Europe, to borrow Dipesh Chakrabarty's term, recording "the ambivalences, contradictions, the use of force, and the tragedies and the ironies" that European histories ignore in constructing their own "master narrative" (27, 43). By directly representing the consciousness of characters such as Maroola, Mrs. Almayer, Nina, and even the "slave girl" Taminah (48), Conrad presents contact zones such as Sambir—spaces where peoples "geographically and historically separated come into contact with each other and establish ongoing relations, usually involving conditions of coercion, radical inequality, and intractable conflict"—in all their complexity (Pratt 6). [24] Like other early postcolonial novels set in contact zones, including Solomon Plaatje's *Mhudi* and A. R. F. Webber's *Those That Be in Bondage, Almayer's Folly* is dialogic in the sense that it sets various languages in relation to one another, making them "live," as Bakhtin might put it (361).

Narratorial Shifts, Dialogism, and Conrad's Postcoloniality

So far I have argued that *Almayer's Folly* exploits the dialogic possibilities inherent in the novel through its representation of the various social voices that exist in Sambir. Not every voice contained within a novel belongs to characters, however: it is important to consider the narrator's voice as well because it, too, represents a particular perspective. In the case of *Almayer's Folly*, ascertaining this perspective is difficult, since, as Allan Simmons notes, "the narratorial perception shifts" as the novel proceeds, gradually moving "from a colonising perspective to a colonised perspective" (Simmons 1997, 163). According to Simmons, this shift in narratorial perception is most evident in the treatment of Nina. Near the beginning of the novel, for example, the narrator describes Nina in a way that reinforces the opposition between Europeans and Malays, noting her "correct [European] forehead" and how her "eyes had all the tender softness of Malay women, but with a gleam of superior intelligence" (166). As Simmons notes, the narrator's description seems "to replicate, and hence endorse, the racial bias of Almayer"—and by extension, those of white imperialists in general (1997, 166). The binary opposition upon which such racism is based, however, is "deconstructed" as the narrative continues (167): the narrator later tells us, for example, that Nina loses "the power to discriminate" between Europeans and Malays and then goes on to suggest that there is, in fact, no significant difference between "the barbarian" and the "so-called civilized man" (Simmons 1997, 168). Moreover, as Simmons demonstrates, the narrator's speech is "gradually infiltrated by the voices of the colonised," and the text becomes "culturally polyphonic" (1997, 170). Finally, Simmons shows how the narrative voice that initially sympathizes with a European perspective "come[s] full circle" and "come[s] to reflect, to empathise with, and to champion the plight of the Orientals" (1997, 172).

The way in which the narratorial perspective shifts from a colonizing perspective to a colonized one clearly challenges British claims of superiority and righteousness. The shift does more than simply contest imperialist ideology, however: to the extent that the narrator's voice becomes "reified" as it enters a dialogic relationship with the other voices in the novel, that voice functions as a subject position within the text, one available to readers through the process of identification (Bakhtin 361). Accordingly, as this narratorial perspective moves from a colonizing perspective to a colonized one, it has the potential to move readers along with it. To put it another way, as the narratorial perspective shifts, it may induce certain readers to shift with it, potentially affecting their assumptions and attitudes.

Although the shift in narratorial perspective that Simmons identifies seems to have a political function, it appears to be as much a product of Conrad's emerging postcoloniality as it is of conscious design. As I indicated earlier, Conrad's attitude toward imperialism and imperialist ideology changed while writing *Almayer's Folly* as a result of his experiences in Congo, leading to an increasingly ironic treatment of Almayer, the development of Nina Almayer as a protagonist, and the dialogic representation of the various social voices present in Sambir. The shift in narratorial perspective appears to be a product of the same process, and *Almayer's Folly* can thus be read as a record of Conrad's developing consciousness: Conrad may not have begun it as a postcolonial novel—that is, as a text that contests imperialist ideology and ongoing forms of colonial domination through the consciousness of subject peoples—but it became one as Conrad's own postcoloniality developed (de Alva 245).

With all this in mind, it is no wonder that *Almayer's Folly* failed to acquire a popular audience: there simply was no market for a novel that not only features a "half-caste" hero but presents a number of alternative perspectives on imperialism through a variety of indigenous characters and even a narrator who ultimately sympathizes with the colonized. As Andrea White suggests, many readers found such "ventriloquism" unacceptably subversive since "the dialogic possibilities permitted by the discrepancies of multiple viewpoints begin to dislodge the authority of the white man's telling" (White 119, 127).[25] In addition, many readers may have been uncomfortable with the novel because it did not affirm their own racist beliefs. As Geoffrey Harpham notes, the novel was "alien" to many of its readers because of "the equality of treatment allotted to all characters, as though absolutely nothing were at stake in noting racial differences" (47). Readers may also have been disturbed by the novel's social and political implications. Even though *Almayer's Folly* closes with the Malay Archipelago still dominated politically, economically, and militarily by the Dutch, British, and Spanish, European hegemony ends as a national identity develops, the anti-imperialist insurgency grows, and an end to imperialism becomes imaginable. As a postcolonial novel published near the peak of British imperialist sentiment, *Almayer's Folly* relates a story most British readers did not want to hear.

An Outcast of the Islands

Conrad began his second novel, *An Outcast of the Islands*, just after submitting the typescript of *Almayer's Folly* to T. Fisher Unwin for publication in the summer of 1894. Superficially, this novel, which is set in Sambir some time before the action of *Almayer's Folly* takes place, resembles Conrad's first novel, if only because it features many of the same characters and addresses many of the same themes. In some ways, however, *An Outcast of the Islands* is even more radical than *Almayer's Folly*, since, in addition to depicting white colonists in a negative manner and representing the formation of a postcolonial consciousness, the novel focuses on subalterns, their subjectivity, and the threat they represent to colonial authority.[26] Whereas in *Almayer's Folly*, subalterns such as the "slave girl" Taminah are represented as having only limited agency, in *An Outcast of the Islands*, subalterns not only speak but act, in Aïssa's case killing the white colonist who betrays her. By depicting subalterns, including Aïssa, a Malay-Arab woman who is one of the novel's central characters, in such a manner, Conrad exposes an important contradiction within the colonial system: subalterns represent a threat to colonial power because they are ungovernable, and they are ungovernable because as subalterns they are excluded from the very institutions that are designed to contain potential insurgents. As a result, *An Outcast of the Islands* not only reinforces the critique of imperialism Conrad offers in *Almayer's Folly* through its representation of Nina and other characters but also supplements it: colonial subjects no longer represent the sole threat to the colonial system; they are joined by subalterns, since they are beyond the control of colonial institutions.

Fools, Thieves, and Megalomaniacs: White Men in the Colonies

Like Robert Louis Stevenson's *The Ebb-Tide* (1894), *An Outcast of the Islands* is, among other things, a study of imperialists at their worst (White 136; Dryden 77).[27] In it, Almayer is an indolent, ineffectual man hoping for an easy fortune just as he is in *Almayer's Folly*. In *An Outcast of the Islands*, he is more of a whiner than a dreamer, however, as evidenced by his long, complaining conversations with Lingard when the latter reappears after a lengthy absence from Sambir (181–96). Peter Willems, in contrast, a protégé of Lingard's who marries Joanna Da Souza, a Malay-Portuguese woman, to improve his fortune, is a talented, arrogant man who believes that scruples are for "the fools, the weak, the contemptible. . . . Where there are scruples there can be no power" (8). For him, power is of the utmost importance. Accordingly, he supports his Malay-Portuguese in-laws even though he regards them as "lazy," because in exchange for his money, "he had their silent fear, their loquacious love, their noisy veneration" (4): as the narrator puts it, "It is a fine thing to be a providence, and to be told so on every day of one's life. It gives one a feeling of enormously remote superiority, and Willems revelled in it. . . . They lived now by the grace of his will. This was power. Willems loved it" (5). Willems, it seems, is a megalomaniac of sorts, a man who enjoys nothing more than domineering those he considers his inferiors, including his "half-caste" wife, Joanna, and his "dark-skinned" brother-in-law, Leonard (25). His attitude towards Aïssa, the Malay-Arab woman who becomes his lover once his marriage fails, is similar: despite his overwhelming attraction to her, he considers her "a complete savage" and takes great pleasure in the idea of having her all to himself "to fashion—to mould" (80, 92). Unlike Almayer, who believes in his own racial superiority but seems to take no particular pleasure in asserting power for its own sake, Willems has been corrupted by the power the colonial system accords him as a white man, and he exercises that power at every opportunity.

Lingard, an Englishman, is very different from the two Dutch colonists, Almayer and Willems. Like them, he is primarily motivated by profit, but he is paternalistic toward Malays rather than contemptuous.[28] To him, Sambir is a private domain of sorts, one in which he controls the trade and rules indirectly through the local rajah, Patalolo (43). Even though he is the one who profits most from the trade, he boasts to Willems, "I brought prosperity to that place. I composed their quarrels, and saw them grow under my eyes. There's peace and happiness there" (45). Despite Lingard's confident assertion of the positive effects of his rule, as the narrative proceeds, it becomes increasingly clear that Sambir is anything but peaceful and happy and that Lingard maintains control by force, quelling rebellions with his "armed brig" (51).

Because Lingard is English—something emphasized repeatedly both in *Almayer's Folly* and *An Outcast of the Islands*—Conrad's ironic treatment of Lingard's self-satisfied paternalism toward Sambir functions as a critique of British paternalism toward its colonies. This critique becomes explicit in a conversation between Lingard and Babalatchi after the "great revolution" occurs and Lingard loses control of the colony (360). Lingard expresses disdain for Dutch imperialist practices and suggests to Babalatchi that he and his allies will regret seeking Dutch protection, telling him "with great earnestness" that in dominating Sambir, he acted "for the good of all" (225, 226).[29] Babalatchi, however, recognizes Lingard's statement as self-serving and hypocritical:

> "This is a white man's talk," exclaimed Babalatchi, with bitter exultation. "I know you. That is how you all talk while you load your guns and sharpen your swords; and when you are ready, then to those who are weak you say: 'Obey me and be happy, or die!' You

are strange, you white men. You think it is only your wisdom and your virtue and your happiness that are true." (226)

Although Babalatchi addresses Lingard here, his words pertain to all imperialists who believed that they best knew what was good for others (200). For all their professed altruism, Babalatchi suggests, British imperialists are limited by their own ethnocentrism: they refuse to accept the possibility that what they consider to be "good" may very well be seen as "bad" by others.

Disparaging depictions of white colonists—even British ones—are not unusual, of course, even in the works of late nineteenth-century British colonialist writers. What differentiates Conrad from writers like Haggard and Kipling is that in Conrad's work, there are no good colonists: even well-meaning Englishmen like Lingard and, as we shall see, Jim of *Lord Jim*, are deluded, hypocritical, and self-serving. Another thing that distinguishes *An Outcast of the Islands* from colonialist novels of the same period is Conrad's pervasive use of irony in his treatment of his white colonists: the narrator even employs sarcasm at times, describing Almayer and Willems as "specimens of the superior race" even as they "glared at each other savagely" and describing Lingard as a "doer of justice" immediately after demonstrating that the actions Lingard contemplates are actually motivated by "revenge" (62–63). As I argued earlier, such use of irony has become part of the postcolonial aesthetic, a means of subjecting white colonists to the kind of ridicule to which colonialist writers subjected the colonized. To white colonists, there is nothing worse than "to be made a laughing-stock of before a parcel of savages," as Almayer puts it (207).

Colonial Subjectivity and Resistance

In addition to disparaging white colonists, *An Outcast of the Islands* explores in detail what it is to be a colonial subject. In *Almayer's Folly*, as we have seen, Conrad depicts the formation of a national consciousness through his representation of Nina, a "half-caste" living in "savage" surroundings who rejects her European heritage to join the rebellion against the Dutch in Bali. In *An Outcast of the Islands*, he focuses on the colonial subjectivity of Joanna and Leonard Da Souza, "half-castes" living in a colonial center who resent being subjugated by Europeans even though they depend on them financially.

As Robert J. C. Young demonstrates in *Colonial Desire: Hybridity in Theory, Culture and Race*, in the nineteenth century, the British generally regarded "half-castes" as racial inferiors, people whose white blood was essentially compromised or polluted. Despite this—or perhaps because of it—they were considered by some to be ideal colonists, particularly in tropical regions when the mortality of white colonists was high. Regarding Jamaicans of African/European descent, Anthony Trollope, for example, writes, "My theory—for I acknowledge to a theory—is this: that Providence has sent white men and black men to these regions in order that from them may spring a race fitted by intellect for civilization; and fitted also by physical organization for tropical labour" (75). In *Ten Years in Saráwak*, Charles Brooke made a similar argument for what Young calls "the breeding of a new strain of mixed-race colonials" in Asia, a belief that, according to Young, "would influence conditions in Sarawak right into the twentieth century" (143–44). To many imperialists, the economic advantages of employing "mixed-race colonials" seemed obvious: the dominant racial stereotypes of their time led them to believe that these half-castes would be hardier than the average European and more intelligent than the average native.[30] Such hybrids, they believed, would also be ideally suited to manage natives even as they themselves were managed by Europeans.[31] This scheme could only work, however, if natives accepted "half-castes" as their superiors, and in turn, half-castes accepted Europeans as theirs. In *An Outcast of the Islands*, Conrad suggests that neither is likely to happen since whites despise half-castes as inferiors, half-castes consider themselves to be white, and native inhabitants treat half-castes as outcasts.

That the whites living in the archipelago despise half-castes becomes evident very early in the novel, not only because of Willems's contempt for his wife but because, as a couple, they will not be accepted into white society because of her mixed blood (9).[32] One reason whites apparently dislike people of mixed race is because they do not accept the place in the colonial social hierarchy that Europeans have assigned them. Rather than assume a subordinate status, half-castes like Joanna and Leonard consider themselves white, something that becomes clear when, just before Willems assaults him, Leonard implores him not to be "brutal" since it would be "unbecoming" for "white men" to fight "with all those natives looking on" (29). As Leonard's words suggest, to half-castes, being white is more than just a matter of blood: acting white is just as important as being white. Indeed, Leonard comes to regard Willems as his inferior because of Willems's actions, at one point telling him that he is "a savage . . . Not at all like we whites" (28).

Conrad's half-castes are not docile, either, even though his white characters expect them to be. When, coming home late on his thirtieth birthday after a night of drinking, for example, Willems wakes Joanna so that he can boast to her of his various exploits and successes, expecting that "she would stand at the further end of the table, her hands resting on the edge, her frightened eyes watching his lips, without a sound, without a stir, hardly breathing, till he dismissed her with a contemptuous: 'Go to bed, dummy'" (9). The passage continues, "She would draw a long breath then and trail out of the room, relieved but unmoved. Nothing could startle her, make her scold or cry. She did not complain, she did not rebel." Much to Willems's "surprise," she does in fact rebel just two days later when she learns that he has embezzled money from her father, Hudig:

> As Willems was looking at Joanna her upper lip was drawn up on one side, giving her melancholy face a vicious expression altogether new to his experience. He stepped back in surprise.
>
> "Oh! You great man!" she said distinctly, but in a voice that was hardly above a whisper.
>
> Those words, and still more her tone, stunned him as if somebody had fired a gun close to his ear. He stared back at her stupidly . . .
>
> "Joanna!" exclaimed Willems.
>
> "Do not speak to me. I have heard what I have waited for all these years. You are less than dirt, you that have wiped your feet on me. I have waited for this. I am not afraid now. I do not want you; do not come near me." (27)

Just as Lingard finds it difficult to accept the fact that the people he dominated in Sambir were anything but grateful to him, Willems cannot believe that Joanna resents him, even though he has systematically abused her since they were first married: "Willems stared motionless, in dumb amazement at the mystery of anger and revolt in the head of his wife. . . . He felt terror at this hate that lived stealthily so near him for years" (27). That Joanna's hatred for Willems was hidden for so long is as significant as the fact that she finally revolts. Colonial subjects like Joanna may hide their hatred, but that does not mean it does not exist and that they will not revolt when they have the opportunity. As if to underscore this point, the narrator dramatizes Leonard Da Souza's rebellion in a similar manner. When Willems first meets him, Leonard is obsequious to the point of being ridiculous, even chalking Willems's "cues when playing billiards" (34). After years of being "Patronize[d] loftily" by Willems, however, Leonard turns on Willems, helping to document his "irregularities" and reporting them to Hudig (3, 33). Willems is stunned when he learns from Lingard what Leonard has done:

> "Why, Captain Lingard," he [Willems] burst out, "the fellow licked my boots."
>
> "Yes, yes, yes," said Lingard testily, "we know that, and you did your best to cram your boot down his throat. No man likes that, my boy." (33)

Lingard's explanation as to why Leonard would ruin the man who supports him and his family seems plausible: people resent being abused even when they are dependent on their abusers. Ironically, Lingard fails to realize that the same dynamic is at work in Sambir: he forces the people there to lick his boots, so to speak, and they rise up against him at their first opportunity.

Governability and the Unspeaking Subaltern

If the narrator's description of Joanna and Leonard Da Souza's actions highlights the tenuousness of imperialist control over the seemingly docile subjects living in colonial centers such as Macassar, Willems's fear of the subaltern "Bajow vagabonds" whom Joanna hires to take her downriver highlights the challenges imperialist control faces on the periphery (309). Although these subalterns do not "speak" in Gayatri Spivak's sense of the term, they do function as "figures of colonial resistance," to borrow Jenny Sharpe's phrase, since their ungovernability exposes the limits of colonial power. As we shall see, Conrad's representation of the men from Bajow does more than just demonstrate that not all subject peoples can be governed. It also suggests that the "vast ideological machinery" of colonization "that silences the subaltern" is the very same machinery that will ultimately bring about the end of colonization, since, in excluding the subaltern, colonial institutions prevent them from being conditioned as subjects (Sharpe 143).

That the men from Bajow have never been subjected to colonial institutions is clear: they are "sea gypsies," to borrow Almayer's term, speaking neither English nor Dutch and knowing little of colonial practices (310, 312). As subalterns they are of no account, at least to white colonists and, as Almayer notes, "could disappear without attracting notice" (310). Even Almayer's servants hold them in contempt: to them, the men are "ill-behaved savages" who "should not be spoken to by white men" (316). Despite their low status—or, perhaps, because of it—they are of great use to white colonists like Almayer, because "they are ready for anything if you pay them" and unlikely to reveal any secrets because "nobody . . . would dream of seeking information of them" (312, 310). Ironically, the unaccountability that makes subalterns valuable to colonists in some ways also makes them a threat. Because they are considered insignificant, at least as individuals, subalterns are never systematically conditioned to accept colonial beliefs and practices, and therefore they are more difficult to control. This becomes evident in the case of Mahmat Banjer, one of the Bajow boatmen, when Almayer threatens to evict him. Even though Banjer abases himself to Almayer, he "made up his mind that if the white man ever wanted to eject him from his hut, he would burn it and also as many of the white man's other buildings as he could safely get at" (318). Subalterns like Banjer are governed by force rather than consent and therefore cannot be expected to follow colonial law when they are not under direct supervision.

The threat that subalterns pose to colonial society becomes even more pronounced in Willems's encounter with the boatmen later in the novel. Like Almayer, Willems strongly believes in his own racial superiority and expects to be treated with deference by subject peoples even as he bullies them, sometimes with "profane violence" (19). At the same time, however, he refuses to travel unarmed with the subaltern boatmen, even though doing so may be his only means of escaping exile: "Couldn't think of trusting himself unarmed with those Bajow fellows," he tells himself (349). As if to emphasize the need for colonists to be armed while among colonial subjects when on the periphery of empire, the narrative reports Willems's desire for his gun three times: when he meets with Joanna upon her arrival (349), when the boatmen land the boat near him (350), and again when he sees Aïssa in the distance (352). Even though he has no particular reason to fear these subalterns, he also seems to know that he cannot rely on racial prestige to protect him from people who have not been conditioned to accept his authority; ultimately, he depends on force to control them.

The novel's climax strongly affirms this point. When Aïssa sees the subaltern boatmen, she arms herself with Willems's revolver to protect him from them. Once she realizes that Joanna has come to take Willems away, however, she becomes angry and refuses to give the gun to him when he demands it (354). Following a confrontation between Aïssa and Joanna in which Joanna slaps her and runs to the boat, Willems tries to reach the gun, which Aïssa has set down. Aïssa grabs it first, however, and puts it behind her back: "You shall not have it. Go after her. Go to meet danger . . . Go to meet death . . . Go unarmed . . . Go with empty hands and sweet words . . . as you came to me . . . Go helpless and lie to the forests, to the sea . . . to the death that awaits you . . ." (359, ellipses in original). As Aïssa's words indicate, she recognizes that Willems can only control the boatmen by force, that "sweet words" will not be enough to control subalterns who have not been conditioned by colonial institutions to accept white authority. The implications of this are important: if, as subalterns, they cannot speak, then they cannot be spoken to and thereby controlled. Their silence is, in a sense, their strength.

The Subaltern Shoots: Aïssa and Willems

If the subaltern boatmen represent a potential threat to Willems, Aïssa proves herself a very real one. It is not savagery that makes her dangerous to him, however, but her ungovernability, something that distinguishes her from subject peoples as they are represented in the colonialist fiction of writers such as Haggard, Kipling, and Cary.[33] Since she has had no contact with whites or colonial institutions until coming to Sambir, she does not realize at first that the racial hatred imperialist ideology fosters—the "contempt of a white man for that blood which is not his blood, for that race which is not his race"—makes a stable, long-term relationship with Willems impossible (152): she cannot comprehend why Willems despises her despite his attraction to her or why Willems comes to despise himself for having an adulterous relationship with someone he considers an "animal" (270). Once she realizes that she has been betrayed by Willems, who never told her he had a wife and child, she recognizes that he is a duplicitous white man who, like most of Conrad's other colonists, acts only in self-interest. Her reaction, as described by the narrator, makes it clear that she represents not just an injured lover but an injured class of people: "Hate filled the world . . .—the hate of race, the hate of hopeless diversity, the hate of blood; the hate against the man born in the land of lies and of evil from which nothing but misfortune comes to those who are not white. And as she stood, maddened, she heard a whisper near her, the whisper of the dead Omar's [her father's] voice saying in her ear: 'Kill! Kill!'" (359).[34] Despite her realization that she has been used by Willems, Aïssa resists her impulse to shoot him, cautioning him not to "come near" (360): unlike the stereotypical savage in an exotic romance, she is not governed by her passions but, rather, shows restraint. Willems, however, decides to risk charging the gun: "Willems pulled himself together for a struggle. He dared not go unarmed [with the boatmen]. He made a long stride and saw her raise the revolver. He noticed that she had not cocked it, and said to himself that, even if she did fire, she would surely miss. Go too high; it was a stiff trigger. He made a step nearer—saw the long barrel moving unsteadily at the end of her extended arm. He thought: this is my time" (360). Willems's final effort to get the gun underscores just how much he fears the men from Bajow: he would rather charge a gun than face them, a decision that costs him his life. That he is killed by a subaltern whom he has sexually exploited is also important, since the narrative holds him accountable for his actions. Although he appears to believe that as a native woman she would be "easy to dispose of," just as Almayer believes of his own wife in *Almayer's Folly*, Willems could not be more wrong (11): it is she, a subaltern, who disposes of him.

Even though Aïssa was originally conceived of by Conrad as a device to advance the stories of Willems and Babalatchi, ultimately she emerges as a fully rounded character through whom Conrad explores not only subaltern consciousness but agency.[35] As we have seen, she is anything but the subaltern who cannot speak or act: she not only shoots Willems but taunts Almayer after the "great revolution" and forces the usually indomitable Lingard to alter his plans through direct confrontation (255).[36] Ironically, despite the directness of her words and actions, white men find her incomprehensible: accordingly, the narrator describes her in paradoxical terms as at once "defiant yet shrink-ing" (244), "timorous and fearless" (245), "savage and tender" (249). She is unknowable even to her lover, Willems, who exclaims at one point, "How can I know what's in her? She may want to kill me next!" (270). In part, Wil-lems fears her because she is a woman and therefore "inscrutable": "You can't believe any woman. Who can tell what's inside their heads? No one. You can know nothing" (268). He also fears her as a racial "other," however, as someone whose "motives, impulses, desires he had ignored, but that had lived in the breasts of despised men, close by his side" (149). As the reference to "despised men" suggests, to Willems, Aïssa has come to represent a whole indigenous underclass, a class of ungovernable subalterns: what "frightened him . . . was the horror of bewildered life where he could understand nothing and nobody round him; where he could guide, control, comprehend nothing and no one" (149). In what amounts to an epiphany, Willems briefly recognizes the threat that subalterns pose to colonial society and is overwhelmed by it.

Dialogism, Difficulty, and British Fiction Market

Taken as a whole, *An Outcast of the Islands* is even more radical than *Almayer's Folly*, something that should not be too surprising since Conrad began his second novel well after his postcolonial consciousness began to emerge. Like his first novel, *An Outcast of the Islands* exploits the heteroglot possibilities of the genre by dialogizing the various social languages present in Sambir and by depicting imperialism and imperialists in a negative manner. In *An Outcast of the Islands*, Conrad pushes his critique of imperialism further, however, targeting British imperialism through a detailed representation of Lingard's misguided paternalism and suggesting that European control of subject peoples is precarious, particularly on the periphery of empire, where subject peoples have not been conditioned by colonial institutions. Indeed, the novel's climax suggests that imperialism is bringing about the conditions of its own destruction: the more Europeans oppress and exploit subject peo-ples, the more these subjects are likely to rebel, as the "great revolution" in Sambir demonstrates. With all this in mind, it should not be surprising that the novel sold poorly: like *Almayer's Folly*, *An Outcast of the Islands* presented multiple perspectives on imperialism at a time when the British reading public was demanding monologic affirmations of its social mission.[37]

Ironically, the complex, dialogic representations of imperialism that lim-ited the novel's popular success were at least partially responsible for the criti-cal acclaim it generally received. Though, as we have seen, many critics disliked Conrad's sympathetic representation of "natives," they recognized the novel's originality and power (Sherry 1973; 55, 60). Here Conrad may have benefited from the same market forces that were to give rise to literary modernism in the twentieth century: Conrad's work was difficult at a time when difficulty was being increasingly appreciated, at least by cultural elitists.[38] Certainly, positive reviews gave Conrad much needed encouragement. As his letters of the period indicate, it was at about this time that Conrad began to seriously consider committing himself fully to a career as a writer, in part because of the difficulty he was having in finding work on a ship.[39]

Notes

1. That the novel violates genre conventions has long been recognized. In his introductory essay to *Conrad's Prefaces*, Garnett, for example, notes that although "Kipling's example paved the way for the 'exotic' Conrad's arrival," the characters of *Almayer's Folly* and *An Outcast of the Islands* must have seemed "beyond the pale" to most English readers (8). See also Dryden 51–52.

2. It is important to note that the concepts *monologic* and *dialogic* do not constitute a binary opposition. Rather, they mark the extremes of a continuum. As Bakhtin indicates, discourse is by definition dialogic; there are, however, degrees of dialogism and monologism (Morson and Emerson 131).

3. For an extended analysis of the conversation Garnett reports, see Firchow 31–37. For discussions of Conrad's changing sensibilities as a result of his experiences in the Congo, see James Clifford's *The Predicament of Culture*. See also Ribeiro de Oliveira 257–58.

4. Regarding his experiences as an Imperial police officer in Burma, Orwell writes, "I gave it up partly because the climate had ruined my health, partly because I already had vague ideas of writing books, but mainly because I could not go on any longer serving an imperialism which I had come to regard as very largely a racket" (quoted in Meyer 68). For detailed accounts of Orwell's change in attitude as a result of his experiences, see Sheldon 79–112.

5. For a detailed discussion of Gandhi's experiences in South Africa and their effects on his consciousness, see Chadha 56–122.

6. It is worth noting that Conrad revisited the Ukraine just before leaving for Africa, particularly since while there, he was forcibly reminded of what it was to be a colonial subject and that it was his duty as a Pole to promote the culture of his birth and act patriotically (Najder 1983, 119–22).

7. The phrase "to his eastern mind" does not appear in the novel's original manuscript. This addition, in concert with other changes Conrad made, tends to highlight Kaspar's race consciousness, while other changes tend to reduce racial stereotyping on the part of the narrator. As an example of the latter, Conrad twice omits the word *asiatic* as an adjective to describe the behavior of indigenous characters.

8. Kaspar's fantasies that "witnessing" Nina's "triumphs" in Europe will enable him to "grow young again" do not appear in the original draft of chapter 1 (5). By detailing Kaspar's absurd fantasies, Conrad makes Kaspar seem more ridiculous.

9. One could argue, of course, that *Almayer's Folly* would not be "nihilistic" even if Kaspar were the only hero, since rather than be "void" of values, in the course of the story Kaspar demonstrates that he has the values and characteristics of late nineteenth-century European colonists.

10. See also Watt 1979, 38–39; and Jones 86–89.

11. One notable exception is the unsigned review in the *Daily Chronicle* that identifies Nina as the "heroine" (Sherry 1973, 49).

12. A number of critics, including Andrea White and Linda Dryden, compare *Almayer's Folly* to Robert Louis Stevenson's *The Beach of Falesá* (1893), a novella that treats one of its main characters, Uma, a "native" woman, sympathetically. Although Uma is never overtly identified as being of mixed descent, the narrator describes her in stereotypical terms that suggest that she is partially European—"very slender for an island maid, with a long face, a high forehead"—and he mentions that Uma's mother was in a long-term relationship with a white man (192, 212). As Barry Menikoff documents in *Robert Louis Stevenson and "The Beach of Falesá,"* for this and other reasons—including negative representations of Europeans—the novel was "received with suspicion and distaste" (4). It is, of course, possible that Conrad was influenced by Stevenson's novella, which first appeared in *Illustrated London News* in July and August of 1892, nearly two years before he completed *Almayer's Folly* and submitted it to Unwin.

13. That *Almayer's Folly* can be regarded as an adventure novel has been ably demonstrated by White in *Joseph Conrad and the Adventure Tradition*. That it can be read as a romance has been demonstrated in Dryden's equally impressive *Joseph Conrad and the Imperial Romance*.

14. The *Times*, for example, put its review of the novel under the heading "An Oriental Romance" (Watt 1994, xlv). As Watt notes, a number of reviews, including those in the *Guardian*, *Academy*, and *Daily Chronicle*, also treated the book as a romance (Watt 1994, xlv).

15. As Hampson indicates, alternatively, "it could be argued, in the language of Homi Bhabha, that she [Nina] finds her identity not through finally choosing (or being forced to choose) her mother's world rather than her father's . . . but rather as a constant performance of identity in the interstices between the different codes and traditions in which she is situated through 'the overlap and displacement of domains of difference'" (106–7). See also Sewlall, who goes even further in applying Bhabha's theory of the Third Space of Enunciation to Conrad's first two novels.

16. Thomas Moser regards Nina and Dain's romance as "the weakest part of *Almayer's Folly*" (52). D. C. R. A. Goonetilleke argues that their romance "is of a conventionally romantic kind" (1990, 19).

17. For an alternative reading of the significance of the novel's "happy end" (259), see Ribeiro de Oliveira (263–71). She argues that, despite her efforts, "Nina cannot totally obliterate her white inheritance" and that ultimately, she transmits "the virus of a hated civilization to infect Dain's comparatively untainted culture" (269). In *Conrad and Empire*, Stephen Ross develops a similar argument (93).

18. For a more detailed account of how Indonesian nationality emerged earlier in the twentieth century, see GoGwilt's *Invention of the West*, particularly pages 83–87.

19. In *Developing Countries in British Fiction*, Goonetilleke argues that none of Conrad's Malay characters "reveal even a semblance" of the "corporate identity" that is a basic characteristic of nationalism. In *Almayer's Folly*, however, it seems clear that at the very least, Conrad represents the emergence of such an identity.

20. Although John Lester argues in "A Fictional Chronology of Conrad's Eastern World" that "since Nina is five at the time of *An Outcast of the Islands* in 1870, the main action of *Almayer's Folly* must occur in 1886" (60), I believe that

the novel must be set in the 1870s since the narrator mentions the beginning of the "Acheen War," which started in 1873, at the beginning of chapter 4. See Watt 1994, 255n38.5. For more on Sulu responses to imperialism, see Hampson 2000, 41–43.

21. As E. S. De Klerck notes in *The History of the Netherland East Indies*, control of Aceh became important when, with the opening of the Suez Canal, international shipping lanes shifted, passing through the Straits of Malacca (2:342). Fearing apparently that another European state would acquire control of Aceh, the Dutch invaded the independent state in 1873 (Ulekke 319). The war continued into the twentieth century.

22. The initial draft of the opening chapter suggests that Maroola's battle with the Dutch was conceived only after Conrad returned from the Congo and decided to focus more on anticolonial insurgencies, since in the original version, Maroola's boat is still intact.

23. Even GoGwilt, whose work is invaluable to understanding the formation of Indonesian national consciousness as it is represented in *Almayer's Folly*, seems to overlook Maroola's significance, treating him as a love object of both Nina and Taminah (GoGwilt 1995, 84).

24. For a discussion of Taminah and her agency, see GoGwilt 1995, 83–85.

25. In White's view, Conrad's "ventriloquism resulted more from his growing technical interest in writerly concerns than from any liberal consciousness" (120). The original author's note to *Almayer's Folly*, which was written in 1895 but not published until 1921, suggests otherwise, however. In this note Conrad focuses on similarities between the British and their colonial subjects rather than differences, declaring that "there is a bond between us and that humanity so far away" and adding that he is "content to sympathise with common mortals no matter where they live; in houses or in huts, in the streets under a fog or in the forests behind the dark line of dismal mangroves that fringe the vast solitude of the sea" (3). Clearly, Conrad had the sort of consciousness that was unlikely to be popular with the imperialistic readers of the 1890s. Indeed, as White herself notes, Conrad intended his author's note as a "disclaimer" of sorts: in it, he attempted to distinguish his work from that of imperialist writers such as Frederick Marryat, G. A. Henty, and Rider Haggard (White 118).

26. As I indicated in chapter 1, for the purposes of this study, I use the term *colonial subject* to denote those who are subjected to colonial institutions directly and the term *subaltern* to denote those who are largely unconditioned by such institutions. I use the term *subject peoples* when referring to both groups.

27. For a discussion of *The Ebb-Tide*, see Sandison, especially pages 317–20.

28. As White argues, "His good intentions amount to 'meddling' and ultimately bring disaster down on the heads of the very people he seeks to protect, contributing to the chaos of the local rivalries and intrigues that plague Sambir and the eventual revolution there" (142). See also Nadelhaft 1991, 15–19.

29. For a discussion of European political and colonial rivalries as they are represented in Sambir, see Hampson 2000, 110–11.

30. Other Europeans believed the opposite, of course—that "half-castes" were hopelessly degenerate and essentially useless. John W. Griffith argues that Conrad shared this view, noting that the narrator of *An Outcast of the Islands* uses the term *degenerate* when describing the Da Souza family (141). Griffith's argument is unconvincing, however, since Conrad develops a "half-caste" character, Nina Almayer, as a protagonist and hero in *Almayer's Folly*.

31. In her discussion of both "interbreeding" and what Benedict Anderson described as "mental miscegenation"—that is, efforts to create "Europeanized natives" through education—Ania Loomba suggests that the belief was that colonial subjects could "mimic but never exactly reproduce English values, and that their recognition of the perpetual gap between themselves and the 'real thing' [would] ensure their subjection" (173).

32. A review of *Almayer's Folly* that appeared in a Singapore newspaper, the *Strait Times*, in 1896 seems to confirm this. The anonymous reviewer writes, "The author has drawn with great power and fidelity the miserable results of a mixed marriage under existing social conditions. . . . The social prejudice against mixed blood, unjust in itself, has been aroused by the narrowing influence of local education and limited interests, and serves to save many foolish lives from mental shipwrecks. Its general utility does not, however, prevent its operating with very cruel harshness against individuals" (quoted in Marle 31). For a discussion of this review and a letter that appeared in the *Strait Times* the next day that vehemently denied that prejudices even existed against people of mixed race, see van Marle's "Jumble of Facts and Fiction."

33. Heliéna Krenn identifies nine instances in which the word *savage* is used to highlight in Aïssa "a total absence of the physical and mental changes that result from exposure to and assimilation of civilization's influences" (64).

34. Like the reference to "sweet words" cited earlier, this passage does not appear in the original manuscript. Such additions tend to amplify Conrad's point about the threat that subalterns pose to the colonial order.

35. For an analysis of Aïssa's function as a "pivot," see Schneider, 49–52. See also Susan Jones's discussion of Aïssa's transcendence of the "role of *femme fatale*" (10).

36. As Nadelhaft (1991) demonstrates, Spivak's studies of subaltern women provide a framework for better understanding the complexities of Conrad's representation of women in *An Outcast of the Islands*, particularly Aïssa. Nadelhaft goes on to analyze Aïssa's encounter with Lingard in detail (32–33). See also Sewall.

37. The role of British fiction in promulgating imperialist ideology has been widely examined. See, for example, Brantlinger's *Rule of Darkness* and Said's *Culture and Imperialism*.

38. In *Who Paid for Modernism?* Joyce Piell Wexler interrogates the relationship between the complexity of texts and their marketability, demonstrating that a market existed for writers who challenged their readers with difficult texts.

39. In a letter to Garnett, for example, Conrad thanks him for attempting to help him to find a ship (*Letters* 1:262). About a month later, he announced to Garnett that he had begun a third novel, "The Rescuer" (*Letters* 1:268). There is little evidence that Conrad seriously considered going to sea again after this date, except for a brief period in 1898 (Najder 1983, 233).

Chronology

1857	Józef Teodor Konrad Korzeniowski born December 3 in Berdyczew, Poland, to Apollo Korzeniowski and Ewelina Bobrowska.
1862	Joseph Conrad's father is exiled to Russia for his part in the Polish National Committee. Conrad and his mother accompany his father.
1865	Mother dies.
1869	Conrad and his father return to Cracow in February. Father dies in May.
1874	Leaves Cracow for Marseilles, intending to become a sailor.
1875	Becomes apprentice aboard the *Mont Blanc*, bound for Martinique.
1877	Part owner of the *Tremolino*.
1878	In February, after ending an unhappy love affair, Conrad attempts suicide by shooting himself. In June, he lands in England. Serves as ordinary seaman on the *Mavis*.
1883	Becomes mate on the ship *Riversdale*.
1884	Second mate on the *Narcissus*, bound from Bombay to Dunkirk.
1886	Becomes naturalized British citizen.
1887	First mate on the *Highland Forest*.

1889	Begins writing *Almayer's Folly*.
1890	In May, leaves for the Congo as second in command of the S. S. *Roi de Belges*, later becoming commander.
1894	Ends sea career.
1895	Publishes *Almayer's Folly*. Writes *An Outcast of the Islands*. Lives in London.
1896	Marries Jessie George on March 24.
1897–1900	Writes *The Nigger of the "Narcissus,"* *Heart of Darkness*, and *Lord Jim*.
1904	Writes *Nostromo*.
1905	Travels in Europe for four months.
1907	Writes *The Secret Agent*.
1911–12	Writes *Under Western Eyes* and *'Twixt Land and Sea*.
1914	Writes *Chance* and *Victory*. In July, visits Poland, where he is caught when the Great War breaks out in August. Escapes and returns safely to England in November.
1916	Son, Borys, fights on the French front.
1917	Writes *The Shadow-Line* and prefaces to an edition of his collected works.
1919	Writes *The Arrow of Gold*.
1920	Writes *The Rescue*.
1924	In May, declines a knighthood. After an illness, dies of a heart attack on August 3 and is buried in Canterbury.
1925	The incomplete *Suspense* is published. *Tales of Hearsay* is published.
1926	*Last Essays* published.

Contributors

HAROLD BLOOM is Sterling Professor of the Humanities at Yale University. He is the author of 30 books, including *Shelley's Mythmaking, The Visionary Company, Blake's Apocalypse, Yeats, A Map of Misreading, Kabbalah and Criticism, Agon: Toward a Theory of Revisionism, The American Religion, The Western Canon,* and *Omens of Millennium: The Gnosis of Angels, Dreams, and Resurrection. The Anxiety of Influence* sets forth Professor Bloom's provocative theory of the literary relationships between the great writers and their predecessors. His most recent books include *Shakespeare: The Invention of the Human,* a 1998 National Book Award finalist, *How to Read and Why, Genius: A Mosaic of One Hundred Exemplary Creative Minds, Hamlet: Poem Unlimited, Where Shall Wisdom Be Found?,* and *Jesus and Yahweh: The Names Divine.* In 1999, Professor Bloom received the prestigious American Academy of Arts and Letters Gold Medal for Criticism. He has also received the International Prize of Catalonia, the Alfonso Reyes Prize of Mexico, and the Hans Christian Andersen Bicentennial Prize of Denmark.

MARTIN PRICE is professor emeritus at Yale University. He is coeditor of *The Oxford Anthology of English Literature* and also published other works, including *To the Palace of Wisdom* and *Forms of Life: Character and Moral Imagination in the Novel.*

ANTHONY WINNER is professor emeritus at the University of Virginia. Aside from his work on Conrad, he has published *Great European Short Novels* and *Characters in the Twilight: Hardy, Zola, and Chekhov.*

MARK A. WOLLAEGER is a professor at Vanderbilt University. He is the author of *Modernism, Media, and Propaganda: British Narrative from 1900 to 1945* and co-editor of two titles on James Joyce. He also is founding co-editor of Modernist Literature and Culture, a new book series from Oxford University Press.

CEDRIC WATTS is a professor at the University of Sussex. He has written or edited numerous books, many of them on Conrad or Conrad's friend Cunninghame Graham, including *A Preface to Conrad* and *Joseph Conrad: A Literary Life*.

CHRISTOPHER GOGWILT is a professor at Fordham University. He is the author of *The Fiction of Geopolitics: Afterimages of Culture from Wilkie Collins to Alfred Hitchcock* and numerous essays on modernism, colonialism, and post-colonialism. He is working on a set of comparative studies of the works of Joseph Conrad, Jean Rhys, and the Indonesian writer, Pramoedya Ananta Toer.

ROBERT HAMPSON is a professor at Royal Holloway, University of London, where he is also head of the English department. He is the author of *Joseph Conrad: Betrayal and Identity* and editor of various works of Conrad. He is also the author of a number of essays and articles on Conrad and is a former editor of the journal *The Conradian*.

TERRY COLLITS has been a professor and head of Chisholm College, La Trobe University, Melbourne, Australia. He is the author of *Postcolonial Conrad: Paradoxes of Empire* and has published several articles on Conrad and other topics.

J. HILLIS MILLER is a professor at the University of California at Irvine. He is the author of many books and essays on nineteenth- and twentieth-century English, European, and American literature, and on literary theory. Among his works are *Poets of Reality: Six Twentieth-Century Writers: Conrad, Yeats, Eliot, Thomas, Stevens, Williams* and *The Disappearance of God: Five Nineteenth-Century Writers*.

TOM HENTHORNE is an associate professor at Pace University. His essays have appeared in various journals, including *Conradiana*.

Bibliography

Adams, David. *Colonial Odysseys: Empire and Epic in the Modernist Novel*. Ithaca, N.Y.: Cornell University Press, 2003.

Ash, Beth Sharon. *Writing in Between: Modernity and Psychosocial Dilemma in the Novels of Joseph Conrad*. New York: St. Martin's Press, 1999.

Baxter, Katherine Isobel, and Richard J. Hand, ed. *Joseph Conrad and the Performing Arts*. Farnham, England; Burlington, Vt.: Ashgate, 2009.

Breton, Rob. *Gospels and Grit: Work and Labour in Carlyle, Conrad and Orwell*. Toronto; Buffalo: University of Toronto Press, 2005.

Carabine, Keith, and Max Saunders, ed. *Inter-relations: Conrad, James, Ford, and Others*. Boulder, Colo.: Social Science Monographs; New York: Distributed by Columbia University Press, 2004.

Chantler, Ashley. Heart of Darkness: *Character Studies*. London; New York: Continuum, 2008.

Cheng, Yuan-Jung. *Heralds of the Postmodern: Madness and Fiction in Conrad, Woolf, and Lessing*. New York: Peter Lang, 1999.

Cousineau, Thomas J. *Ritual Unbound: Reading Sacrifice in Modernist Fiction*. Newark: University of Delaware Press; Cranbury, N.J.: Associated University Presses, 2004.

DiSanto, Michael John. *Under Conrad's Eyes: The Novel as Criticism*. Montreal: McGill-Queen's University Press, 2009.

Dryden, Linda. *Joseph Conrad and the Imperial Romance*. Houndmills, Basingstoke, Hampshire; New York: Palgrave, 2000.

Erdinast-Vulcan, Daphna, ed. *Joseph Conrad: The Short Fiction*. Amsterdam, Netherlands: Rodopi, 2004.

———. *The Strange Short Fiction of Joseph Conrad: Writing, Culture, and Subjectivity.* Oxford; New York: Oxford University Press, 1999.

Fincham, Gail, and Myrtle Hooper, ed. *Under Postcolonial Eyes: Joseph Conrad After Empire.* Cape Town: UCT Press, 1996.

Firchow, Peter Edgerly. *Envisioning Africa: Racism and Imperialism in Conrad's Heart of Darkness.* Lexington: University Press of Kentucky, 2000.

Glendening, John. *The Evolutionary Imagination in Late-Victorian Novels: An Entangled Bank.* Aldershot, England; Burlington, Vt.: Ashgate, 2007.

GoGwilt, Christopher. *The Fiction of Geopolitics: Afterimages of Culture, from Wilkie Collins to Alfred Hitchcock.* Stanford, Calif.: Stanford University Press, 2000.

Hampson, Robert. *Joseph Conrad: Betrayal and Identity.* London: St Martin's Press, 1992.

Hand, Richard J. *The Theatre of Joseph Conrad: Reconstructed Fictions.* Basingstoke, England; New York: Palgrave Macmillan, 2005.

Harpham, Geoffrey Galt. *One of Us: The Mastery of Joseph Conrad.* Chicago: University of Chicago Press, 1996.

Hawthorn, Jeremy. *Joseph Conrad: Narrative Technique and Ideological Commitment.* London: Edward Arnold, 1990

Henthorne, Tom. "An End to Imperialism: *Lord Jim* and the Postcolonial Conrad." *Conradiana* 32, no. 3 (2000): 203–27.

Houen, Alex. *Terrorism and Modern Literature from Joseph Conrad to Ciaran Carson.* Oxford; New York: Oxford University Press, 2002.

Jayasena, Nalin. *Contested Masculinities: Crises in Colonial Male Identity from Joseph Conrad to Satyajit Ray.* New York: Routledge, 2007.

Karl, Frederick R. *A Reader's Guide to Joseph Conrad.* Syracuse: Syracuse University Press, 1997.

Kauhl, Gudrun. "Strategies of Reappraisal: Joseph Conrad's *The Secret Agent.*" *Conradiana* 26, no. 2 (1994): 103–18.

Knowles, Owen, and Gene M. Moore. *The Oxford Reader's Companion to Conrad.* Oxford; New York: Oxford University Press, 2000.

Krapp, John. *An Aesthetics of Morality: Pedagogic Voice and Moral Dialogue in Mann, Camus, Conrad, and Dostoevsky.* Columbia: University of South Carolina Press, 2002.

Levin, Yael. *Tracing the Aesthetic Principle in Conrad's Novels.* New York: Palgrave Macmillan, 2009.

Lindner, Christoph. *Fictions of Commodity Culture: From the Victorian to the Postmodern.* Aldershot, Hampshire, England; Burlington, Vt.: Ashgate, 2003.

Moore, Gene M., ed. *Joseph Conrad's Heart of Darkness: A Casebook.* Oxford; New York: Oxford University Press, 2004.

Moore, Gene M., Allan H. Simmons, and J.H. Stape, ed. *Conrad Between the Lines: Documents in a Life*. Amsterdam; Atlanta: Rodopi, 2000.

Panichas, George A. *Joseph Conrad: His Moral Vision*. Macon, Ga.: Mercer University Press, 2005.

Paris, Bernard J. *Conrad's Charlie Marlow: A New Approach to* "Heart of Darkness" *and* Lord Jim. New York: Palgrave Macmillan, 2005.

Peters, John G. *Conrad and Impressionism*. Cambridge; New York: Cambridge University Press, 2001.

Quick, Jonathan. *Modern Fiction and the Art of Subversion*. New York: Peter Lang, 1999.

Roberts, Andrew Michael. *Conrad and Masculinity*. New York: St. Martin's Press, 2000.

Ross, Stephen. *Conrad and Empire*. Columbia: University of Missouri Press, 2004.

Schwarz, Daniel R. *Rereading Conrad*. Columbia: University of Missouri Press, 2001.

Segal, Alex. "Deconstruction, Radical Secrecy, and *The Secret Agent*." *Modern Fiction Studies* 54, no. 2 (Summer 2008): 189–208.

Simmons, Allan. *Conrad's* Heart of Darkness: *A Reader's Guide*. London; New York: Continuum, 2007.

Simmons, Allan, and J. H. Stape, ed. Lord Jim: *Centennial Essays*. Amsterdam; Atlanta: Rodopi, 2000.

———. Nostromo: *Centennial Essays*. Amsterdam; New York: Rodopi, 2004.

———. The Secret Agent: *Centennial Essays*. Amsterdam; New York: Rodopi; UK: Joseph Conrad Society, 2007.

Stape, J. H. "'The Dark Places of the Earth': Text and Context in *Heart of Darkness*." *Conradian: Journal of the Joseph Conrad Society* 29, no. 1 (Spring 2004): 144–61.

Strychacz, Thomas. *Dangerous Masculinities: Conrad, Hemingway, and Lawrence*. Gainesville: University Press of Florida, 2008.

Watt, Ian. "Conrad's *Heart of Darkness* and the Critics." *North Dakota Quarterly* 57, no. 3 (Summer 1989): 5–15.

Yeow, Agnes S. K. *Conrad's Eastern Vision: A Vain and Floating Appearance*. Basingstoke, England; New York: Palgrave Macmillan, 2009.

Acknowledgments

Martin Price, "Conrad: Satire and Fiction." From *The Yearbook of English Studies* 14 (1984): 226–242. © 1984 by the Modern Humanities Research Association.

Anthony Winner, "*The Secret Agent*: The Irony of Home Truths." From *Culture and Irony: Studies in Joseph Conrad's Major Novels*, pp. 70–91, 128–29. © 1988 by the Rector and Visitors of the University of Virginia. Reproduced by permission of the University of Virginia Press.

Mark A. Wollaeger, "'Heart of Darkness': Visionary Skepticism." From *Joseph Conrad and the Fictions of Skepticism*. Copyright © 1990 by the Board of Trustees of the Leland Stanford Jr. University.

Cedric Watts, "Conrad and the Myth of the Monstrous Town." From *Conrad's Cities: Essays for Hans van Marle*, edited by Gene M. Moore. © 1992 by Editions Rodopi B.V.

Christopher GoGwilt, "Subversive Plots: From *Under Western Eyes* to *The Secret Agent*." From *The Invention of the West: Joseph Conrad and the Double-Mapping of Europe and Empire*. Copyright © 1995 by the Board of Trustees of the Leland Stanford Jr. University.

Robert Hampson, "Absence and Presence in *Victory*." From *Cross-Cultural Encounters in Joseph Conrad's Malay Fiction*. © 2000 by Robert Hampson. Reproduced with permission of Palgrave Macmillan.

207

Terry Collits, "Anti-Heroics and Epic Failures: The Case of *Nostromo*." From *Conradian* 29, no. 2 (Autumn 2004): 1–13. © 2004 by the Joseph Conrad Society.

J. Hillis Miller, "'Material Interests': Conrad's *Nostromo* as a Critique of Global Capitalism." From *Joseph Conrad: Voice, Sequence, History, Genre*, edited by Jakob Lothe, Jeremy Hawthorn, and James Phelan. © 2008 by Ohio State University.

Tom Henthorne, "'There Will Be Fighting': Insurgency and Postcoloniality in Almayer's Folly and An Outcast of the Islands." From *Conrad's Trojan Horses: Imperialism, Hybridity, and the Postcolonial Aesthetic.* © 2008 Texas Tech University Press. Reprinted by permission of Texas Tech University Press.

Index